HANNAH ARENDT: THE RECOVERY OF THE PUBLIC WORLD

HANNAH ARENDT: THE RECOVERY OF THE PUBLIC WORLD

EDITED BY *Melvyn A. Hill*

ST. MARTIN'S PRESS · NEW YORK

For information, write:

St. Martin's Press, Inc., 175 Fifth Ave.,

New York, N.Y. 10010.

Manufactured in the United States of America
Library of Congress Cataloging in Publication Data
Main entry under title:
Hannah Arendt, the recovery of the public world.
Bibliography / Includes index.
1. Arendt, Hannah. 2. Political science—Addresses,
essays, lectures. I. Arendt, Hannah. II. Hill, Melvyn A.
JC251.A74H36   310.5'3'0924   78–19393
ISBN 0–312–36071–1

This book is dedicated to the memory of

HANNAH ARENDT

sad is Eros, builder of cities

W. H. Auden
"In Memory of Sigmund Freud"

Contents

INTRODUCTION

When I first began to edit this collection of essays, Hannah Arendt protested: "Please, don't make me the excuse for another book that is not really a book." She was referring to those volumes of papers in which the authors are not engaged in the coherent dialogue that would justify their work being published together. I believe the reader will find a real dialogue in this volume of essays, but for me to specify its themes and define its unity would be unnecessary—or, if I am wrong, an idle invention. Therefore, by way of introduction, I shall discuss only the background to the project as a whole: the point behind the years of work, care, and attention that have gone into its conception and realization. (The essays were written at various times between 1972 and 1978, and while one or two of them deal with questions of thinking, willing, or judging, they were almost all written before the posthumous appearance of Hannah Arendt's Gifford Lectures, *The Life of the Mind.*) Confronted with the plethora of books on social and political theory, the reader has every right to ask: "Why should I read this book on the work of Hannah Arendt?"

There is no school of Arendtians and this volume was not intended to create one, nor to sketch its possible outlines. Far from attempting an orthodox interpretation of Hannah Arendt, each of the contributors views her work as controversial. And it is precisely the controversial quality of Hannah Arendt's thinking that the book is meant to clarify.

It has been evident for some time that Hannah Arendt's thinking is at odds with the major schools of thought that prevail today. She was, of course, fully aware of this herself, and had she wanted the kind of consideration and acceptance that comes from belonging to a school of thought, or from founding one, there is no doubt that she could have made the necessary accommodations. She preferred to remain an independent thinker and to expect the same from her students and friends. As a consequence she enjoys a peculiar reputation: while her books are respected, few people feel comfortable with the way she argued or with the conclusions she reached. Her recognition takes the form of a *succès d'estime*, where the sheer originality of her thinking is acknowledged at the same time that it is agreed that a sustained dialogue with her would distract one from the significant debate on the left or the right in our time. The contributors to this volume believe that a consideration of Hannah Arendt's positions can illuminate various issues that otherwise remain obscure or neglected because of the assumptions made by those who swim in the mainstream.

I would argue that the reason for Hannah Arendt's *succès d'estime* does not lie so much in her originality as in the paradigmatic status of her work as a thinker. And in the end this quality is likely to determine whether, in fact, her contribution remains repected and gains influence. Unlike theorists in the mainstream, Hannah Arendt does not so much tell us what to think or what to do, as she offers an example of how we might engage in thinking given the conditions of our world. This paradigmatic quality of her thinking is rooted in the way she understood the task of the thinker. And here we can begin to grasp what set her apart from the major schools of thought in her time. There are two basic points to be made. The first concerns Hannah Arendt as a political theorist, and the second concerns her view of thinking, as such.

One might attribute to Marx the definition of the task of the theorist that has come to be generally accepted in modern times; he declared that hitherto the philosophers have attempted to understand the world but the time has come to change it. The task of social and political theory ever since has been taken to be to bridge the gap between thinking and acting—to tell us what to think so that we can know how to act. Hannah Arendt regarded this view of political theory as suspect. She believed that it is up to the actors themselves to judge how to act, and to persuade each other on the best course to follow. The political theorist was in no position to tell the actor what to do. In part this was because she did not believe there was any political theory that could eliminate the need for judgment by offering in its place a certain knowledge of the consequences of different courses of action. But it was chiefly because she believed that the uncertain course of action is a condition of freedom that the actor embraces in company with his peers. And she viewed the search for a political theory to tell us how to act as a profound symptom of our alienation from that condition of freedom, and, indeed, from the others with whom we constitute a world.

Hannah Arendt argued that the philosophers have themselves been alienated from the world insofar as they distrusted the uncertainty that characterizes action, and that their typical response, since Plato, has been to think up ways to order the world in conformity with the kind of certainty and predictability to be found in logical thought. Thus political theory has repeatedly sought a new principle of rule whose authority would make the world of action give way to a set of correctly thought-out premises. For Hannah Arendt this meant that these political theorists simply built on their own alienation from the world of action. She tried to overcome her alienation, and ours in turn, by revealing how attractive the exercise of freedom can be, and how disastrous its disappearance has been. She saw thinking about politics as ancillary to the freedom of political action, and she saw her task as showing us how to understand and appreciate the possibility of freedom in the world, not as teaching us how to change it. Changing it she considered to be the collective task of those who act, not the solitary work of the theorist.

What is it about Hannah Arendt's political thinking that gives it a paradigmatic quality, which shows us how to recover the meaning of the public world? It is quite simply that she started from the fact of her own alienating political experience as a Jewish refugee—one who was considered superfluous and excluded from participating in a world—and in order to grasp its meaning, she found it necessary to recover the political experience she was denied: what it means to participate freely in the affairs of a world. Her experience of superfluousness and world alienation—as she later called it—has become typical for the average citizen in a mass society, so that the manner in which she thought her way back to the reality of the world offers each one of us an example of how it can be done. Her thinking offers to reclaim our capacity for action for us. But it does not try to tell us what to think or what to do.

If Hannah Arendt's contribution to the dilemma of political thinking and acting finds a permanent place, it will be because the radical, participatory implications of her view of the world are recognized—not as another attempt to find an appropriate set of principles by which to reconstitute the ruling system, but as a recovery of what the world is meant to be. In every instance where she extended her admiration to political actors, it was to those who loved to act together *but had no ambition to rule*. For she was concerned with the freedom to participate in action not as a means to some political end, but rather as an end in itself: as the possibility for realizing "public happiness." And it was this and no other meaning of the public realm that she tried to reveal and defend, even at the price of disagreeing with those whose dedication to the cause of social justice made them view politics as a subordinate means to that end. As a political thinker Hannah Arendt believed that social programs belong in the sphere of administration, and she insisted that the *raison d'être* of the public realm was above all to realize freedom as an end in itself.

Then there is the other controversial and paradigmatic side to Hannah Arendt's work: her attitude toward thinking, as such. I have mentioned her refusal to join or to found any school of thought. In part this was because she objected to the view of thinking that obtains in the modern schools in general: it is supposed to serve as a means to certain knowledge in various fields, just as in political science it is supposed to enable us to know how to act. She also objected in principle to the notion of a school of thought, since this requires that thinking become an orthodox body of thought that then exercises authority over what others think. Here again she took her stand against ruling principles that are meant to govern and preempt the activity they address, and defended a Socratic notion of thinking that constantly unravels by night the conclusions to which it has come by day.

For Hannah Arendt, thinking was an ongoing activity—again, an end in itself—since it was constantly faced with the protean forms of experience and the need to discover their meaning. For her the justification for thinking was not the knowledge it confers, but the possibility of meaning that it holds out. Unlike so many philosophers, she did not look to thinking as a way of overcoming experience, but of embracing it. Consequently she could hardly understand how anybody who loved to think in order to find the meaning of his experience could be expected to submit to the conclusions of somebody else's thinking. Far from wanting to contribute an orthodox body of thought, and far from wanting to claim the authority of certain knowledge for her thinking, she hoped to play a part in the ongoing dialogue of those who think about experience and saw this as the only real justification for her writing.

Living at a time when people were alienated from the capacity to act and had lost the tradition that once informed thought, she offered an understanding of what it means to act and what it means to think, as activities that are viewed without the help of prior assumptions, "without bannisters," as she once put it. However much the various contributors to this book disagree with her sense of acting and thinking, they have found some point of illumination in her work that they believe deserves the reader's serious consideration. To attempt to discover Hannah Arendt's real contribution by examining the major aspects of her controversial and unconventional career as a thinker is precisely the point of this book. In editing it, I hoped to show the reader why it is that anyone who is concerned with thinking and acting in our time may benefit from a dialogue with Hannah Arendt.

Melvyn A. Hill
Toronto, 1978

HANNAH ARENDT: THE RECOVERY OF THE PUBLIC WORLD

Elisabeth Young-Bruehl

FROM THE PARIAH'S POINT OF VIEW: REFLECTIONS ON HANNAH ARENDT'S LIFE AND WORK

> On attache aussi bien toute la philosophie morale à une vie populaire et privée qu'à une vie de plus riche étoffe: chaque homme porte la forme entière de l'humaine condition.
>
> —Montaigne

Hannah Arendt finished her doctoral dissertation, *St. Augustine's Concept of Love*, in 1929. Soon afterwards she began her biography of a late eighteenth-century Berlin salon hostess, *Rahel Varnhagen: The Life of a Jewess*. But she did not complete this manuscript until 1938, when she was living in Paris, and she did not publish it until 1958, when she was living in New York. *Rahel Varnhagen* was the book of her exile, and its theme, Rahel's development into "a self-conscious pariah," was the theme of Arendt's exile years.

Even after her work was well known and her years of displacement and poverty were well past, Hannah Arendt continued to think of herself as a pariah. In 1959 she was honored with a visiting professorship to Princeton University, and prepared there the lectures which became her fourth American book, *On Revolution*. But the comfortable surroundings and the genteel society of Princeton made her uneasy and restless. She wrote to her old friend Kurt Blumenfeld, the president of the German Zionist Organization during her youth and one of her favorite Berlin café companions, that the gentility of Princeton was "nicht für meiner Mutters Tochter. Ich schreibe über Revolution, nämlich über Revolution überhaupt. Das hier! Est ist eigentlich von einer makabren Komik."[1]

Regardless of her circumstances, Hannah Arendt worked with a furious energy, a startling intensity—an intensity which she converted, with startling abruptness, into listening-energy at the behest of "history." She could have said after every crisis she lived through—and there were many—what she said in a letter to Mary McCarthy after the 1973 October War in the Middle East: "I have some trouble to get back to work chiefly, of course, because of this unexpected outbreak of 'history.' "[2] The pariah's task, in Arendt's understanding, was to be alert to the unexpected, to look at how things and events appear without preconceptions about history's course or pattern, to avoid sacrificing the outsider's perspective for the parvenu's comforts. The personal ideal of pariahdom which Arendt framed in her youth was transformed in her later years into a political idea: she was able to generalize on the basis of her experience about the conditions of political action and the nature of good judgment.

Hannah Arendt's mother's daughter learned her first lessons in social and political independence while she was growing up in Königsberg, East Prussia. Her grandparents on both sides of the family were comfortably middle-class synagogue-goers. The Cohns, her maternal grandparents, were Russians by birth, refugees from Russian anti-Semitism, who made a good living in Königsberg importing tea. The Arendts were both from established Königsberg families. Max Arendt, Hannah Arendt's grandfather, was a wealthy and prominent man, a member of the Königsberg

Jewish community council and a leader of the city's branch of the *Centralverein deutscher Staatsbürger jüdischen Glaubens*. Both he and his wife, who made a career of philanthropy, were assimilated Jews, Jews who sought a reconciliation in their lives between the claims of *Judentum* and the claims of *Deutschtum*. Both of Hannah Arendt's parents had left behind the claims of *Judentum,* and both were, unlike their parents, politically concerned. They joined the reformist branch of the Social Democratic Party and ardently read Eduard Bernstein's *Sozialistischen Monatsheft*. But Martha Cohn Arendt was also a great admirer of the revolutionary branch of the SPD, the group which became the Spartacists, and particularly of the woman who led the Spartacists, Rosa Luxemburg.

Martha Arendt was not troubled by her own Jewishness, and she hoped that her daughter would learn the lesson she had to teach: the fact of having been born a Jew is undeniable and any attempt to deny it is undignified. Recalling the atmosphere in her childhood home, Arendt remarked: "You see, all Jewish children encountered anti-Semitism. And the souls of many children were poisoned by it. The difference with us was that my mother always insisted that we never humble ourselves. That one must defend oneself! When my teachers made anti-Semitic remarks—usually they were not directed at me, but at my classmates, particularly at the eastern Jewesses—I was instructed to stand up immediately, to leave the class and to go home. . . . My mother would write one of her many letters, and, with that, my involvement in the affair ended completely. . . . There existed house rules by which my dignity was, so to speak, protected, absolutely protected. . . ."[3]

Maintaining her dignity was Arendt's task from childhood. And there were many trials in the face of which to undertake the task. The Arendts' household, comfortable but not genteel, equipped with a fine library but decidedly provincial, was broken apart by a great grief when Hannah Arendt was five years old. Her father, Paul Arendt, was institutionalized with tertiary syphilis, and he died two years later, in 1913. A year after that, with the unexpected outbreak of the First World War, Martha Arendt and her daughter fled to Berlin fearing that the Russians, then advancing into East Prussia, would capture Königsberg. During the war years, Martha Arendt and her daughter lived in financially strained circumstances, and Hannah Arendt suffered through a series of illnesses and absences from school that left her nervous and ill at ease in public. In 1920, when Martha Arendt remarried, they found domestic peace and financial security in the household of Martin Beerwald and his two teenage daughters. But financial trouble came again in the mid-1920s. Martin Beerwald's small manufacturing firm went bankrupt and was absorbed into one of the huge manufacturing concerns that became typical of Germany in the 1920s, when two percent of all businesses employed over fifty-five percent of all workers. During these years Arendt continued her university studies, aided by an uncle.

The years during which Arendt studied at Marburg, Freiburg, and Heidelberg, 1924 to 1929, were relatively peaceful, politically. Arendt herself was not concerned with politics, and neither were the philosophers with whom she studied—Martin Heidegger, Edmund Husserl, and Karl Jaspers. Her doctoral dissertation, written under Jaspers' supervision, was not a politically aware work, though it did contain seeds of concepts which later became central to Hannah Arendt's political philosophy. The concept of "natality" is a particularly important example, and it is also the one concept in the dissertation that does not bear the stamp of Heidegger's seminars, where Arendt had cultivated her interest in St. Augustine. She questioned in the dissertation how it was possible to live in the world, to obey the commandment "love thy neighbor as thyself," while adhering to an unworldly or extra-worldly Christian vision. In her biography of Rahel Varnhagen, an equally difficult conflict posed a question even more personally pressing: how is it possible to live in the world, to love one's neighbors, if one's neighbors—and even you yourself—will not accept who you are? Arendt struggled with this question—which can become a political question, though in Rahel Varnhagen's life it was a social one—until she herself was brought to politics by an unexpected outbreak of history: the rise to power of Adolf Hitler.

The Varnhagen book had resulted from the prelude to this unexpected outbreak, the rising anti-Semitism in Germany in the late 1920s, and the rising influence of the National Socialists. Hannah Arendt had met Kurt Blumenfeld while she was studying in Heidelberg and had been astonished by this extraordinary man, if not converted to his cause, Zionism. When she moved with her first husband, Gunther Stern, to Berlin in 1931 to work on the Varnhagen biography with support from the *Notgemeinschaft für deutscher Wissenschaft,* she renewed her acquaintance with Blumenfeld and came to know his Zionist friends and associates. With these friends and in those times, she began to be aware of what it meant politically to be a Jew in Germany. But before 1933 her awareness was still largely tied to Rahel Varnhagen's social struggle with her Jewishness. Arendt's biography concentrates on how Rahel dealt with what she called on her deathbed "the thing which all my life has seemed to me the greatest shame, which was the misfortune and misery of my life—having been born a Jewess," and the biography questions how Varnhagen came to conclude that "this I should on no account now wish to have missed."

The Zionists Hannah Arendt encountered in Berlin wanted to maintain their dignity as Jews, but they considered the task of reconciling *Judentum* and *Deutschtum* both impossible and undesirable, and they looked forward to the day when Jews could be Jews with pride in Palestine. Hannah Arendt did not become a Zionist; she was a pariah even among pariahs. But she was grateful for the opportunity they presented her with in 1933—the opportunity to act. She accepted a political task: she went to the Prussian State Library, where she had been working on her Varnhagen book, to make excerpts from official anti-Semitic tracts, which the Zionists wanted to use as "horror propaganda" at the 18th Zionist Congress scheduled for August 1933. The Zionists wanted to inform the German Jews and all others of the true nature and extent of German anti-Semitism. At the same time, Arendt made another gesture of resistance: she harbored in her apartment German Communists who were preparing to flee from Germany. Both tasks came to an end when Arendt was arrested by the Gestapo and imprisoned. Because of the helpfulness of one of her German guards and the efforts of her friends, she was released after eight days. She left Germany soon afterwards without papers, and went to Prague, to Geneva, and then to Paris, in the company of her mother.

The German refugees in Paris were culturally, linguistically, socially, and politically isolated from the French. They lived where they could—in hotels, rented rooms, or borrowed apartments— moving from place to place, struggling to secure identity papers. Many were caught in the vicious circle so well known to modern refugees: jobs were available only to those with identity papers, and identity papers were available only to those with jobs. Unlike many, Arendt was able to find jobs with Jewish organizations. When she left Germany, she had resolved to work for the Jews, to do practical work for the Jews, and also to have nothing further to do with the intellectual milieu in which she had lived. She had been deeply shocked when close German friends—including Martin Heidegger—had been infected by the Nazis' propaganda, and she had concluded that intellectuals were more inclined to collabora- tion with the Nazi regime than most: "The problem, the personal problem, was not what our enemies might be doing, but what our friends were doing."[4] This conclusion became subject to revision in France, where Arendt's circle included intellectuals like Walter Benjamin, intellectual friends of long standing like her Königsberg schoolmate Anne Weil, who had studied philosophy with Ernst Cassirer in Hamburg, and Anne's husband Eric Weil, who later became one of the most important philosophers in France. But these intellectuals were Jews. With a very few exceptions, the non- Jewish refugees with whom she became friends were not intellec- tuals. Chief among these was a Communist from Berlin, Heinrich Blücher, a man of working-class origins with almost no formal edu- cation, who later became Hannah Arendt's second husband. Later, in America, Arendt was less skeptical about intellectuals, but her pariah standards remained the same. She could say in 1948 that "social non-conformism as such has been and always will be the mark of intellectuals. . . . intellectually, non-conformism is almost the *sine qua non* of achievement."[5]

In the spring of 1940, as Hitler's army approached Paris, the "enemy aliens" in Paris were ordered to report for transport to the French-run internment camps in the south of France. Hannah Arendt reported to a sports palladium, the Velodrome d'Hiver, where she stayed for a week before being transported by rail to Gurs, a camp that had been built for refugees from the Spanish Civil War. After the occupation of Paris, there was a brief period of administrative confusion in Gurs, and the women interned there were presented with a dreadful choice: to escape from the camp with, as Arendt put it, "nothing but a toothbrush," or to stay and hope for the best. "After a few days of chaos, everything became regular again and escape was almost impossible."[6] Many of those who chose what they thought was the safer alternative were shipped, after three horrible years, to Auschwitz, where they were killed. Arendt secured liberation papers and left the camp. She was more fortunate than most of the escapees, for she had a place to go—a house rented by non-Jewish friends near Montauban—and she was able to rejoin her husband, Heinrich Blücher, who had also escaped from a camp. After six months of living here and there in southern France, the Blüchers were able to secure visas for themselves and for Arendt's mother to go to America. They left France as quickly as possible; those who waited longer fared less well. Repeatedly, during her last year in Europe, Hannah Arendt learned a lesson she was never to forget: when a choice between uncertain freedom and the precarious security of unfreedom comes, when a "unique chance" for action presents itself, hesitation can be fatal.

During the war years in New York, the Blüchers' acquaintances consisted largely of German Jewish refugees—that is, of people with whom German could be spoken. Arendt knew that she had to acquire English, and she endured a period with an

American family in Connecticut to that end, but she was in no rush to assimilate. In a caustic, ironic article, written in a style that presaged the controversial style of her later *Eichmann in Jerusalem*, she sounded the theme which had given her strength since her childhood and which became one of the mainstays of her political theory: to reject the identity you are born with, the identity which your natality bestows upon you, is to reject the possibility of a dignified existence.

> Man is a social animal and life is not easy for him when social ties are cut off. Moral standards are much easier kept in the texture of a society. Very few individuals have the strength to conserve their own integrity if their social, political and legal status is completely confused. Lacking the courage to fight for a change of our social and legal status, we have decided instead, so many of us, to try a change of identity. And this curious behavior makes matters much worse. The confusion in which we live is partly our own work. . . . It is true that most of us depend entirely on social standards; we lose confidence in ourselves if society does not approve us; we are—and always were—ready to pay any price in order to be accepted by society. But it is equally true that the very few among us who have tried to get along without all these tricks and jokes of adjustment and assimilation have paid a much higher price than they could afford: they jeopardized the few chances even outlaws have in a topsy-turvy world.
>
> All vaunted Jewish qualities—the "Jewish heart," humanity, humor, disinterested intelligence—are pariah qualities. All Jewish shortcomings—tactlessness, political stupidity, inferiority complexes and money-grubbing—are characteristics of upstarts [or parvenus]. . . .
>
> [The pariahs] have one priceless advantage: history is no longer a closed book to them, and politics is no longer the privilege of Gentiles. . . .[7]

During the war years, Arendt was first and foremost a Jew; and she understood her tasks as a Jew to be: to speak to the European emigrant Jews about Jewish identity, to urge the creation of a Jewish army to fight against Hitler's army, and to call for the founding of a bi-national Arab-Jewish state in Palestine. She called upon the Jews to resist new forms of the old assimilationist *mentalité,* to resist Hitler militarily, and to forego the temptation of forming a state that would make another group of people, the Palestinian Arabs, into refugees. All that she hoped for failed to materialize. In her opinion, the population of Jewish parvenus increased; she saw no Jewish army, only isolated resistance groups and Jewish brigades of Allied armies; and she watched what she considered a reversion to nineteenth-century nationalism as the State of Israel was founded as a Jewish state. The book of history was not opened to the Jews as she hoped it would be.

After the war, Hannah Arendt made an enormous effort to open the book of modern European history to the Jews and to all who would learn from their suffering, and she called the result of this effort *The Origins of Totalitarianism.* This book, like all of Arendt's work in the 1940s, was an act of resistance. "I felt as though I dealt with a crystallized structure which I had to break up into its constituent elements in order to destroy it. This image bothered me a great deal, for I thought it an impossible task to write history not in order to save and conserve and render fit for remembrance, but, on the contrary, to destroy."[8] Arendt's aim, as she described it, is reflected in the passionate, relentless tone of the book, which bothered many critics at the time of its 1951 publication, and which bothered many more later critics of the "revisionist" sort who felt that the book had contributed to the Cold War brand of American anti-totalitarianism. And it is true that Arendt's book, along with *Totalitarian Dictatorship and Autocracy* by Carl Friedrich and Zbigniew Brzezinski, "went far toward shaping lay and academic understandings of totalitarianism in the 1950s."[9] The book provided fuel for the Cold Warriors, but it also provided a call to resistance for those who feared not just the excessive anti-Communist attitude of McCarthy, but his tactics. For example, the founders of the National Committee for an Effective Congress, the spearhead of the 1953 anti-McCarthy lobby, saw in Arendt's analysis of Stalin's totalitarian regime an analysis of McCarthyism.

The feature of *The Origins of Totalitarianism* that particularly excited "revisionist" criticism in the 1960s—other than its tone—was its claim that the Nazi and the Soviet forms of totalitarian government were basically the same. Critics argued that Arendt had developed her "unitotalitarianism" thesis by analogically extending her analysis of the Nazi regime to the less well known, less fully documented Soviet regime. More recent studies of Soviet history have revealed inadequacies in her treatment of Stalin's regime, and particularly of that government's social and economic policies. But most of the revisionist critics have missed the specifically political dimension of Arendt's claim: she was concerned with the similarity of the *form of government* in Nazi Germany and Bolshevist Russia; she did not claim that the forms had come into being in the same way, on the basis of the same ideologies or policies, in the two countries. One of Arendt's great contributions to political theory was her revival of the traditional discussions—from Plato to Montesquieu—of forms of government and her attempt to add to the traditional types a new, an unprecedented type—totalitarianism.

Shortly after the 1951 publication of *The Origins of Totalitarianism,* Arendt applied to the Guggenheim Foundation for a grant to support her next project: a study of the Marxist elements of totalitarianism. This book was to address the imbalance in *The Origins of Totalitarianism,* to fill out the analysis of Soviet totalitarianism, and also to take up the differences that she perceived between the Nazi and Soviet ideologies: the Nazis' racism was not, she felt, connected to the "Great Tradition" of European thought, but the Soviets' Marxism was—for Marx was still a part of this "Great Tradition." Arendt spent a year in Europe working on her Marxism study, but her research led her to reformulate her task. It became clear to her that throughout the "Great Tradition" of European thought there were modes of conceiving the activities of what she called the *vita activa* that reflected a blindness to the political realm, to what is specifically political—action and speech. Arendt found much more important and much more amenable to her creative spirit the possibility of writing a non-destructive history, of writing a book that would "render fit for remembrance" the capacities she had come to understand as the only ones on which men of the problematic modern age can place any hope—action and speech. Instead of the proposed study of the Marxist elements of totalitarianism, she wrote the essays contained in *Between Past and Future* and then *The Human Condition*, and she planned another book, *Introduction to Politics*. This last was never written. Its program called for more than Hannah Arendt could produce. It called for the consideration of thinking, willing, and judging to which Arendt turned her attention in the last years of her life and about which she began to write in an unfinished work called *The Life of the Mind*.

In the 1950s, despite the tumult of the McCarthy era, despite the continuation of the Cold War and the ominous development of nuclear arsenals and space programs, and despite numerous unexpected outbreaks of history, Hannah Arendt's anguished need to destroy the "crystallized structure" of the past abated. And one unexpected outbreak of history gave her grounds to hope that her concern for man's political capacities would not prove a dreamer's concern. She added to the 1958 edition of *The Origins of Totalitarianism* an epilogue in which she discussed this unexpected outbreak, the Hungarian Revolution of 1956.

There is in this chapter a certain hopefulness—surrounded, to be sure, with many qualifications—which is hard to reconcile with the assumption of [the last section of *The Origins of Totalitarianism*] that the *only* clear expression of the present

age's problems up to date has been the horror of totalitarianism. . . . [The Hungarian Revolution] has brought forth
once more a government which, it is true, was never really
tried out, but which can hardly be called new because it has
appeared with singular regularity for more than a hundred
years in all revolutions. I am speaking of the council-system,
the Russian soviets, which were abolished in the initial stages
of the October Revolution, and of the central European Räte,
which first had to be liquidated in Germany and Austria before
[those countries'] insecure party democracies could be established. . . . While not unaware of the role which the council
system had played in all revolutions since 1848, I had no hope
for its re-emergence. . . . The Hungarian Revolution had
taught me a lesson.[10]

What the Hungarian Revolution suggested to Hannah Arendt was
that the problems of the age—the rise of mass societies, technological changes of unprecedented sorts, and the breakdown of the
nation-state—could lead to two different sorts of forms of government: totalitarianism or the council system. She put all of her hope
on the council system, which is to say that she put all of her hope
on the human capacity to act, to begin something new, to open, as
she put it, "a political space."

Readers of *The Human Condition*, Hannah Arendt's study of
labor, work, and action, the modes of the *vita activa*, have been
troubled by her notion of action. All hope rests with this capacity,
and yet Arendt gives no specific modern examples of it and no
specific program for action—indeed, she lifts action right out of
the means-ends categories she finds appropriate only for work.
Even more troubling, she removes action from the sphere of what
she calls "the social" and also from the scope of moral judgments.
To anyone whose primary concern is with socio-economic
reordering or with religious or moral renewal, such removals may
seem completely impractical and reactionary—"Burkean Toryism,"
as one reviewer put it—or dangerously relativistic. These two
reactions, if taken seriously—as they should be—and taken in

conjunction, will perhaps bring into relief the challenge of Arendt's thought.

To moralists, passages in *The Human Condition* like the following were startling:

> Unlike human behavior—which the Greeks, like all civilized people, judged according to "moral standards," taking into account motives and intentions on the one hand and aims and consequences on the other—action can be judged only by the criterion of greatness because it is in its nature to break through the commonly accepted and reach into the extraordinary, where whatever is true in common and everyday life no longer applies because everything that exists is unique and *sui generis*.[11]

The procedure of moral judgment, subsumption of a particular case under a general rule, is inappropriate for action. Each action must be judged on its own, in its uniqueness, without reference to an external standard or measurement. As Arendt commented in a footnote to this passage, Aristotle said in the *Poetics* that action in a drama, which imitates actions in life, should be judged by its greatness, by its distinction from the commonplace, as beauty, also, is to be judged. Arendt thought that a deep tie exists between esthetic judgment or taste and the judgment appropriate to action, and "Judging," the third part of her unfinished work, *The Life of the Mind*, was intended as an exploration of this deep tie.

We do not, unfortunately, have this exploration, but the sort of experiences that propelled Arendt to think in this direction, that led her to follow suggestions from Aristotle and from Kant's *Critique of Judgment*, are recorded in several essays. One of these, written after she attended the trial of Adolf Eichmann in Jerusalem, was called "Personal Responsibility under Dictatorship." In it she considered those Germans who were able to live in Hitler's Germany without collaborating or participating in public life, even though they could not rise in rebellion against the regime. And she implicitly extended her concept of the pariah into a concept of the nature of good judgment.

> The non-participants, called irresponsible by the majority, were the only ones who were able to judge by themselves, and they were capable of doing so not because they [had] a better system of values or because the old standards of right and wrong were still firmly planted in their mind and conscience but, I would suggest, because their conscience did not function in [an] as it were automatic way—as though we [had] a set of learned or innate rules which we then apply to the particular case as it arises. . . . Their criterion, I think, was a different one: they asked themselves to what extent they would still be able to live in peace with themselves after having committed certain deeds. . . . The presupposition for this kind of judging is not a highly developed intelligence or sophistication in moral matters, but merely the habit of living together explicitly with oneself, that is, of being engaged in that silent dialogue between me and myself which since Socrates and Plato we usually call thinking. . . . The total moral collapse of respectable society during the Hitler regime may teach us that those who are reliable in such circumstances are not those who cherish values and hold fast to moral norms and standards. . . . Much more reliable will be the doubters and sceptics, not because scepticism is good or doubting wholesome, but because [these people] are used to [examining things and making up their own minds]. Best of all will be those who know that, whatever else happens, as long as we live we are condemned to live together with ourselves. . . .[12]

Hannah Arendt's admiration for those who can, rising above moral standards, judge for themselves is everywhere apparent in *Eichmann in Jerusalem,* which was published in the spring of 1963 and quickly became a *cause célèbre.* In this book she described

Adolf Eichmann as a banal man: his evil was banal, she claimed, because it arose not from some unfathomable or psychopathological depths but from thoughtlessness, from the complete absence of the "habit of living together explicitly with oneself." To Hannah Arendt, "banal" meant "commonplace" (which, let it be noted, is not the same as "commonly occurring"—she did not think that Eichmann was Everyman) and "commonplace" was the opposite, in her terms, of greatness.

This banal man was a typical parvenu—in Arendt's terms the very opposite of a pariah. Eichmann initiated nothing new; he did what he was told to do by those whose approval he wanted, and obeyed the law of the land in doing so. He behaved; he did not act. "He did not need to 'close his ears to the voice of conscience,' as the judgment had it, not because he had none, but because his conscience spoke with a 'respectable voice,' with the voice of respectable society around him."[13] By the prevailing "moral standards" of Hitler's Germany, he behaved well; by the moral and legal standards prevailing when and where he was tried, he behaved abominably, and deserved to be punished as a man who was responsible for his deeds.

Arendt's portrait of a non-demonic, thoughtless Eichmann outraged many, and her portrait of the leaders of the Jewish councils who collaborated with the Nazis after 1941 during the "Final Solution" outraged many more. She claimed that for those Jewish leaders and members of Jewish police forces who knew what was in store for the Jews they registered and rounded up: "There was no possibility of resistance, yet there existed the possibility of *doing nothing*. And in order to do nothing one did not have to be a saint, one needed only to say: I am just a simple Jew, and I have no desire to play any other role. . . . These people still had a certain limited degree of freedom and of action. Just as the SS members, as we now know, had a limited choice of alternatives. . . ."[14] Arendt never called for resistance when resistance was clearly impossible; she spoke of the possibility of non-participation and of not denying one's birth-given identity. And, addressing her contemporaries, she spoke against a tendency to treat "such matters as though there existed a law of human nature compelling everyone to lose his dignity in the face of disaster. . . ."[15]

Judgments that touch on matters so agonizing to remember —matters of life and death, of dignity and lack of dignity—are of the utmost difficulty. Hannah Arendt's judgments on the matter of Jewish collaboration with the Nazis were not only difficult, many felt, but "heartless." What makes her judgments seem "heartless" is the criterion—never made explicit—by which they were made, namely, "greatness." She contrasted what she took to be the heart's mode of relation to men—pity—with solidarity, and she rejected pity in favor of solidarity: ". . . because it partakes of reason, and hence of generality, it is able to comprehend a multitude conceptually, not only the multitude of a class or a nation or a people, but eventually all mankind. . . . Compared with the sentiment of pity, it may appear cold and abstract, for it remains committed to 'ideas'—to greatness, or honor, or dignity—rather than to any 'love' of men. . . . Solidarity is a principle that can guide and inspire action. . . ."[16]

No respect would be paid to Hannah Arendt's hope for action or her attempt to understand judgment if the questions they pose were not raised. One can ask of one's self the extraordinary, but can one ask of another, in the present tense or in reflection on the past, the extraordinary? One can say, "Here I stand, I can do no other," but can one say, "Stand here, you can do no other"? Can one person say, under any circumstances, disastrous or not, what the extraordinary should be? Does this criterion, "greatness," allow for any specification? Surely the deeds which allow one thoughtful man to live explicitly together with himself will not always be the same as those that allow another man to do the same. Each man's actions are, as she put it, "ontologically rooted" in the conditions of natality, but each man's birth-given identity is his own. One may say, "I am just a simple Jew, and I have no desire to play any other role," but each simple Jew is an individual.

On the very grounds on which Hannah Arendt challenged traditional morality, she is challengeable—that is, insofar as she judged, implicitly or explicitly, as though greatness were a rule, a standard by which to measure particular cases. But, on the other hand, if her challenge is abstracted from the realm of what individual Jewish leaders, facing dreadful dilemmas, did and did not do, it carries a message of political importance.

In the funeral oration that Thucydides attributed to Pericles, praising those who had fallen in battle against the Spartans, the Athenian statesman charged his people: "It is for you to try to be like them. Make up your minds that happiness depends on being free, and freedom depends on being courageous. . . . . . . Any intelligent man would find a humiliation caused by his own slackness more painful to bear than death, when death comes to him unexpectedly in battle, and in the confidence of his patriotism." Judgments that do not appeal to a general rule can appeal only to deeds called exemplary by general agreement. What is presumed—and was presumed by Pericles—is a community, a solidarity of the like-minded. Each, confident in his fellowship in the community, will follow the community's exemplary figures to the best of his abilities. Calls to greatness made in a community context, and particularly those made when the community is threatened as a community, do not shock us—indeed, we call them "great." Hannah Arendt's criterion, greatness or dignity, was posed to a community—the community of mankind, a multitude greater than any class or nation or people. If there was general agreement among the members of this community about the criterion "greatness" (as she, perhaps naively, assumed), her hope for mankind rather than her lack of pity would have been recognized.

Hannah Arendt wrote *Eichmann in Jerusalem* when her hope for action, and for the council system, was at its apogee. She did not write as, so to speak, a belligerent, trying, as she did in *The Origins of Totalitarianism,* to destroy the "crystallized structure" of totalitarianism. She strove for the impartiality she so much admired in Homer, Herodotus, and Thucydides. She strove to relate how the collapse of respectable society in Nazi Germany affected all who had tied their lives to it—persecutors and victims.

She strove to tell the best and the worst men are capable of when such a collapse has occurred, to face the facts without flinching or waxing sentimental. The ironic tone of her book is shocking, just as the ironic tone of Thucydides' book is, after centuries, still shocking. The books are not comparable in artistry, but Arendt did amass her information, weave her statistics, observations, opinions, stories, and witnesses' accounts together with a reckless fervor comparable to that which is palpable on every page of Thucydides' history. For many of those who lived through the events Arendt told, her ironic speech was pure pain. But her book is a *ktema es aei*, a possession for all times; it tells the story of a "disturbance," as Thucydides said, "affecting all mankind"—though hers does so, as she constantly reiterated, because what she wrote about was a "crime *against humanity*."

When generations other than hers, or perhaps even ours, have corrected the book's factual errors and gained the distance that comes not only as an effort of the intelligence but as a gift from time, the message of her book may be clearer. It is very difficult for us not to feel as the ancients felt about Thucydides' history, that, in the words of Dionysius of Halicarnassus, "he wrote about a war which was neither glorious nor fortunate—one which, best of all, should never have happened, or [failing that] should have been ignored by posterity and consigned to silence and oblivion."

Simone Weil said of Homer's *Iliad* that its true central character was Force—the Force that reduced Greeks and Trojans alike to less than their human stature. The true central character of *Eichmann in Jerusalem* is not Adolf Eichmann, nor his victims, but the Force of individual human thoughtlessness and lack of judgment, which totalitarian regimes, more quickly than any other sort, are able to mold and which is capable of "laying waste the earth."

Hannah Arendt's hope for action, and for the council system, was tied to an exemplary historical occurrence—the very city which Pericles addressed. She argued, in *The Human Condition*, that: "One, if not the chief reason for the incredible development of gift and genius in Athens, as well as for the hardly less swift decline of the city-state, was precisely that from beginning to end its foremost aim was to make the extraordinary an ordinary occurrence of everyday life."[17]

Hannah Arendt hoped that the council system would provide modern men with what the city-state had provided the Greeks—a space for action, an opportunity for the extraordinary. But she knew that the council systems that have existed, that have appeared in the course of revolutions, have been notoriously short-lived, and she also knew that they have arisen *spontaneously*. She knew these things, and she wrote *On Revolution* to ask how the legacy of revolutions, the council systems, could be preserved, how the "swift decline" that has characterized the council systems could be forestalled.

On Revolution offers a comparative study of revolutions, and particularly of the French and American revolutions. It is rapturous in its praise of the American Revolution as a political revolution, a revolution that culminated in a duly constituted republican form of government, as it is severe in its criticism of any call for a social revolution that neglects the key action of revolutions, constitution-making. She tried to understand why the men of the French Revolution did not appeal to the American political achievement, but only to the pre-revolutionary American social condition that Jefferson called "the lovely equality the poor enjoy with the rich." She suggested that concern with "the Social Question," the problem of poverty, diverted them from the goal of founding political freedom—the very weight of the misery they confronted was overwhelming. What troubled her was that during the subsequent century, "It was the French and not the American Revolution that set the world on fire . . ."[18] And it was the problem of poverty and not the problem of forming a government which set European theoretical discussions on fire.

Arendt set her schematic contrast of social and political revolutions in the context of her concern with how little Americans themselves remember of the story of their republic's founding and with how uncomprehending American governments have been of revolutions, particularly in the post–Second World War world— "Fear of revolution has been the hidden *leitmotif* of post-war American foreign policy." Her task was to retell the American story, to render it fit for remembrance, and to warn that: "In the contest that divides the world today and in which so much is at stake, those will probably win who understand revolution. . . . And such understanding can neither be countered nor replaced with an expertness in counter-revolution. . . ."[19]

This context was not troubling to readers whose primary concern was for "social justice," and neither was Arendt's praise of the council system at the end of the book. But Arendt's distinction between social and political revolutions most certainly was. The book was greeted with amazement by most of its reviewers. The socialist Michael Harrington, for a typical example, could not understand how such a conservative and such a radical could coexist in one person, so he concluded that there must be "two Arendts."

Harrington's assessment points to the central political challenge of Arendt's thought. Since the French Revolution, Right and Left, reactionary and progressive, conservative and liberal, have been standard oppositions. Arendt, because she did not accept these oppositions, because she did not embrace one alternative and attack the other but insisted on her own way, her *Selbstdenken,* has bewildered adherents of both sides. She was, as a thinker, a pariah—and she never wanted to give up her pariahdom to become a parvenu. Her reaction to the supposedly opposite alternatives of socialism and capitalism is characteristic of her stance:

All our experiences—as distinguished from theories and ide-ologies—tell us that the process of expropriation, which started with the rise of capitalism, does not stop with the expropriation of the means of production; only legal and political institutions that are independent of the economic forces and their automatism can control and check the inherently monstrous possibilities of this process. . . . What protects freedom is the division between governmental and economic power, or, to put it in Marxian language, the fact that the state and its constitution are not superstructures.[20]

Brecht's ironic imperative "first bread, then ethics" is recognizably of the genre we call *épater le bourgeois*. "First politics, then socioeconomic matters"—which at first glance seems to be Hannah Arendt's imperative—is less easy to classify. Is it not heartless to place the "public happiness" of acting and speaking, or participating in politics, before the needs of the hungry, the economically and socially unenfranchised? Is not an opposition of the social and the political just as simplistic as the oppositions Arendt rejected?

Hannah Arendt did not call for "politics first, then socioeconomic matters," for she knew very well that only those who have been liberated from dignity-destroying worry about how to put food on their tables or clothe themselves are free to participate in politics. In her terms, liberation *precedes* revolution, which is constitution-making, a people's action of constituting a government, of instituting a balance of powers. Her point was that: "While it is true that freedom can come only to those whose needs have been fulfilled, it is equally true that it will escape those who are bent upon living for their desires."[21] She distinguished between the slogan of liberation from poverty—"to each according to his needs"—and the slogan she thought she read above the door of failed revolutions—"to each according to his desires." Her distinction is, surely, right, for it is obvious that a limitless quest for abundance can lay waste the earth, destroy what Arendt called "the world," the sum of relatively permanent artifacts, and subserve the human capacities for action and speech to its exigencies. In short, Hannah Arendt did not want revolutionaries to become parvenus. But in her ardent concern for the political, for action and speech, for "public happiness," she left unanswered two crucial questions: What, exactly, are the *needs* of each, and *how* shall the injunction "to each according to his needs" be followed? What she hoped for was a solution to the problem of poverty "through technical means," through a "rational, non-ideological economic development." What this might be, she did not say. Her assumption was that technology can be "politically neutral"—a very problematic assumption. However, her hope is clear: she wanted a solution to the problem of poverty that did not, does not, dictate a form of government.

One of the grave weaknesses of *On Revolution* is that the two questions posed—What are men's basic economic needs? and, *How* shall these be met?—are neither raised nor answered. Its strength is that it highlights how basic the need to appear in public (to discuss, to debate, to act) is to men; it gives the examples of human speech and action that *The Human Condition* lacked. And it presents to those who think of conservation and revolution as opposites a powerful image of revolutionary conservatism, of the American Founding Fathers' concern for a new political science, one utilizing the traditional discussions of forms of government, with which to forge, in John Adams' phrase, "institutions that last for many generations." Hannah Arendt's mother's daughter addressed our worn-out political categories in the manner of Hannah Arendt's mother's idol—Rosa Luxemburg —who was a pariah among the socialists and Marxists of her time because she called for people's councils and for the founding of a republic.

Since Plato proposed that the ideal city-state should be a man writ large, there have been in the "Great Tradition" many ways in which model communities have been used to picture what man might become in the future or what he has been in the long-forgotten past. What emerges from Hannah Arendt's reflections on man's thinking and judging and on action is an analogy that is—to borrow the title of one of her books—"between past and future." It is an analogy that is not tied to a hierarchical ideal or standard, but must vary from particular instance to particular instance. The checks and balances existing within an individual, who "lives together explicitly with himself" and can thus judge for himself, are rooted in his natality, as is his capacity for action, for freedom. Of the plurality within us—the me and myself—and the autonomy of the human faculties, we can constitute a free self. The checks and balances existing within a community, which allow men to live freely with each other, are rooted in its natality, as is the community's capacity for action, for freedom. Of a plurality of autonomous individuals, a free republic can be constituted. When an individual forgets or denies his original uniqueness, his newness by virtue of being born, he forecloses the possibility of independent judgment and action—of greatness. When the people of a community forget or deny the community's origins, the impulse for freedom that brought the people together in action, they foreclose the possibility of further action—of greatness. The Greek poet Pindar's maxim holds both for men as individuals and for free communities: "Become what you are."

NOTES

1. Letter to Blumenfeld, 31 March 1959. "Not for my mother's daughter. I am writing about revolution, namely, about revolution in general. That here! It's really something out of a macabre comedy."

2. Letter to McCarthy, 16 October 1973.

3. Adelbert Reif, ed., *Gespräche mit Hannah Arendt* (Munich: Piper & Co., 1976), p. 17.

4. Ibid., p. 20.

5. From an unpublished manuscript (on which Arendt noted "Lecture—Rand School—1948 or 49") in the Library of Congress Arendt Collection.

6. Letter in response to Bruno Bettelheim, *Midstream* (Summer 1962), p. 87.

7. Hannah Arendt, "We Refugees," *The Menorah Journal*, Vol. XXXI (January 1943), pp. 69–77.

8. Hannah Arendt, "Totalitarianism," *The Meridian*, Vol. II, no. 2 (Fall 1958), p. 1.

9. Robert Burrowes, "Totalitarianism: The Revised Standard Version," *World Politics*. Vol. XXI, no. 2 (January 1969), p. 272.

10. Arendt, "Totalitarianism," p. 1.

11. Hannah Arendt, *The Human Condition* (Chicago: University of Chicago Press, 1958), p. 205.

12. Hannah Arendt, "Personal Responsibility Under Dictatorship," *The Listener* (August 6, 1964), pp. 187 205.

13. Hannah Arendt. *Eichmann in Jerusalem: A Report on the Banality of Evil* (New York: The Viking Press, 1965), p. 126.

14. Arendt, "Personal Responsibility Under Dictatorship," p. 207.

15. Arendt, *Eichmann in Jerusalem*, p. 131.

16. Hannah Arendt, *On Revolution* (New York: The Viking Press, 1965), p. 84.

17. Arendt, *The Human Condition*, p. 197.

18. Arendt, *On Revolution*, p. 49.

19. Ibid., p. 219.

20. Hannah Arendt, "Thoughts on Politics and Revolution," *Crises of the Republic* (New York: Harcourt Brace Jovanovich, 1972), p. 212.

21. Arendt, *On Revolution*, p. 136.

Bernard Crick

ON REREADING
THE ORIGINS OF
TOTALITARIANISM[1]

*So many quibble at the word and so few will look at the
thing itself.*

To understand a concept, it is necessary to consider it in its
context; but to judge its usefulness for general theory is not simply
to reduce a concept to a particular context. *The Origins of
Totalitarianism* is, in many ways, Hannah Arendt's greatest
achievement, but the one most misunderstood. Margaret Canovan,
in a thoughtful introduction to Arendt's political ideas, recently
wrote that *The Origins*, although her first major political work, "is
also the one for which she is most widely known and has been both
highly praised and much criticised."[2]

The context is that she wrote it in 1949 and it was published
in 1951, exactly a year later in each case than George Orwell's
1984, a book written in much the same mood, also a warning not a
prophecy, but to which she oddly never refers in much-revised (indeed over-revised) later editions. The preface to the first edition
began: "Two World Wars in one generation, separated by an un-
interrupted chain of local wars and revolutions, followed by no
peace treaty for the vanquished and no respite for the victor, have
ended in the anticipation of a third World War between the two
remaining world powers."[3] And to force herself and her readers to
see that she was writing with relevance for humanity and not pro-

fessionally for political scientists, she put as a legend over all a quotation from her old Heidelberg teacher, Karl Jaspers: "Weder dem Vergangenen anheim fallen noch dem Zukünftigen. Es kommt darauf an, ganz gegenwärtig zu sein." ("To give in neither to the past nor to the future. What matters is to be entirely present.")

However, it is as crude as it is stupid, therefore, to treat the origins of the whole concept as either wartime propaganda or as a device of the Cold War—as does, for instance, the entry under "Totalitarianism" written by Herbert J. Spiro in the *International Encyclopedia of the Social Sciences* (1968):

> The word, which first gained currency through anti-Nazi propaganda during World War II, later became an anti-Communist slogan in the cold war. Its utility for propaganda purposes has tended to obscure whatever utility it may have had for systematic analysis. . . . As the social sciences develop more discriminating concepts of comparison . . . and as, hopefully, the more glaring differences between the major parties to the cold war begin to wither away, use of the term "totalitarianism" may also become less frequent. If these expectations are borne out, then a third encyclopedia of the social sciences, like the first one, will not list "totalitarianism."

It is an almost Orwellian thought that the offensive word will simply be removed from the vocabulary of a political science of such dubious predictive value. But what is intellectually disreputable is that Spiro can ignore the evidence, either because it does not suit his thesis or possibly simply through ignorance, that the term was current before the Second World War. From about 1936, very much a product of the behavior of the Communist Party in the Spanish Civil War, several well-known, or to become well-known, political writers or literary intellectuals began to take over Mussolini's unrealistic and bombastic term, if applied to Italian fascism, and to apply it to something that they saw independently of each other and at first found hard to believe. They saw with unwelcome horror that there were astonishing similarities between the style, the structure of thought, and the key institutions of the Nazis and the Russian Communists. Borkenau, Gide, Koestler, Malraux, Orwell, and Silone all saw this.[4] Even some political scientists began to discuss it heavily, earnestly, and professionally.[5] The concept used in this sense was, certainly, that of a minority, but they made it a commonplace nonetheless, long before the Cold War. Some people, however, still do not want to face the past. I am sure that Arendt would have liked what Orwell wrote in an introduction to *Animal Farm* which he never used: "Liberty is telling people what they do not want to hear."[6] Or else people think that totalitarianism was not an assault on humanity that failed, but is simply a concept with which professional games of classification can be played. Since so many political scientists have used or "defined" it so idiosyncratically and often overschematically, it can be declared meaningless. Political science will then, like economics presumably, confine itself to concepts that can be defined precisely and used to build quantifiable models, thus escaping from the mess of the real world.[7]

A Peculiar Explanation

To begin in such a way is, of course, partly defensive. For I think Arendt was a great thinker although she certainly never wrote in a way either familiar to or pleasing to social scientists— much the same as Orwell, even though he was on a lower philosophical plane and far closer to immediate practice than she. He was saved from banality by not having gone to university; and she was saved from the internalizing routines of the social scientists by writing her great book on her own, coming into the university only when already mature, famous, and independent. On the other hand, she herself was either less than generous or not perceptive about the prewar fashioners of the concept. In fact, she spent no time in the first edition justifying the term at all. She simply accepted its existence, both as a worthwhile concept and as a phenomenon of our times, and got down straight away to her peculiar explanation of its origins. She did not make the claim to be the first to use the concept analytically, even if perhaps one may infer such a claim from her ignoring literary progenitors. For otherwise she used literary sources well when she wished to establish the *plausibility* of the concept. Only in the second and later editions did she become self-conscious about the concept, responding both to criticism of the whole concept and to a sudden plethora of rival characterizations and models.[8] But she could never believe that scholars living in freedom could be so insensitive as to claim that something historically unique and world-shaking had not been attempted.

I said "her peculiar *explanation*" of its origins. Strictly speaking, there is no explanation of the origins of totalitarianism. Indeed, she did not believe from her general philosophical position that there could be any unique and necessary line of development toward what occurred. This is where the "model-builders," with their pretense at causality, go astray in reading her, or rather with their very abstracted notion of causality. Things occur because of antecedent "causes"—events, conditions, and beliefs—but they need not occur. To find the causes of a phenomenon is not, strictly speaking, to explain it but simply to understand it better. Above all, it is to understand why a secular ambition to transform society totally became plausible. Became plausible, that is, to bands of resolute, determined, and yet to a large extent lucky fanatics and adventurers ("armed bohemians," she said once) when conditions were ripe; and conditions were ripe not in terms of these men preparing for, still less making, the revolution, but in terms of the breakdown of the previous social order. The breakdown, she argued, was of something far more fundamental than any one form of social order. The breakdown was of all settled expectations, of any possibility of ordinary people seeing the world as reasonable and predictable.

So with Arendt, it is necessary to distinguish sharply between her account of the growth of the ideology of Nazism and her account of the breakdown of traditional bourgeois values and expectations. There can be a true historical account of each of these, but it is only the ideologist himself who claims either that he (or even his opponents, getting trapped into accepting his concepts) caused the breakdown, or that he foretold its character and could always prove that when it came it would uniquely and necessarily benefit him. Strictly speaking, the two accounts have no logical connection. But what is to be explained, then, is not the necessary preconditions of the rise of Nazism and of Stalinism, respectively, but how these two groups ever picked up, long before they came to power or power came to them, the astonishing concept that they held "the key to history" and possessed a total and comprehensive explanation and prophecy of *everything*, not simply of political phenomena—what she calls simply "ideologies."[9]

This accounts for her seeming arbitrariness, both to the generalizing social scientist and to the nominalist historian, in moving from one event to another and one country to another, leaving her critics giddy and gasping that there is no connection between the Dreyfus Affair and the imperialism of Cecil Rhodes, or between either Britain and France and German Nazism, nor between racialist Pan-Slavism and Stalin. But that seems to her (though it would have helped to have said so more clearly) not the point. The point is simply (if such a word can be used of such a person—occasionally) to establish the existence and plausibility of ideologies (in her special sense).

In fact, her methodology is not at all unlike that of Tocqueville. In the first chapter of his *Souvenirs*, Tocqueville says that he detests equally those literary men remote from public affairs who produce vast, abstract, and all-embracing iron laws and first causes of human history and those politicians and men of affairs who believe that everything is, on the contrary, just a matter of pulling strings or of accident. He believes, he says, that both are equally mistaken. Nothing can happen without antecedent social conditions changing and giving an opportunity, but nothing actually happens without the actions of men; and many different sorts of actions and inactions can occur in changing social conditions, some better, some worse, some good, some evil, some successful and some unsuccessful—"although I firmly believe that chance does nothing that has not been prepared beforehand."[10] So she sets out the broad "causes" and *also* the particular conditions that led to the breakdown of traditional expectations of government in Germany, whether authoritarian or republican; but her main effort goes into demonstrating the intense if terrible plausibility of Nazism.

This explains the much criticized lopsidedness of the book: 300 pages on anti-Semitism and then imperialism (neither on the face of it very relevant to Stalin's communism) before 150 pages on totalitarianism, on the character and working of totalitarian society, which suddenly embrace both Russia and Germany. In the second edition, in the famous epilogue "Reflections on the Hungarian Revolution," she first admits hope that a totalitarian regime can, once established, be destroyed from within, not simply, as happened to Hitler, from without; and she first clearly links the short-lived workers' councils of Budapest to the soviets that Lenin first stirred up and then suppressed, to the Commune of Paris, to Proudhon rather than Marx as the great *social* theorist, and to the historical fame and some of the actual practices of fifth-century Athens—themes to become very important, the anarchist twist to her conservatism (a marriage, as it were, of Tocqueville and Prudhomme), in *The Human Condition* and in *On Revolution*. She concentrates on Germany surely because, though without sufficient explanation, few people would then, perhaps even now, concede that the Nazis had a full-blown ideology, irrational in its power to comprehend the real world but rational in terms of a broad internal consistency. For two arguments are going on in parallel. Many who deny that the Nazis ever had an ideology or that it was important, such as A. J. P. Taylor in his accounts of the origins of the Second World War on Bertolt Brecht caricaturing Hitler as a mere gangster in politics, cheerfully concede or firmly claim that communism is an ideology—in something very close to Arendt's sense of "a key to history."[11] This Arendt has to refute, but not merely in terms of showing the origins of Nazism but of showing how a racialism with exterminatory inferences (beyond *mere* racial prejudice, like *mere* anti-Semitism) could emerge even in a relatively benign imperialism, like the British, the French, or the Belgian. See what can happen, she is saying, in unprecedented and dehumanizing circumstances; she is talking about a new kind of human imagination, as when Cecil Rhodes "dreamed in centuries and thought in continents" and "would annex the planets if I could";[12] or as when ordinary Frenchmen during the Dreyfus Affair became convinced that there was an international Jewish conspiracy aimed both at the Church and at the safety of the Republic.

Arendt certainly knew more about Germany than about Russia. But this does not explain the strategy of the book. The first point for her to settle was that the Nazis had such an ideology and that it had precedents elsewhere. Only then could the parallel argument be developed, that the Russian Communist ideology once in power (and it needs less or no explanation of what it is) behaved remarkably similarly in its mode of government to that of the Nazis. Certainly when compared to any previous "mere" autocratic regimes or military dictatorships, they had, as the times had, much in common. And she never said anything as foolish as that they were the same way, as death on the road can be by different kinds of vehicles, not necessarily by the same kind. However, the modern age was not simply characterized by technology, by new instruments of power; it was characterized by a new mode of thought, a new way of perceiving things, which she called ideological.

If the book does seem unbalanced in the space it gives to Germany, perhaps this is a fault, but to see it as a gross fault would be to misconceive the whole purpose and strategy of the book. It would be rather like, having been able to grasp that Tocqueville's *Democracy in America* is really meant to be about the whole of Western European civilizations, to then say that he should have given equal and explicit space to France and to England. He assumed that his readers knew more about them already, whereas America was both unfamiliar and represented a projection of the European future. But the second volume is completely generalized, about democracy in general or, rather, about the general character of the social effects of holding a democratic doctrine—like the last section of Arendt's *Origins*.

Ideological Superstition

In other words, Arendt is the most rational of the revolt-against-reason theorists. Small wonder that those who still cannot grasp the enormity of the events, the scale and the utter economic irrationality both of the camps and of the purges, either accuse her of making abstract models or, as a leading British political philosopher says in his table talk, of "metaphysical free association." She does move from one thing to another, but she is not trying either to write a complete history or to give a complete causal explanation of why Nazism and Stalinism arose precisely in the form they did (that she would hold, in light of her views on freedom and on action, to be anyway impossible). She is rather a historical sociologist, trying to show why certain crazy ideas could become plausible. She deals in the rationality of the irrational, something that empiricists are often ill-equipped (both frightened and incompetent) to touch.

While the totalitarian regimes are thus resolutely and cynically emptying the world of the only thing that makes sense to the utilitarian expectations of common sense, they impose upon it at the same time a kind of supersense which the ideologies actually always meant when they pretended to have found the key to history or the solution to the riddles of the universe. Over and above the senselessness of totalitarian society is enthroned the ridiculous supersense of its ideological superstition. Ideologies are harmless, uncritical and arbitrary opinions only as long as they are not believed in seriously. Once their claim to total validity is taken literally they become the nuclei of logical systems in which, as in the systems of paranoiacs, everything follows comprehensibly and even compulsorily once the first premise is accepted. The insanity of such systems lies not only in their first premise but in the very logicality with which they are constructed. The curious logicality of all isms, their simpleminded trust in the salvation value of stubborn devotion without regard for specific, varying factors, already harbors the first germs of totalitarian contempt for reality and factuality.[13]

Again like Tocqueville and Hegel, she starts from the shattering effect of the French Revolution. Even amid injustice, there was a clarity about social relationships in the old regime, she asserts. Once masses of people became detached from clear class allegiances, they became not class-conscious workers but rather classless and massified, open to superstitions, but now political superstitions more than religious, available for mobilization. Her famous distinction between the mentality of "the mob" and of "the masses" emerges: the "mob" the active and aggressive residue of classes, the ready followers of political adventurers; the "masses" inert and hopeless, until stirred in times of desperation.

The specific desperation that created the immediate conditions for ideologists to gain mass support was, Arendt argues, the experience of the First World War—mass slaughter—followed almost immediately by mass unemployment and inflation. She talks of war and mass unemployment as being like "two demons" who completely refuted and destroyed the rationality of liberal political and economic expectations.[14] The statelessness of so many people thrust out of nation-states seemed suddenly to create a condition even before the camps, but in some ways a foretaste of the camps, in which all "normal" human rights seemed to be removed from human beings if they were not securely citizens of a state. The man without a political homeland became a man without rights: the whole message and understanding of the Enlightenment reversed. Even within nation-states, men came to be declared not merely not-citizens but anti-citizens, corruptive of the society, if they were, in one instance, of the wrong social class and, in the other instance, of the wrong race.

For racialism as a principle of allegiance cut right through nations. It was no longer enough to be, as most Jews in Germany were before and during the First World War, "a good German": to be a citizen and to have rights one had to be an Aryan, or what the party said was an Aryan. And imperialism, in seeking "the expansion of political power without the foundation of a body politic," needed not merely a justification such as racialism (for "improvement" would doom the imperialists eventually to hand over or to share power) but also needed an excuse to treat mere subjects, seen as never fit for citizenship, as less than men. Precedents were set, as in the Congo and South Africa, as to what could be done when rulers were liberated from the normal constraints of politics. Arendt is almost obsessed to convince her readers that racialism is an authentic ideology, something to be taken seriously as an original and irreducible mental force, however factually wrong, however irrational. It cannot be reduced to economic circumstances, even though these can exacerbate it:

> an ideology differs from a simple opinion in that it claims to possess either the key to history, or the solution for all the "riddles of the universe," or the intimate knowledge of the hidden universal laws which are supposed to govern nature and man. Few ideologies have won enough prominence to survive the hard competitive struggle of persuasion, and only two have come out on top and essentially defeated all others: the ideology which interprets history as an economic struggle of classes, and the other that interprets history as an economic struggle of races.[15]

This is simple, but surely convincing. To call this kind of thing "ideology" need not be to deny that the word is well used in other contexts. This is not *the true* meaning of ideology.[16] But it is one possible meaning which cannot reasonably be denied and which functions, in many ways, like a secular religion.[17] Perhaps she is incautious in always talking about "ideology" as a comprehensive world view, seeking transformation, engendering terror out of its very irrationality and out of its hostility to the spontaneity and unpredictability of free human actions.[18] It may well be, as I have argued elsewhere, that the notion that ideas are products of circumstances (be circumstances conceived as biological or economic) dangerously inclines toward a contempt for human freedom, to a belief that justice can be obtained only by reforming circumstances by force rather than by reasoning and acting among men. But not everyone who speaks the language of causation in fact means what he says. Usually these causal statements of "necessity" and "determination" are scientific rhetoric for more conditional assertions: circumstances *condition* ideas, ideas are *not unaffected* by circumstances—relative statements and negative formulations can make the study of *how much* ideas are "products" of circumstances almost innocent of any totalitarian implications (while not making "ideology" so empty as to mean simply that all ideas about politics imply practice, as Martin Seliger has recently argued at length[19]).

However, Arendt is simply not concerned with the debate about usages of ideology. She is concerned simply to establish that ideologies, in her sense, have existed and have done uniquely terrible things. But done them by the opportunity of wielding power, not by any special prescience in knowing how to or ability in actually overthrowing conventional society.

An Element of Accident

Here we are close to the two great confusions in the whole debate about "totalitarianism." Accounts of how they came to power and of what they did when they were in power are often confused, and, as I have already argued, they are not logically related. And accounts of what they intended to do when in power and of what they actually did are often confused; or rather (where I find Arendt herself is confusing) their actions were not as systematic as the ideologies would lead us to suppose. Both Hitler and Stalin were selective, but grimly selective: not selective by the normal political mechanisms that engender compromise, but selective by fanatical pursuit of what they thought to be the most important parts of the ideology.[20] So to claim that there was, indeed that there ever could be, a fully and literally totalitarian system of government is to claim too much. But to use a theoretical or logical refutation of this rhetorical claim to deny the uniqueness of the two regimes, particularly the massive horror and uniqueness of the Nazi extermination camps and of Stalin's purges, this is to miss the point and to trivialize "the burden of our times" (which was the morally apt, if uninformative, title of the first English edition of *Origins*).

Let a historian prefer Bracher's, Bullock's, or even A. J. P. Taylor's account of how Hitler came to power to Arendt's. But this still does not meet her main point. What did Hitler do when he came to power? Hitler was (in part) a clever nationalist politician (*vide* Taylor), he was also (in part) a cunning demagogue who pursued a "tactic of legality," saying one thing to the party and another to the public (*vide* Bullock); but neither seems to give an adequate account either of what happened when Hitler came to power or of his motives.[21]

Strictly speaking, the historian is on firmer ground to claim that Arendt gives no clear explanation of how the Nazis came to power. She virtually says so herself: "There is an abyss between men of brilliant and facile conceptions and men of brutal deeds and active bestiality which no intellectual explanation is able to bridge."[22] Nazism and Marxism might have been as futile as Freemasonry and Single Tax had conditions not proved ripe. There is an element of terrible accident about—not "it all," for something terrible would have happened amid such breakdown—what actually happened. The formation of ideologies can be described. The breakdown of old systems can be described. And what then happens can be described. But there are no inevitable connections between them. Arendt never implies that there are. Her critics have either not read her closely or else are just using other formulations of the origins and conditions of totalitarianism, often crude, rigid, and deterministic, as sticks to beat both her and the concept. Or often they are angered, even if not Marxist, by the comparison: of course Marxism is nothing at all like Nazism, has no totalitarian qualities, and is, of course, a much more comprehensive and total view of human history than was ever Nazism, and it happens either to be true or to be the only ideology scientific enough for liberal tolerance or respect.

An appearance of determinism could be given to Arendt's argument because, quite naturally, she concentrates on an account of the growth in the nineteenth century of those elements of thought that became important in Nazism in the twentieth century; and she gives all too few glimpses of the nonstarters and the less successful ideologies of the *salon* and of the gutter. She is, quite properly, writing history backwards: she selects what is relevant to understanding the mentality of the Nazis and of the Communists under Stalin; and she is not writing a general account of nineteenth-century extreme political sects. She should have said this more explicitly, or a few examples of the "also rans" would have shown the historian that she was not arguing a direct causal connection between the thought of Gobineau and the deeds of Hitler or between the thought of Marx and the deeds of Stalin, but only showing how it was, given power, that they were able and eager to think in world-transforming terms rather than—like traditional autocrats—in power-preserving and power-enjoying terms. One example from elsewhere:

> What have these Saints achieved? In the midst of a free peo-
> ple, they have founded a despotic power. In a land which
> repudiates state religions, they have placed their church above
> human laws. Among a society of Anglo-Saxons, they have in-
> troduced some of the ideas, many of the practices of red
> Indian tribes, of Utes, Shoshones and Snakes. . . . Putting
> under their feet both the laws of science and the lessons of
> history, they preach the duty of going back, in the spirit and
> in the name, to that priestly and paternal form of government
> which existed in Syria four thousand years ago; casting from
> them, as so much waste, the things which all other white men

have learned to regard as the most precious conquests of time and thought—personal freedom, family life, change of rulers, concurrence in laws, equality before the judge, liberty of writing and voting. They cast aside these conquests of time and thought in favor of Asiatic obedience to a man without birth, without education, whom they have chosen to regard as God's own vicar on the earth.

With them to do any piece of work is a righteous act; to be a toiling and producing man is to be in a state of grace.

What need is there to dwell on the political value of such a note?[23]

Indeed this intelligent English traveler, watching in 1866 a large wagon train of converts from South Wales pouring down into Salt Lake City, worried himself profoundly, for a moment, at what might happen if Mormonism were to increase its appeal to the poor (the white poor, anyway) everywhere. Forgive this digression. The Mormons were not serious starters in the twentieth-century totalitarian stakes—though perhaps more due to their lingering cultural realism when faced by an ultimatum from the U.S. Senate or the U.S. cavalry-on-the-move than by self-willed political constraints. But this traveler saw in them something of the logic of plausibility of what Arendt was to call totalitarian ideology. That is the main point that Arendt sought to establish.

If criticized for being digressive, she might have done better to be more digressive and seemingly "irrelevant" to the plain tale of development from Gobineau to Hitler that so many mistakenly expect, as in those absurd and terrible old attempts to jazz up or give a kind of pornographic interest to political thought by titles like *From Luther to Hitler* (usually, with almost wicked ignorance and superficiality, via Hegel).[24] She should have shown more instances of new lights that failed. For she is sustaining the claim that ideologies (in her sense) arose at all, not that the two that won out and came to power themselves explain how they came to power, nor even that the movements associated with them created the revolutionary situations. When in power they made history, but not until then.

What She Has Said

Certainly there are many questionable judgments, irrelevancies, mistakes, and eccentricities in Arendt's analysis.[25] Her prefaces establish the sense of the problem, to comprehend how the attempt at totalitarian government was possible, but say nothing helpful to the reader faced with a work so large, so unusual, so diverse, so outside the Anglo-American scholarly tradition, about her presuppositions. The student reader is, I find, awed, bewildered, and enthralled all at once. But bewildered more than a bit, like all of us on first reading, because her premises and preconceptions are not made clear, at least not in the prefaces or in any one place in the text. They become clear in her later books. *The Human Condition* (1958) makes clear her assumptions about the political, human freedom, and the capacity for action. *On Revolution* (1963) makes clear her assumptions about the possibilities of deliberate social change. *Eichmann in Jerusalem* (1963), while a *livre d'occasion*, extends her account of freedom in relation to totalitarian power and exemplifies what freedom should be in practice, particularly in the lack of a political tradition. And in the shortest and clearest of her works, *On Violence*, she answers those who preach the necessity of, or who would even make a cult of, violence; but more fundamentally she makes clear her views on the nature of power and of authority.

If these books are read as each taking up a theme that emerges in *The Origins of Totalitarianism*, but is left unresolved or insufficiently clarified, then we see her writings in true perspective and as constituting a whole.

I think that what she has said is something like this: "Power corresponds to the human ability not just to act but to act in concert." So it is never the property of an individual: an individual must persuade others to follow or obey. Violence, "which is distinguished by its instrumental character," cannot be wielded by one person to create more than a momentary power among very few people. So violence reaches its height in the breakdown of power rather than through power. Acting in concert means some minimal respect for human freedom, even if only of an elite. But since the time of the Greeks in the fifth century, an ideal and a memory has always been living with us: of men treating each other as equals in a public realm of argument and dispute, politics. So to her, politics and freedom are virtually the same thing. Freedom is "the ability to begin," action which is not necessary or predetermined and whose consequences cannot be predicted. Basically it arises from the double aspect of humanity: nothing more like one man than another, but each man absolutely individual. Freedom is not, as liberals began to maintain, being left undisturbed by power, particularly the power of the state: on the contrary, freedom is the mutual exercise of power. Governments which try to suppress public politics are actually weaker than political regimes, unless they go to inhuman and (while they last) irreversible lengths of terror. It is this negativism of liberalism which rendered it so weak both in preventing total war, mass unemployment, and inflation, and in dealing with the ideological terrorists who could take advantage of the revolutionary conditions. Ordinary people lost the capacity for action and despaired of being able to influence things at all.

Minorities, like the Jews, at first thought it enough to be emancipated from formal restraints; it took them long to realize that, as it were, the price of freedom-from-restraint is not just vigilance but constant activity. The breakdown of liberalism explained the sudden plausibility to masses of people of the ideologists' belief, not in human action, but in world-changing, qualitative transformation. The unity of ideology, however, contradicts the facts of human nature: it can grasp the commonness but not the individuality of men. So terror is piled upon terror to convince people that freedom of action for individuals is impossible but that "everything is possible" to the party. *Eichmann in Jerusalem* (whether historically right or wrong—was there more Jewish resistance than she believed?) is at least a terrible parable about what can happen when the totalitarian assumptions of inevitability are accepted even by the victims. Here her pagan, humanistic, existentialist ethics become quite clear: to be human is to act freely, even if effective resistance is impossible. When prudence and compromise break down or are impossible, compliance and hopeless resignation only feed the irrational belief of the new oppressors that some objective necessity, not man, rules. Thus the *need* for the extermination, not just concentration camps, as she sees it, to degrade people before they were killed anyway; something as economically and governmentally irrelevant as Stalin's purges, in order to prove to the elite and their followers that individuals cannot sustain themselves outside social relationships of a specific kind. And hence the need even for hopeless resistance to such things and for her grim reminder (which comes right to the edge of what one human being may ever say to another) of Cicero's dictum that a free man, if captured in war and taken into slavery hopelessly, irredeemably, and with no chance of escape, *should* commit suicide: the last free action possible to prevent degradation.

Slightly crazy to think that one can compress all of Arendt into a nutshell of even a long paragraph. For she is such a profound wide-ranging writer, and at times both richly and irritatingly digressive. Each of her books, except *On Violence*, could have been so much shorter. The essential theory is clear, and to add so many examples was to create the appearance of writing history and to attract simple and obvious empiricist objections. But I offer a summary, however abstract, poor, or unbalanced, simply to establish the point that her works should be looked at as a consistent world view in which the later books establish and sometimes modify the premises about the human condition underlying her greatest, but most pell-mell and least philosophical work, *The Origins of Totalitarianism*.

Arendt sees the continuities as well as the discontinuities more clearly than Marx between the consciousness and conditions of the ancient and the modern worlds. If her sociology of the modern state is far less developed than Marx's, yet she sees that it is easily possible—both in liberal and in Marxist economic theory—to exaggerate the unique effects of industrialization. The struggle is not between capitalism and communism, it is between the political or republican tradition and its totalitarian caricatures. If we are ever to establish the republic for all, she implies, it will be through drawing on, yet transcending, the past, not repudiating it utterly. Yet, of course, the most likely alternative now seems, from all her works and all the events that came after the first publication of *The Origins of Totalitarianism,* that we fear so much the perversion of the political tradition that was totalitarianism, that we do not dare try for the republic, so we stay with or lapse into the banal evils (and the banal welfare goods) of autocracies, open or concealed, better or worse. (The nastiest and most plausible prophecy may now not be that we will reach 1984 but that we will continue much as we so shoddily and inadequately are—without even fear of worse to scare us into action for far better and with all conventional wisdom saying, so impressive to the young, "run no risks.") Certainly her message is not that of a J. S. Talmon who, after his studies of the origins of totalitarianism, to guard against the abuse of political lapses, though an Israeli, into a kind of Burkean and elitist conservatism. If totalitarianism showed that "anything is possible," good government as common citizenship and social justice is still, to her, among those possibilities. This became more and more clear in her later writings.

Rereading her, I am convinced that even yet her stature has been underestimated. There is a view of political and social man just as comprehensive as those of Hobbes, Hegel, Mill, and Marx; and, to my mind, one far more flattering to humanity.

NOTES

1. This essay appeared previously in *Social Research,* Vol. XLVI, no. 1 (Spring 1977).

2. Margaret Canovan, *The Political Thought of Hannah Arendt* (New York: Harcourt Brace Jovanovich, 1974), p. 16.

3. Hannah Arendt, *The Origins of Totalitarianism* (New York: Harcourt Brace, 1951).

4. See Franz Borkenau, *The Totalitarian Enemy* (London: Faber and Faber, 1940); André Gide, *Retour de l'U.R.S.S.* (Paris: Gallimard, 1936); Arthur Koestler, *Arrival and Departure* (New York: Macmillan, 1943); Ignazio Silone, *The School for Dictators* (London: Jonathan Cape, 1939); and George Orwell, *The Collected Essays, Journalism and Letters,* 4 vols. (New York: Harcourt, Brace & World, 1968), Vol. I, pp. 332, 376, 459, and in Vol. II his review of Borkenau, *The Totalitarian Enemy,* pp. 24–26—thus all references within the period 1936–40. William Steinhoff's recent *George Orwell and the Origins of 1984* (Ann Arbor: University of Michigan Press, 1975) makes clear that most of the fundamental ideas in Orwell's totalitarian thesis were formed in this earlier period, not in the Cold War and above all not as a combination of Cold War and death wish, as if he hadn't thought about it before he wrote in 1948. In my biography of Orwell (in progress) I will be able to prove this point conclusively.

5. See Carlton J. H. Hayes, ed., "Symposium on the Totalitarian State, 1939," *Proceedings of the American Philosophical Society,* Vol. LXXXII (Philadelphia: American Philosophical Society, 1940).

6. George Orwell, "Freedom of the Press," *Times Literary Supplement* (September 15, 1972), together with my note "How the Essay Came to be Written," pp. 1037–40.

7. See Benjamin Barber's contribution to Carl J. Freidrich *et al., Totalitarianism in Perspective: Three Views* (New York: Praeger, 1969).

8. Notably Carl J. Friedrich, ed., *Totalitarianism: Proceedings of a Conference Held at the American Academy of Arts and Sciences, March 1953* (Cambridge: Harvard University Press, 1954); and his and Zbigniew Brzezinski's *Totalitarian Dictatorship and Autocracy* (Cambridge: Harvard University Press, 1956), a book which, it is fair to Brzezinski to say, became more and more Friedrich's in the second American edition (indeed, Brzezinski vanished from the title page of even the German edition), and more and more conceptually rigid ("my model is . . .") and less and less historical.

9. See Arendt, *The Origins of Totalitarianism,* p. 159, for her clearest definition.

10. Alexis de Tocqueville, *The Recollections of Alexis de Tocqueville* (London: Harvill Press, 1948), pp. 67–68.

11. See A. J. P. Taylor, *The Origins of the Second World War* (New York: Atheneum, 1962) for a picture of Hitler as a normal politician; and see Bertolt Brecht's play *Arturo Ui* for a picture of Hitler as simply a political Al Capone seizing power by force and fraud alone.

12. Arendt, *The Origins of Totalitarianism,* p. 124.

13. Ibid., pp. 431–32.

14. Ibid., Chapter 9, "The Decline of the Nation State and the End of the Rights of Man," pp. 266–98.

15. Ibid., p. 159.

16. I discuss various possible senses of "ideology" in "Ideology, Openness, and Freedom," in Dante Germino and Klaus von Beyme, eds., *The Open Society in Theory and Practice* (The Hague: Martinus Nijhoff, 1974). pp. 217–37.

17. Arendt has somewhere remarked that there is, indeed, a functional equivalent between religion and ideology, but the content, she mildly remarks, is somewhat different: it does make a difference whether one believes in Jesus Christ or in Adolf Hitler or in Joseph Stalin either as teachers or as models of behavior.

18. See Hannah Arendt, *The Origins of Totalitarianism*, 2nd enlarged ed. (New York: Meridian Books, 1958), p. 468:

Ideologies—isms which to the satisfaction of their adherents can explain everything and every occurrence by deducing it from a single premise—are a very recent phenomenon and, for many decades, played a negligible role in political life. Only with the wisdom of hindsight can we discover in them certain elements which have made them so useful for totalitarian rule. Not before Hitler and Stalin were the great political potentialities of the ideologies discovered.

I believe that she was correct and that her remark about "only with hindsight" shows that she did not believe in a causal chain of explanation anyway, which she is alternately criticized for having and for not having. But there are other valid senses of "ideology"—the term arose from a common set of needs, but has crystallized into several different, clear, and useful meanings. See my "Ideology, Openness, and Freedom."

19. Martin Seliger, *Ideology and Politics* (New York: The Free Press, 1976). This is a very scholarly book in the sense of identifying and summarizing scores of different usages of ideology, but weird in its banal resolve to show that they all merely mean that even to think about politics is to have practical implications, which I don't think is true anyway—except in very trivial senses.

20. Under interrogation in captivity Goering said that the liquidation of the Jews was a vast political blunder; many would have made good nationalists and joined in the liquidation of the Communists. If only Hitler had not confused these two issues, he said (G. M. Gilbert, *The Psychology of Dictatorship* [New York: Ronald Press, 1950], p. 246). But this only shows how important racialism was to Hitler, a matter of faith, whereas to an immoral adventurer like Goering it was simply a matter of expediency.

21. Taylor, *The Origins of the Second World War*, and Alan Bullock, *Hitler: A Study in Tyranny* (New York: Harper and Row, 1952). A perspective that sees the importance of the ideology even while it studies the effect abroad of "the tactic of legality" is Brigitte Granzow's brilliant and neglected *A Mirror of Nazism: British Opinion and the Emergence of Hitler, 1929–1933* (London: Gollancz, 1964).

22. Arendt, *The Origins of Totalitarianism*, 1st ed., p. 159.

23. William Hepworth Dixon, *New America* (London: Hurst & Blackett, 1867), pp. 171–72, 200. Superficially this is an ordinary travel book, but Dixon (a barrister who became a judge of the High Court) had as his traveling companion Charles Dilke, Gladstone's political heir (if scandal had not ended his career), a keen political mind.

24. William Montgomery McGovern, *From Luther to Hitler: The History of Fascist-Nazi Political Philosophy* (Boston: Houghton Mifflin, 1941).

25. Canovan, *The Political Thought of Hannah Arendt*, is a judicious repository of these.

Mildred Bakan

HANNAH ARENDT'S CONCEPTS OF LABOR AND WORK

Nowhere in *The Human Condition* is Hannah Arendt's thought so open to criticism as in her concept of labor. The chapter on labor begins apologetically. Though she intends to criticize Marx, she would not, for all that, be identified with those who, she expects, would welcome her remarks—the avowed anti-Marxists.[1] She explicitly acknowledges her respect for Marx, describing him as the greatest of the "labor philosophers." But she does even more than that: she seems to ally herself, implicitly, with the central direction of his thought.

In a footnote,[2] she expresses the opinion—and it is avowedly no more than an opinion—that Marx was as much influenced by Aristotle as by Hegel. It is clear from *The Human Condition* that Hannah Arendt's own concept of political thought stands firmly rooted in Aristotle. It is as though she sees her criticisms as still, at least in some ways, in the Marxist tradition. And yet her critique of Marx is devastating!

The very basis of her hierarchical differentiation among the activities of the *vita activa*—labor, work, and action—is drawn from Aristotle. According to Arendt, action, like speech, is its own end, and in that sense an end in itself. Action, like speech, is precisely actuality, which contains its own end, in just the Aristotelian sense that the very act is the realization of its potentiality. Aristotle himself uses seeing, touching, and the like as examples of an act containing its own end.[3] The perfection of seeing is precisely seeing and not some other end. In the same sense, action and speech are, for Arendt, their own ends, not means to other ends.

In this respect, action is radically different from work. Work is inescapably part of a means-end series. Work establishes a world of things through products. Work is instrumental, producing things for use. Yet, through this production a human world is opened in which speech and action can appear. Man-made things take us out of a simply natural environment into a world we are collectively concerned to keep against the ravages of time.[4] Labor, on the other hand, participates neither in the fully human actuality of speech and action—which are ends unto themselves—nor in the world-building end of work. Labor is simply on a par with nature, which must be held at bay. Nature is relentlessly incessant, without beginning or end, and so is labor.

Only speech and action originate as ends unto themselves. The end of speech and action, being contained in speech and action itself, is its own appearance in the world. Speech and action, containing their own ends, display the personality—identity—of speaker and actor. But appearing, "being-in-the-world," is fragile.[5] It cannot last. The *polis*—the political arena—is precisely the domain which persons in their collective plurality establish to show who they are and to remember their appearing being.

According to Arendt, "what all Greek philosophers took for granted is that freedom is exclusively located in the political realm,"[6] freedom being taken in the sense of freedom from coercion by either life's necessities or human forces and violence. For Arendt, as for Aristotle, only what originates out of itself as its own end is free in this sense.[7] Correlatively, only the participation of men who are free in this same sense can constitute a political realm in which no one is more ruler than ruled and in which, accordingly, all are equal.[8]

Arendt, in criticizing Marx, argues that he is contradictory. On the one hand, he acknowledges that freedom begins where the necessity of labor ends; on the other hand, he attributes to labor the differentiation of man from animal. It would seem that she attributes to Marx a concept of freedom like her own, an Aristotelian (and Greek) concept of freedom that is also political, indeed constitutive of the political. It is by virtue of sharing this concept of freedom that she ventures to criticize Marx's concept of labor. To do so she returns to Aristotle, and, further, to what informs his thinking—the pre-philosophical experience of the Greeks.

Indeed, some of the strongest aspects of *The Human Condition*—her emphasis on the political importance of assembly, her sense of the essentially collective, or cooperative, dimension of action, even her concept of power as resting on, at least, tacit collective consent—are also to be found in Marx's writing, though Arendt does not say so.[9]

The core of her criticism concerns Marx's concept of labor. It is interesting to note that beyond casual, off-hand remarks, she pays no attention whatever to the Hegelian origins of Marxist thought. The Marxist concept of labor is directly drawn from Hegel, which as Arendt briefly notes, Marx himself acknowledged. If, however, one goes back to Hegelian sources, it is abundantly clear that Arendt has seriously misconstrued the Marxist concept of labor.

Neither Hegel nor Marx differentiated between labor and work in the manner of Arendt. Both Hegel and Marx aim to tie work, in precisely the sense used by Arendt, i.e., as world-building, to labor in terms of the bodily expenditure of energy, as effort. Since Hegel makes this connection before Marx, he could be said to share Marx's materialist emphasis in this respect.[10] Hegel, by relating work as world-building to labor, in the sense of bodily energy expenditure, grounds our world concept dialectically in natural necessity. The relation of work to labor is a particularly important instance of the more general Hegelian conception of the dialectical relation of form (as work) to its material content (as labor).

Whereas some differentiation may be in order, the sharpness of the distinction drawn by Arendt serves to obfuscate rather than clarify labor and work. Without labor, no work as world-building would be possible. If labor were not tied to work in this way, what distinction could be drawn between labor and such animal activity as nest-building? Labor is surely not a matter of instinct as nest-building, for example, is. Instinctual activity is governed by heredity, and takes place in an environment which is restricted to what is present. Labor, unlike instinctual activity, takes place in a world opened up as an arena for possible activity. Though Marx and Hegel do tie labor to metabolism, labor is never taken as a matter of instinct, nor even as something simply natural. Indeed, labor can be separated from world-making only to the degree that one labors in the service of another. As Arendt notes, among the Greeks it is another's home that is kept by the laboring slave. Labor in this sense is no longer simply natural, for it establishes the world location of another by keeping his home. To keep one's own home, even in the Greek sense of the relation of home to *polis*, would be to labor to establish one's own location in the world by virtue of which one is entitled to membership in the *polis*.

What Arendt misses totally is the dialectical relation of labor to nature that is the cornerstone of Hegel's and Marx's concept of labor. Animals don't labor; they are simply driven by appetite. The gratification of appetite—desire—by its object amounts to Hegel's way of analyzing instinctual activity.[11] Hegel's distinction between labor and simple appetite puts a radical hiatus between the two. Appetite is incapable of knowing the object on which it is dependent for satisfaction because it destroys its object in gratifying itself. Therefore, indeed, according to Hegel, appetite is insatiable, ceaselessly driven to further sources of gratification. Appetite, incapable of knowing the object on which it is nevertheless dependent, cannot know itself either. Yet the ultimate aim of subjectivity is precisely self-knowledge.

To account for our uniquely human control of appetite, Hegel places a power struggle between master and slave at the origin of human consciousness. For this analysis, labor is crucial as a uniquely human relation to objects in terms of deferred rather than immediate desire (simple animal appetite). According to

Hegel the slave must be forced to defer desire, precisely because deferred desire is not simply natural. Because the slave defers desire—or appetite—he is open through labor to the object as independent of his desire. So labor, by virtue of its dialectical relation to nature, as split from *and* related to nature, is at the origin of the transformation of animal desire to human want. Wants are open to a world; wants can be cognized and criticized, recognized as shared by others, and gratified through collective action that is initiated and planned.

The critical point here is that labor takes place in the context of a future opened as possible, whereas animal gratification does not. A future opened as possible is a future which is paradoxically present, as thought. According to Hegel, it is the transformation of appetite itself into thought in the context of deferred desire that allows laboring work in a world to occur.[12] Thus labor lies at the origin of the very appearance of mind as thought. In just this sense, labor lies at the origin of freedom as well. For freedom is precisely determination by thought—possibility—rather than appetite. For Hegel, as for Arendt, human freedom is absence of determination by natural necessity, but Hegel retains a dialectical relationship between freedom and natural necessity, which Arendt cuts off.

Analogously, Arendt cuts off the dialectical relation of labor to nature. So Arendt loses the distinction between animal hunting and devouring, on the one hand, and human preparation and consumption of food, on the other. While Arendt draws on Marx's concept of labor, relating labor to metabolism, she fails to recognize that labor, for both Marx and Hegel, are related to metabolism through a transformation of appetite to human want. But the breakthrough on this point was made by Hegel, not Marx. Hegel takes labor as that split from nature by virtue of which desire is itself transformed into thought. Indeed, labor that can appear only in the context of deferred desire is itself the primordial appearance of thought, as the intention of an object independent of itself. Labor is a decisive stage in the objective realization of the idea. Instead of merely appetitive destructive relations to objects, labor negates its objects by transforming them so as to embody intent. For this reason also, the laboring transformation of objects embodies the laborer's own will. It is just through this primordial embodiment of will that nature is humanized, and the odyssey of freedom in the world begins. Through his labor, the slave comes to know himself as potentially free in a world that stretches beyond his environment.

For Hegel—and for Marx also—it was a question of the origins of human consciousness. Both recognized that human consciousness is not, and, indeed, could never be—simply appetitive. It is not labor that reduces the slave to the appetitive, as Arendt argues, but torture and pain. Quite incredibly, Arendt takes as her model of labor exploited, dominated labor, insofar as labor is dominated, not insofar as it is laboring. Marx can take labor as differentiating man from animal and, without contradiction, look to historical freedom from unnecessary labor (and from interpersonal domination) precisely because labor is the concretely material relation of man to nature by virtue of which man surpasses instinctual determination and, also, makes that world (through work) where he must find himself.

The second point that Arendt misses in the Hegelian-Marxist conception of labor is that labor is taken as the origin of the achievement of human self-consciousness through self-objectification. The master in the master-slave power struggle becomes master because he is ready to die, whereas the slave is not. The significance of being ready to die is that it marks the bare emergence of a sense of self that is not simply bodily. In other words, it marks the bare emergence of a self as distinct from the simply natural.[13] Though the master rules out of his sense of freedom, won through battle, the slave, terrified by the prospect of his death, has at least faced the possibility of death. But up to this point, neither master nor slave know themselves as human. Neither has won an identity. To know themselves as human, they must objectify themselves in the eyes of each other, in terms of a world. In the Hegelian account, only a subject which is also objective to itself is self-conscious, as humans indeed are.[14] The master's attempt to objectify himself by winning recognition from the slave is doomed to failure: recognition by dominance of another is self-defeating. Only recognition which is freely given provides that acknowledgment of self which establishes personal identity. The slave, on the other hand, by refashioning the object so as to gratify the master's desire, embodies his thought of the intended future object in the real object. Thus the slave gains what the master cannot, self-consciousness through self-objectification by embodying his will in the object. For Hegel, this is not the end of the odyssey of self-consciousness, but it lies at its foundation. The slave has yet to dare to die to win his freedom.

What is to the point in this context is that Marx fully accepts the Hegelian concept of self, or identity, as inseparable from concrete objectification. He agrees that labor lies at the origin of self-consciousness.[15] In his essay, "Alienated Labor,"[16] this concept of self-objectification through labor is implied in his account of the alienation of the laborer under the factory conditions of capitalism. The species-being Marx refers to in that same essay is Feuerbachian. Feuerbach had argued against Hegel that human species-being involves the recognition of oneself as akin to one's fellow man through love rather than thought. But the concept of mutual recognition, as the *telos* of man's evolving species-being, is strictly speaking, Hegelian. Marx argues in the essay that the exploitation of labor under capitalism deprives *both* laborer and capitalist of their species-being. But species-being is hardly their being as simply natural in the sense that Arendt asserts. (In the same essay, Marx claims man has all of nature as his object.)[17] Through exploitation, both laborer and capitalist are deprived of their sense of kinship with each other as human.[18] Furthermore, the world that is made through capitalist-exploited labor is no longer one in which man can find himself. The world, though it is man-made, is now against man, alien to man. Nevertheless, the exploitative situation does engender a difference in personal identity—and interest—between capitalist and laborer, by virtue of the different mode of objectification available to exploiter and exploited.

For Marx, the contemporary world alienation that Arendt

takes as central to our current situation is rooted in a mode of production whose engine is the exploited surplus productivity of labor.
By tying work as world-building to labor, Marx is able to relate the
world we live in to our mode of laboring as a mode of relation to
nature, in terms of its resources, and as a mode of relation to
one another, in terms of domination—an avenue of understanding
simply cut off by Arendt.

Yet Arendt retains the decisive aspect of the Hegelian
concept of identity: mutual recognition. So she restricts self-
objectification to speech and action which others recognize.
Though Hegel also takes speech and action as self-objectifying in
relation to others, he insists that this self-objectification takes place
in a world that labor has fashioned and appropriated historically.
Space, according to Hegel, is congealed time,[19] as capital is, for
Marx, congealed labor.[20]

Arendt's position with respect to labor affects her position
with respect to work and with respect to speech and action as well.
Labor, as the point of the relation of work to nature, does indeed
provide a space for human action and speech, but this space is
both continuous with and limited by nature. Furthermore, the tool
that work creates is neither simply its own end, nor a means to
other ends.[21] The development of the tool is a part of the
humanization of our environment as man's dwelling place. The
world as dwelling place is a place to live. And if the context of life
is lost, what is left of the sense of world as man's home? Does
nobility of action mean excellence for excellence's sake regardless
of activity? Is the world to be taken as an arena for privileged
esthetic enjoyment? No doubt that is an unfair assessment of
Hannah Arendt's sense of world. But it is not altogether off the
mark to say that, for Arendt, the world takes on an essentially
theatrical aspect. We are heroes—or cowards—and the cowards
may have more sense of the life at stake. A theater must be set
apart from nature to provide a place in which survival is not at
issue.[22] A theater is a place in which, after all, the play's the
thing.

But even self-objectification through speech and action takes place in a world that is neither identical with the story about it, nor simply made, but rather (even as made) continuous with what is found. Political speech is still addressed to others situated in a real world. Language must take account of objective possibilities, as must action. Objective possibilities change as the world is materially transformed. The very possibilities for assembly change. As our interdependence on each other changes with our mode of work and labor, policy becomes more problematic. Indeed, one of Marx's central points concerning capitalism is that its mode of production is socialistic, though the relations of production are not. The change in the mode of production effects a change in the possibilities for human action through a change in the possibilities for assembly.

Arendt's separation of speech and action from labor and work, by obscuring the real possibilities for action, also obscures the relation of speech to reality. According to Arendt, speech and action engender reality. One *becomes* real by appearing to others through speech and action. The relation of speech and action to a reality with which one is in touch and which transcends one's speech and action, not merely as something made, but as something found, cannot even be raised—except as a question of shared common sense. There is after all a point to Plato's insistence against Protagoras, which Arendt cites, that God is the measure of even the things man makes, and indeed of all things. For Plato's point speaks to the recognition of an objective world—an everlasting universe. The things about us are not merely made. Things as found, though they are given a place in our world, are there (even if transformed) as a transcendent power, not fully known or possessed, on which we are dependent, and to which we belong.

Even for Plato *nous* orders the appetitive part of the soul (through the intermediary of spirit).[23] *Nous* provides the paradigm, for both the state and the soul, through the sight of the *eidos,* which itself brings harmony into nature, allowing it to be. It is not nature that is held at bay, but rather *chaos,* and *chaos* cannot even be. Chaos *informed,* is nature. For, according to Plato—and the Greeks—nothing can be without a principle of being that harmoniously relates its elements.[24] On this point, Aristotle does not differ from Plato.

It is important to note that Plato's philosopher-king needs freedom from interest to see the whole, so as to give each his due. Though the Platonic freedom from interest is something like Hegel's and Arendt's freedom from natural determination, for Plato, freedom from interest opens one to the *eidos* of things themselves. As Arendt points out, it is not idle that Plato relies on the model of the craftsman for his concept of the *eidos.* The *eidos* allows the thing itself to be.[25]

Arendt takes the Platonic *eidos* as the domination of nature. But without the participating *eidos,* there would, according to Plato, be no nature at all. And it is through sight of that same *eidos* that human passions are ordered. The *eidos* that orders nature, orders our passions as well, bringing us into harmonious relation to nature. It is indeed puzzling how the *eidos* can be in nature, but the Aristotelian conception of form, as the release of potentiality inherent in shaped matter itself, never leaves the Platonic context of nature as essentially informed. The Platonic *eidos,* no less than the Aristotelian form, allows the thing itself to be. To recognize the *eidos* as form is to know what is due the thing, as a matter of justice. And for both Plato and Aristotle to rule wisely is to rule justly.

Divorced from this Greek relation to nature, freedom, for Arendt, loses its ground. Speech and action arise out of a freedom that is no longer Greek. Freedom seems to be unfounded caprice. Hegel, who returns to Aristotle as a post-Kantian, introduces development into form itself through a dialectical relation with its content. The form itself develops. Thus Being takes on a historical dimension, inseparable, however, from the things of the world and nature. Arendt, unlike the Greeks, has a post-Hegelian historical sense. For Arendt, history is informed by ideology—by meaning—without, however, a grounding material base. (So

Arendt goes back to Greek pre-philosophical experience to unpack our sense of the political, because according to Arendt, our own ideology has its historical origin in Greek experience.)

Hegel, however, shares the Platonic (and Aristotelian) hope that politics will be informed by rationality. This rationality is in things themselves for Plato and Aristotle, as unchanging *eidos* or form, and for Hegel, as historically developing form. But Arendt divorces politics from rationality. The political domain is the domain for the display of character. Taken at its best, the political domain is the domain for the display of excellence of character. Politics shows the ethical, in the sense of what the Greeks meant by *aretē*. Indeed, for Arendt, as for the Greeks, politics allows what is ethical to appear. As Arendt herself notes, for the Greeks, "courage was the political virtue par excellence."[26] But "excellence itself, *aretē* as the Greeks . . . would have called it, has always been assigned to the public realm where one could excel, could distinguish oneself from all others."[27] Taken at its worst, politics in this sense can become the display of idle heroism, "noble deeds" unfounded in anything beyond their own display.

For Aristotle, no less than Plato, only actuality is Being. The potentiality for Being is a deficiency of Being. So the slave is not human as the free man is. But rather than Plato, it is Aristotle, seeking a resolution of the Platonic problem of the participation of Being in the things of our world, who nevertheless studied in depth the potentiality for Being in things themselves. The potentiality for Being, though the deficiency of Being, is the disposition to, or for, Being. So according to Aristotle, the disposition for virtue, in the sense of excellence, is a matter of habit that can be acquired by the development of judgment in practice, whereas, according to Plato, virtue, if it is to be learned at all, must be learned by recollecting excellence. To moderns, that the deficiency of Being can nevertheless be a disposition to Being may make little sense. But the Aristotelian conception of the nature of things puts the deficiency of Being in things, as well as the actualization of Being. The deficiency of Being, as potentiality, belongs to the material cause of things, as the potentiality for form itself. The other causes

of the actualization of form—efficient, formal, and final—participate with the material cause in bringing form to its realization.
What Plato ignores—the relation between ruler and ruled as the
disposition to realization of the *polis*—is precisely the potentiality
for the *polis* as community, in terms of its deficiency. According to
Aristotle, the deficiency nevertheless allows (but does not neces-
sitate) the *polis* to be realized, a political perspective Plato cannot
gain and that of course Arendt shares.

Though the Aristotelian scheme of things allows for development in the world, it does not allow for the development of form
itself. Hegel, to whom Marx is at least as close as he is to Aristotle,
explicitly remains in the Aristotelian tradition in his emphasis on
the developmental aspect of things as their potentiality. But in the
Hegelian scheme of things, potentiality, though still the deficiency
of Being, itself develops. The development of potentiality is precisely history. Marx, of course, retains this concept of the development of potentiality itself (in terms of the development of productive forces). But it is just this aspect of Hegelian Marxism that
Arendt discards. The Hegelian-Marxist orientation remains in the
Platonic-Aristotelian rationalist tradition. It is through the development of potentiality that reason itself develops. (In this connection, there is a sense in which Marx is to Hegel what Aristotle is to
Plato. For Marx puts his stress on material potentiality for form,[28]
just as Aristotle brings into significance the material potentiality
for form as the worldly disposition for its realization.) According to
Hegel, history moves to the worldly actualization of Being as the
actualization of reason. The Platonic-Aristotelian sense of potentiality as deficiency remains. For Marx, too, history has a *telos*—
the worldly actualization of rationality. But this *telos* is no longer
grounded only in reason as form. Matter, as the potentiality for the
actualization of reason, takes on primacy, rather than developing
form as reason itself. In just—and only—this sense, Sartre is
correct in maintaining that Marxism is itself an existentialism.

For Arendt (as for Sartre) history has no *telos* to be realized.
And in just this sense, Arendt's political philosophy has contemporary appeal. But Arendt, though rejecting Platonic-Aristotelian

reason as the final form for all that there is in the world, neverthe-less retains the Aristotelian—and I would say also Platonic—con-ception of the *polis* as the domain for the actualization of character —virtue.

Having rejected Plato's and Aristotle's conception of reason, can Arendt's political philosophy escape falling into irrationality? Arendt distrusts reason. She would replace reason by humanity as the ground of political life. But persons in their collectivity can be destructive as well as constructive. And to simply say, as Arendt does, that tyranny cannot last, has something of the ring of the talk one hears on occasion in the propaganda of the radical Left: tyranny will surely die. But this is hardly enough to assure us. The remarkable capacity for bureaucratic organization that makes our contemporary multi-national corporations possible also makes to-talitarianism possible.

It was out of concern for the problem of tyranny that the Platonic political philosophy espoused reason as the guide for political life. What it needed is not the surrender of reason, but the expansion of reason to provide a place for the relation of person to person.

The contemporary ring of Arendt's political philosophy stems from this distrust of reason. But her political philosophy leaves us with a sense of helplessness and impotence, because it gives no credence to any analysis of our political situation that might provide some hope for change. For Arendt there are no analyses that provide programs for change.

But though she is not a liberal, she is not a pessimist either. Arendt communicates a message: People will find a way and there is no substitute for participation in the struggle.

It is important to note, however, Arendt's thesis that the confirmation of reality demands shared appearance betrays a dubious conflation of meaning and being. This conflation of meaning and being is central to her position. She cannot avoid that conflation, because she has lost that unspoken sense of reality that comes from nothing else than a laboring or—I would prefer to say —a working relation to things. It is through labor that our bodies are effectively engaged with things in a transforming way. Through labor, things are disclosed as a transcendent and enabling power on which we are dependent. This sobering reality of things, which is to some extent accessible in gymnastics and battle as well, supplies a context for our senses, without which, indeed, the distinction between dreams and reality disappears. Beyond storytelling, the world, through its transformation, remembers as well. Indeed, what the world does not remember through its transformation, the stories won't keep alive either.

Marx went far beyond Hegel in pointing to the problems of exploitation inherent in our modes of working and laboring. Marx's great contribution was to point to the concealed conflicts of interest in our modes of being in the world, by virtue of its being a world in which we live and must labor to live. Conflicts of interest of this sort generate conflicting worlds in Arendt's sense. A hero in one world may be a nobody in another. In the end, Arendt gives us nothing on which to base criticality of those interests that bring us together in one way and separate us in another. Being critical of our interests would require surpassing the world as it appears to us in order to reach real possibilities beyond. For Arendt this makes no sense. The collapse of meaning and being locks us into appearance as it is shared.

Despite these shortcomings, which are indeed important, and perhaps even vitiating, *The Human Condition* makes a point with respect to speech and action and persons that we forget at our peril. The essential open-endedness of the human situation, the sense of the person as an originating ground, as introducing the principle of *beginning* into the world through speech and action, is described with a clarity and precision not exceeded in any contemporary political writing that I know of. She states more clearly, and with less jargon, what has made Sartre famous. Indeed, she even shares with Sartre the nagging problem of the fragility of cooperative action. What she implies concerning the rights and power of assembly is perhaps enough to found a political philosophy. Her point on the crucial political significance of workers' councils is as relevant as ever. Our personal identity *is* tied to appearance and a common world. But for that very reason a critique of what we take as our world in terms of its real structural features is indispensable.[29] But what Arendt attributes to the ideological dominance of man's lowest aspect—*animal laborans*—Marxists attribute to historically relative human relations of production that can be changed through our actions. The difficulty lies precisely in a concept of action and speech which is cut off not merely from work, but from labor itself.

Precisely because we are speaking and acting creatures, labor cannot be simply natural. According to Hegel and Marx, it is originally through labor that our future is opened up as an arena for action. But labor itself could not occur except in a context of work and thought, which is moreover interpersonal. After all, work realizes *initiated* ends. Only a creature that can initiate ends is capable of action that begins. And to be able to begin, to originate, is also to be able to bring into question—to wonder, in the Greek sense—and to be open to anxious doubt in the modern sense.[30] What Hegel and Marx remind us of is important: speech, labor, work, and action, even in Arendt's sense, belong together, not in any hierarchical order, but in mutual dependence.

NOTES

1. Hannah Arendt, *The Human Condition* (New York: Doubleday/ Anchor Books, 1959), p. 71.

2. Ibid., p. 365. See also, in this connection, ibid., pp. 142, 163, and 351, note 8.

3. Hippocrates, G., Apostle *Aristotle's Physics* (Bloomington: Indiana University Press, 1969), p. 141.

4. For Arendt's distinction between natural environment and world see, in particular, *The Human Condition*, p. 48. Her concept of world as a realm of shared appearance relative to the "human artifact" is very close to Heidegger's concept of world as that in which *Dasein* has its being. See, in this connection, Martin Heidegger, *Being and Time* (New York: Harper & Row, 1962), Part I, chapters II and III. Her concept of thought as properly unproductive and recollective is also Heideggerian. See Martin Heidegger, "A Letter

on Humanism," in Henry Aiken and William Barrett, eds., *Philosophy in the Twentieth Century*, Vol. II (New York: Random House, 1962).

5. Heidegger, *Being and Time*, pp. 174–78. The expression "being-in-the-world" is used to suggest an affinity of Arendt's sense of personal identity with Heidegger's concept of man's *Dasein* as being-in-the-world.

6. Arendt, *The Human Condition*, p. 29.

7. Ibid., pp. 13–14.

8. Ibid., p. 30.

9. See, for example, Marx and Engels, "Manifesto of the Communist Party," in Robert C. Tucker, ed., *The Marx-Engels Reader* (New York: Norton, 1972), especially pp. 342–45, 353.

10. Hegel's emphasis on labor is an important point of difference with Shelling, whose analysis of labor, like Arendt's, stops at natural necessity.

11. G. W. F. Hegel, *The Phenomenology of Mind*, J. B. Baillie, tr. (New York: Macmillan, 1955), p. 225.

12. Ibid., pp. 238–40.

13. Ibid., pp. 232–33.

14. Ibid., p. 229 and pp. 236–37.

15. Karl Marx, *Capital*, Vol. I (New York: International Publishers, 1939), p. 57.

16. Karl Marx, *Early Writings*, T. B. Bottomore, ed. and tr. (New York: McGraw-Hill, 1964).

17. Ibid., pp. 126–27.

18. Ibid., p. 129.

19. Hegel, *The Phenomenology of Mind*, p. 21.

20. Marx, *Capital*, Vol. I, pp. 50, 154. Marx, in effect, takes expended labor-power as concrete time.

21. Lukacs emphasizes Hegel's recognition of the importance of the tool. According to Hegel, the tool belongs to the objective spirit, the world transformed by thought. See Georg Lukacs, *The Young Hegel*, Rodney Livingstone, tr. (London: The Merlin Press, 1975), pp. 344–50.

22. Johan Huizinga, *Homo Ludens* (Boston: The Beacon Press, 1930), pp. 9–10.

23. Plato, *The Republic*, in *The Dialogues of Plato*, B. Jowett, tr. (New York: Random House, 1937), pp. 702–09. Spirit, the Greek *pneuma*, is closely related to *aretē*, excellence in the sense of aristocratic honor. *Pneuma*, as spirit, it should be remembered, is the part of the soul expressed by the guardians in particular. On this point, I am particularly indebted to André Dekker, my colleague at York University.

24. See J. N. Finlay, "The Three Hypostases of Platonism," *The Review of Metaphysics*, Vol. XXVIII, no. 4 (June 1977), pp. 66, 67.

25. Ibid., p. 69.

26. Arendt, *The Human Condition*, pp. 33, 311.

27. Ibid., p. 44.

28. See, in this connection, my comments on labor and work at the beginning of this essay. Labor as the bodily expenditure of energy gives us the *potentiality* for the human actualization of reason. See Marx, "Alienated Labor," *Early Writings*, pp. 128, 129. See also Marx, *Capital*, Vol. I, pp. 42–44, 177*ff*. It is interesting to note that Marx often speaks of nature itself, insofar as it is the material potentiality for form as body, or, at the very least, as extension of the human body. For Aristotle, matter is to form as body is to soul.

29. The work of the contemporary Czechoslovakian philosopher Korel Kosik is an interesting and, I think, important attempt to establish a theoretical basis for such a critique. Kosik, avowedly following Marx and Hegel, takes work as man's ontological opening to Being.

30. Unfortunately, Arendt simply ignores that unsettling interplay between personal identity and work taken in the broadest sense as self-objectifying project—that Sartre's major writings explore with such painstaking detail and brilliance.

Bikhu Parekh

HANNAH ARENDT'S CRITIQUE OF MARX

My concern in this essay is to examine Hannah Arendt's critique of Marx. Unlike many other critics of Marx, Arendt's critique is launched from the perspective of a clearly worked-out alternative philosophy of man and society. Accordingly I begin with a brief outline of Arendt's position. In the second section I outline her criticisms of Marx, and, in the third, assess their validity. In the final section I briefly draw together some of the general conclusions arising from the preceding sections.

Arendt distinguishes two fundamental modes of life: the *vita contemplativa* and the *vita activa*. By the term *vita contemplativa,* which is a Latin version of the more familiar and accurate Greek concept of the *bios theōrētikos,* she refers to the life devoted to theoretical pursuits.[1] As we shall see, the *vita activa* refers to the life devoted to practical activities, meaning those that deal with the problems thrown up by the nature and conditions of human existence. In this essay I shall ignore her discussion of the *vita contemplativa* both because it is not directly relevant to her critique of Marx and because the posthumous publication of her writings on the subject is still awaited.

Under the term *vita activa,* Arendt subsumes three "fundamental human activities," namely labor, work, and action. Labor is a biological necessity which man shares with the animal. Man must eat before he can do anything else, and therefore he must labor to produce the objects of his need. He produces objects, which he consumes and which he must produce again. The cycle of production and consumption goes on with its rhythmic regularity as long as human life lasts. Labor produces nothing permanent; it only feeds objects into the consumptive furnace of the human organism. It is therefore at once a necessary and a futile activity, necessary because without it man ceases to exist, futile because the expenditure of effort involved produces nothing permanent to show.

Work, the defining characteristic of the *homo faber*, is a distinctively human activity. Arendt understands work as if it were craft, and subsumes under it all activities in which man works upon nature and produces durable objects ranging from a tool to an everlasting work of art. Work is man's response to the destructiveness and fluidity of nature. It creates lasting objects that collectively constitute the world. The world is the wall man builds both to protect himself against the relentless destruction of nature and to create a home, a stable framework of social existence that relates him to others and creates conditions for a human community. Arendt's distinction between labor and work is not very clear and has been a subject of considerable controversy. The distinction broadly corresponds to Marx's well-known distinction between abstract and concrete labor.

First, while the products of labor are meant to be consumed, those of work are meant to be used.[2] Arendt acknowledges that the distinction between consumption and use is not "absolute," as use "does contain an element of consumption." Her point is that destruction "though unavoidable, is incidental to use but inherent in consumption." Unlike the objects of consumption, such as bread and butter, objects of use, such as a coat and a chair, are not meant to be used up the moment they are produced but are expected to last. Hence every society develops ways of preserving, mending, and servicing them. Second, labor assimilates man to nature, whereas work distinguishes him from it. Labor is a mechanical and cyclical activity in which man produces and consumes like all other natural beings, and adjusts himself to the rhythm of processes outside himself, be they natural or imposed by machines; in work he distances himself from nature, freely forms his projects, and gives the natural material a new shape and form. In labor man accepts the external nature as given; in work he "measures" up to it, works it over, and puts his distinctive stamp upon it. Third, since labor is undertaken to serve human needs, it is judged by the subjective and instrumental criteria of human desires. By contrast work produces objects that stand over against man and enjoy a measure of independence. They are public and objective entities and are subject to esthetic and other considerations.

Action is one of the most interesting and yet the least clearly defined categories in Arendt's thought. "To act, in its most general sense, means to take an initiative, to begin, to set something into motion."[3] To act is to begin "new and spontaneous processes," to "start processes on our own." As opposed to behavior and habit, action is self-conscious, freely undertaken, breaks through the bounds of the predictable pattern of the natural and social life, and begins something new. A scientist who in the course of his experiment sets off new processes in nature is engaged in action; and so is a politician who by words or deeds initiates a chain of consequences that disturbs the prevailing configuration of events. Although Arendt's concept of action appears rather romantic (as her examples of Achilles and other Greek and Roman heroes suggest), it is not. It covers any action, whether in a town hall meeting or in a workers' council, in which a man does and says what no one else could have done or said. It is, at bottom, an expression of the agent's uniqueness or individuality.

Action, so understood, has several features. First, since it expresses what is unique, it is a medium of freedom. Freedom is the ability to take charge of events, to shape one's destiny. Obviously, action is its most appropriate vehicle. Second, action is the sole medium through which an agent can reveal his individuality. In labor man reveals his bodily needs; in work, his craftsmanship; in action, "himself," that is, the totality of his unique being. Unlike work, and to some extent labor, which reveal "what" a man is, action reveals "who" he is. Third, action is the sole source of meaning in human life. For Arendt, as for Sartre, neither God nor human essence nor history nor the universe can confer meaning on human life. Each individual must confer it on his life himself, and he can do so only by means of action. By beginning something new and by revealing his identity an individual distinguishes himself from others, demonstrates that he is a unique individual and not an anonymous and uniform atom, leaves behind a distinct story, and saves his life from the futility to which all things natural are sentenced. Further, by means of action, men draw the worldly objects into their orbit, make them part of the story which their actions inevitably generate, and give them a meaning. The world, which is in itself a heap of unrelated objects, acquires significance when made an object of human speech and a theater of human action. Fourth, although action can take a number of forms, political action is its paradigmatic form, and the organized public space its ideal home. In political life man acts amongst his peers, whose very presence and critical judgment bring out his full potential. What is more, political life is especially designed for action, and gives it a sense of reality and permanence that no other area of life can give.

For Arendt the activities of labor, work, and action collectively constitute the world of human *praxis*. Each is indispensable. Without labor neither the individual nor the species can survive; without work and the world it builds, man is lost in the cosmos and does not develop a distinctive human identity; without action, his life lacks meaning and he does not develop a sense of personal identity.

All three activities, further, are interdependent. Without labor neither work nor action is possible; without work men lack the tools to ease labor and increase its productivity, as well as to record the achievements of human speech and action; and without action life lacks meaning and the world remains a mere heap of unrelated objects. They are interdependent in another way also. Arendt frequently invokes what I might call a contrastive theory of identity.[4] The theory is neo-Hegelian in inspiration and asserts that each activity defines itself and comprehends its distinctive identity in contrast to some other activity. The world is a world in opposition to nature. We define and appreciate the permanent and rock-like objectivity of the world in opposition to the cyclical, repetitive, and transient character of the natural processes. Similarly freedom has meaning and significance; that is, we value it and indeed become conscious of it only in opposition to necessity. Political life becomes "shallow" and loses its distinctive character if it "loses the quality of rising into sight" from the "dark" background of private life. When any one of the three activities disappears or loses its characteristic form, the others lose their framework of reference and suffer a loss of, or at any rate a confusion of, identity.

Moreover, each activity is autonomous and has its own distinctive mode of operation. Labor cannot be performed as if it were work, as Marx imagined, nor as if it were action, as the champions of the workers' council imagined. Labor exists to produce articles of consumption. To treat it as work is to expect its products to conform to standards demanded of a work of art, and this is to invite collective suicide. And to treat it as action is to seek freedom in the realm of necessity, a foredoomed enterprise. Similarly work cannot be performed as if it were labor as is the case in the modern society, since its products will then be articles of consumption and cannot build the objective world; nor as if it were action, for it then becomes a vehicle of meaning and loses its instrumental character. Finally, for reasons we shall see, action cannot be treated as if it were labor, as Marx thought, nor as if it were work, as most political philosophers since Plato have thought.

Fourth, although all three activities are important, they are not equally important. For Arendt "each human activity points to its proper location in the world." Labor is the lowest and action the highest of the three. Work occupies an intermediate position. Arendt justifies her view in several fascinating ways which, although not well coordinated, are full of stimulating suggestions. Sometimes she appeals to the degree of freedom involved in an activity, and argues that labor permits no freedom at all, work some degree of freedom, and action the highest. On other occasions she invokes the degree of self-sufficiency of an activity.[5] Although all three are interdependent, labor depends upon work far more than work does upon labor, and work depends upon action far more than action depends upon work. On yet other occasions she appeals to the sense of reality offered by an activity. At the minimal level the existence of the worldly objects is the source of the human sense of reality; however, the reality of the worldly objects themselves is ultimately dependent upon the common consensus among men. As Arendt puts it, "the presence of others who see what we see and hear what we hear assures us of the reality of the world and ourselves."[6] Since labor is essentially a private activity, although it may be performed in a group, and produces no worldly objects, the *animal laborans* lacks the assurance of his reality. For reasons we saw, labor offers a minimal sense of reality, and action the highest. To put it differently, the reality that action confers is everlasting. The reality offered by work lasts as long as the objects created by it last, whereas that offered by labor disappears once its objects are consumed.

For Arendt, then, the three activities stand in a determinate relationship to each other. If any one of them were to be eliminated, or practiced in an inappropriate manner, or given an inappropriate place in the hierarchy, that activity itself, as well as the others, would suffer and the human life would be seriously distorted.

It is Arendt's basic thesis that Western political philosophers have, to a man, failed to appreciate the autonomous and hierarchical structure of the three fundamental human activities. The Greek philosophers, who created the discipline of political philosophy, and the Christian thinkers who followed them, extolled the beauty and dignity of contemplation, and viewed the world of *praxis* as merely a means to creating and maintaining the necessary conditions of contemplative life. Inevitably they blurred the distinctions between the three activities. What was more, they almost completely neglected action. Unlike the other two, it introduces the element of unpredictability in human affairs which philosophical contemplation finds disturbing and disquieting. Plato reduced the entire realm of the *vita activa* to work and understood both action and labor in terms of it. Marx took an even more decisive step. He glorified labor, traditionally considered to be the lowest human activity, and reduced both action and work to it. As if this subversion of the Western intellectual tradition were not enough, he even reduced the *vita contemplativa* to labor. He understood contemplation as a form of labor and subordinated it to labor. When Plato reduced the *vita activa* to work, he did so in the interest of contemplation. And while he distorted the *vita activa,* he at least respected the integrity of the *vita contemplativa.* By contrast Marx indiscriminately reduced both types of activity of labor. His thought therefore represents a radical subversion of the Western intellectual tradition. Marx, however, had not worked out a clear alternative to the tradition and was therefore led to subvert it in terms of its own categories. His paradoxical enterprise inevitably resulted in a series of fundamental and flagrant contradictions, none of which could be resolved within the framework of his thought.[7]

The emphasis on labor is not unique to Marx. Locke was one of the first to advocate the labor theory of value, and his view was shared by Adam Smith and other classical economists. All of them, however, recognized that the labor theory of value was subject to qualifications and that some forms of labor produced no value. Further, nearly all of them acknowledged the distinction between work and labor, which they generally expressed as a distinction between productive and unproductive labor. The former produces durable objects, whereas the latter "seldom leaves any trace," as Adam Smith put it.[8] What is more, none of them glorified labor.

Marx took over their views and gave them an entirely new twist. He advanced the most radical and extraordinary thesis—that labor is the essence of man. As he put it: "Men begin to distinguish themselves from animals when they begin to produce their means of subsistence." For Arendt this "indeed is the very content of the definition of man as *animal laborans*." Marx's definition implies that labor and not God created man, that man's humanity is the result of his own activity, and that not reason but labor is his *differentia specifica*. In taking this view Marx challenged the entire Western tradition that defines man as *animal rationale* and views labor as the lowest of all human activities. He treated with "contempt" the traditional distinction between productive and unproductive, mental and manual, and skilled and unskilled labor.[9] He reduced diverse human activities to their "common denominator in laboring," and interpreted work, action, and thought as forms of labor. He argued that man "produces" social institutions and philosophical systems in the same way that he produces articles of consumption and the silkworm produces silk.

Marx used the term "labor" to refer to both material production and the reproduction of the species, one ensuring the survival and the other the continuance of the species. Labor so understood was for him a "natural biological force."[10] Since Marx viewed labor as a natural force, he reduced labor to labor-power. Labor is a human activity and implies an element of initiative and purpose. The concept of labor-power removes the residual human link and assimilates human labor to a natural force. Labor-power in Marx is "the force of the life-process itself." Even as natural force is inherent in a natural body and is activated by its interaction with other natural bodies, labor-power is inherent in the human body and is activated by its inescapable metabolic interaction with nature. Marx described man-made tools and social cooperation as productive forces, an appropriate naturalistic expression. Productive forces exist to increase the productivity of man's own natural bodily force and produce abundance, Marx's highest ideal.

For Marx life is "the highest good," abundance the highest goal, and labor the highest human activity. Worldly objects are nothing more than articles of consumption, crystallizations of labor-power created only to satisfy human needs. Marx's men have one common and overriding interest, namely abundance, and therefore one will and one opinion.[11] They are creatures of the same kind, namely mankind. The inherent logic of the *animal laborans* leads Marx to replace human plurality by a single subject, as is evident in his concept of species-being or socialized mankind. For Marx, man's species-being represents his human essence. Mankind is a species like any other natural species, and man, a species-man, is a specimen of his species. The species is the subject of the life-process of society, "the gigantic subject of the accumulation process."[12] The species, however, cannot be a subject in the same way that an individual human being can be, and therefore all that we are left with in Marx is a subjectless process, the cycle of production and consumption grinding on relentlessly as it does in nature. Marx assimilates man to nature, and human life to a cyclical natural process.

Marx's thoroughgoing "naturalism" prevented him from appreciating the significance of the objective world.[13] He sees the world in the image of "becoming" and not "being," motion and not permanence. For him, man is a consuming being who builds the world only to dismantle and recreate it to suit his constantly changing needs. There is therefore neither permanence nor continuity. Nothing is accepted as "given," "as it is," but only as a challenge and an opportunity to periodic destruction. For Marx the very independence and solidity of an object is a source of alienation. Accordingly he aims to destroy the objective world by reducing it to a mere extension or the "inorganic body" of man. Marx's project of the humanization of nature springs from an "extreme" anthropological "subjectivism" and represents an attempt to create a world where man, having destroyed the "solid objectivity" and "sheer otherness" of nature, everywhere encounters only himself.[14] Arendt acknowledges that Marx from time to time recognizes the importance of the objective world, but insists that these moments of recognition are not systematically pursued and play an exceedingly minor role in his thought.

In Arendt's view the destruction of the world spells the destruction of man himself. She invokes the contrastive theory of identity referred to earlier and argues that man knows himself to be a distinctive being only in contrast to nature. Once the world's objectivity is destroyed, the protective wall that separates man from nature is destroyed, and man's humanity is seriously endangered. As Marx himself acknowledged, although without realizing the full implications of his view, the humanization of nature involves naturalization of man, that is, the assimilation of man to nature. According to Arendt, the destruction of man's distinctive human identity is evident in Marx's vision of the communist society, in which men spend part of their life laboring and the rest in such activities as fishing, painting, literary criticism, and artistic work that are really private "hobbies."[15] Neither their labor nor most of their hobbies are distinctively human, and in any case neither has the capacity to release man from his subjectivity. Labor can produce only consumable objects, and hobbies only private pleasures. Neither can create a world, a public and communally shared human dwelling place, that outlasts its inhabitants, preserves their achievements, and gives them a sense of stability, permanence, and historical continuity. In the ultimate analysis, Marx's communist society is not a genuine community but a collection of socially homogeneous species-men mutely sharing common social goals and distinguished by nothing more edifying than their hobbies.

Marx's philosophy of labor, Arendt goes on to argue, prevents him from appreciating not only the objectivity of the world but also of such activities as politics, revolution, and history, to the understanding of which he claimed to have made the most original contribution.

For Arendt,, politics is an activity in which men collectively take charge of their destiny and reshape the world. In acting and initiating new processes, they experience freedom, disclose their unique individual identity, and give to their lives and their world a meaning and a sense of significance. Politics is therefore an arena of speech and action, of noble words and great deeds. As such it can be conceptualized only in terms of such categories as freedom, individuality, speech, action, principle, and the world.

In Arendt's view Marx fails to see this. Since he assimilates man to nature and makes life-process the center of social life, he reduces freedom to necessity, and politics to economics. For him, men are motivated by material interests. Now material interests are uniformly shared by groups of men, and therefore Marx is led to make classes, not individuals, the chief agents of political life. Further, since abundance is the highest ideal of the proletariat, its political actions are not motivated by principles but by a desire to remove the human obstacles to the full development of the productive forces. The communist society does not therefore represent a new beginning but only the continuation of the old one. Furthermore, since Marx takes material interest to be the spring of human action, he is unable to see the importance of argument and discussion. For him ideas are mere ideological rationalization and not worth taking seriously. The proletariat is therefore left with no other means of action save violence. Violence, traditionally the *ultima ratio* of political life and a symbol of the animal nature of man, is for Marx not only the paradigmatic but the sole form of political action.[16] It not only overthrows the bourgeoisie but also prepares the proletariat for the new society. As Marx put it, a revolution is necessary "not only because the ruling class cannot be overthrown in any other way, but also because the class overthrowing it can only in a revolution succeed in ridding itself of all the muck of ages and become fitted to found society anew."

Even as Marx misunderstands the nature of political activity and its relation to the realm of necessity, he misunderstands the nature of revolution. For Arendt revolution is a political rather than an economic phenomenon whose purpose is to found freedom, that is, to create a form of government in which men can enjoy freedom as a way of life and collectively determine their destiny. The new society may and does aim to eliminate poverty. As long as men are haunted by necessity, they neither seek nor enjoy freedom, and therefore necessity must be conquered. However, its conquest is only a precondition of freedom and best secured by "technical, non-political" rather than political means. In

Arendt's view "the whole record of past revolutions demonstrates beyond doubt that every attempt to solve the social question with political means leads into terror, and that it is terror which sends revolutions to their doom."[17] Poverty has the urgency inherent in necessity and is impatient of the slow processes characteristic of political debate and discussion. Since its elimination is a technical matter, a revolution motivated by economic considerations is forced to place the technological and administrative above the crucial political considerations of the organization of public space and the creation of democratic and participatory political institutions. Poverty, further, generates the inherently limitless emotions of pity and compassion for the poor, and rage and hatred against the rich, and these emotions breed blindness to reality, lack the restraints of common sense, and do not have the power to create a lasting political system. For Arendt the French Revolution failed, whereas the American Revolution succeeded, principally because one was motivated by the economic and the other by political considerations.

Marx makes the mistake of the leaders of the French Revolution.[18] For him a revolution is a means to solve poverty and create abundance. To be sure, this view was more characteristic of his later than his earlier writings. The young Marx defined poverty as a political rather than an economic phenomenon, a result of exploitation and oppression by the ruling class. The older Marx was different. For him poverty and political oppression were alike products of scarcity, and material abundance an answer to both. Consequently for him the aim of revolution is "to liberate the life process of society from the fetters of scarcity so that it could swell into a stream of abundance."[19] Revolution belongs to the realm of necessity. It is a natural event that bursts forth with irresistible force from the hidden recesses of the human life-process and sweeps aside all legal and political obstacles in its way. It is not designed to found a society based on freedom as is evident in Marx's "total neglect" of the political structure of the communist society.[20] Predictably, Lenin, the first successful Marxist revolutionary, placed more emphasis on electrification than on the soviets and ended up establishing the dictatorship of the Bolshevik party.

It might be argued that the Russian Revolution perverted Marx's aim, which was to create a fully free society. Arendt disagrees. In her view Marx's communist society does not and cannot create the necessary conditions of freedom. First, Marx's society is dominated by one overriding interest, namely material abundance, and therefore its central concerns are necessarily administrative rather than political. Its management therefore can be best left to periodically elected and removable administrators.

Second, Arendt cannot see why Marx's communist men should at all be interested in freedom. They are interested in discharging their share of socially necessary labor and in private hobbies. They define themselves in terms of personal fulfillment, and not historical immortality achieved through words and deeds. Consequently negative liberty rather than positive freedom is their overriding concern. Third, men value and cherish freedom when they constantly win it in the face of necessity, which Marx aims to abolish. For reasons already discussed, Arendt thinks that the disappearance of necessity spells the disappearance of freedom as well.[21]

Finally, Marx's view that when men are freed from necessity they will devote their time to higher activities rests on "the illusion of a mechanistic philosophy, which assumes that labor-power, like any other energy, can never be lost, so that if it is not spent and exhausted in the drudgery of life it will automatically nourish other, 'higher' activities."[22] We know from experience that the free time of the *animal laborans* is never spent in anything but consumption, and that the more free time is left to him, the greedier become his appetites. Instead of paving the way for freedom and higher activities, the increase of leisure in Marx's ideal society poses the "grave danger" that consumption will reach unprecedented proportions, "annihilate" the objective world altogether and, with it, man's very humanity.

Since Marx misunderstood the nature of politics, he misunderstood the nature of history also. Even as he could not accept nature as "given," as "the other," he could not accept the past as "given." In both cases he reduced the "solid objectivity of the given" to a mere means to serve the present needs.[23] For Arendt politics is the essence of history. History is a story of the memorable words and deeds of political actors who had the courage to emerge from the security of their lives, to show their concern for the world, and in so doing to leave something of themselves behind. In Arendt's view Marx reversed the relationship between history and politics. Hegel had already prepared the ground for the reversal. He saw history as the story of the *Geist* realizing its own "higher" intentions through the "narrow aims" of concrete political actors. For Hegel history had an author, namely the *Geist,* as well as a plot, and identifiable trends and patterns. Unique individual actions had meanings only as parts of these trends. Their meaning was located neither in themselves nor in the intentions of their agents but in an impersonal entity called history. In short, Hegel historicized politics and, in so doing, misunderstood both history and politics.

Marx took over Hegel's view of history and reversed it. Hegel had reduced politics to history; Marx politicized Hegel's historicist view of politics.[24] Hegel had argued that the historian's task was to discover "higher" aims in the exoteric aims of specific historical actors. Marx agreed, but unlike Hegel, he turned these higher aims themselves into the ends of political action. For Marx the political actor's task is to bring historical patterns or trends to fruition. Marx's proposal has disastrous consequences. It makes future necessity the goal of present politics, and identifies freedom with necessity. Further, Marx's proposal locates meaning not in unique deeds but in historical trends, and judges political actions instrumentally rather than in terms of the character, political principles, and the capacity for judgment of the actors involved. Again Marx ends up repeating the age-old fallacy of reducing acting to making. For him the historian's job is to elicit models of action that the political craftsman is to realize in practice. Such a view destroys both politics and history. It reduces political discourse to disputes about the correct implications of the laws and models of history, and replaces the creative process of political argument by rigorous political deductions. It distorts history also. Since history has a pattern which can be fully realized, Marx is led to argue that a paradise can be established on earth and that history can be used to put an end to history. What is more, since the realization of a pattern is all that matters, the past has at best only an instrumental value. Past historical actions are absorbed into and cancelled out by future goals, and are therefore hardly worth remembering. Unique historical facts are not worth investigating, and their meaning is not worth elucidating. Marx's view of history renders history meaningless and futile. Arendt observes: "In the classless society the best mankind can do with history is to forget the whole unhappy affair, whose only purpose was to abolish itself. It cannot bestow meaning on particular occurrences either because it has dissolved all of the particular into means whose meaningfulness ends the moment the end-product is finished: single events and deeds and sufferings have no more meaning than hammer and nails have with respect to the finished table."[25]

We have so far outlined Arendt's criticisms of Marx's theory of labor, work, and action. We should now briefly expound her criticism of Marx's epistemology. According to Arendt, Marx subjects thought to the "inexorable despotism of necessity" and reduces it to logical reasoning, to little more than spelling out the logical implications of the laws of history.[26] For Marx, human thought is necessarily end-directed and operates within a rigid historicist framework. Such a functional and instrumental view deprives thought of such powers as imagination, creativity, disinterested contemplation, intellectual wonder, and playfulness. The playful and imaginative exploration of the interrelations between ideas plays no part in Marx's epistemology. Further, since human thought in Marx is tied to life or "necessity" and does little more than solve its practical problems, it lacks the capacity to transcend the exigencies of life and create imaginative systems of ideas. What is more, Marx's epistemology destroys the objectivity and transcendence of truth. For Marx man does not discover truth but "makes" things come true by means of *praxis*. On such a "pragmatist" view, for which truth is not given but manufactured, one can no longer distinguish between truth and opinion, between *episteme* and *doxa*, and the very idea of truth is rendered meaningless.

In Marx, then, thought remains postivistically enchained to the prevailing reality. Since human reason for Marx is activated and developed by labor, it accepts the ends and values of the *animal laborans*. It cannot even imagine, much less criticize, the inadequacy and futility of the life devoted to material abundance. In Arendt's view this is evident in the fact noted above that Marx's communist society differs little from the society as it already exists. It eliminates poverty, eases the life of the laborer, and creates free time, but it does not in any way transcend the world-view of the laborer.

It is Marx's pragmatist and instrumental view of thought that informs his desire to realize philosophy in practice. For Arendt, philosophy is inherently contemplative and theoretical. It deals with "eternal verities" and is "not of this world." Marx's proposal to realize philosophy is feasible only if philosophy is made worldly, that is, reduced to the level of *praxis*. Hegel had already paved the way for this by turning philosophy in its old metaphysical sense into a philosophy of history. Marx carried the process further and turned Hegel's philosophy of history into a historicist philosophy of politics. For Marx philosophy is concerned with nothing more than prescribing the rules of political action.[27] In taking this view he distorted philosophical consciousness and deprived thought of one area where it can rise above the clamor of the world of necessity and experience "highest" freedom. Not only the philosophical thought but also the world of politics, in whose interest philosophy was dragged down to the marketplace, suffered. Politics lost its autonomy and became merely a vehicle for the realization of abstract and *a priori* ideas.

Let us sum up Arendt's criticisms of Marx. Marx completely failed to understand the nature of, and the relationship between, the *vita contemplativa* and the *vita activa*. He one-sidedly emphasized labor, and in so doing misunderstood both it and the other two activities. One consequence of this was that both his diagnosis of the modern society and his proposed remedy remained utterly inadequate. His diagnosis did little more than uncritically reiterate at the theoretical level the modern age's obsessive preoccupation with material interests and its reduction of all activities to labor. As for his ideal society, it represented nothing more than the age-old dream of the *animal laborans,* "which can have a charm of its own so long as it is a dream, but turns into a fool's paradise as soon as it is realized."[28] In Marx's communist society men, devoid of a shared objective world and an organized political space, and lacking a sense of individuality and freedom, spend their time in labor and private hobbies. We are already close to Marx's quite "unutopian" ideal, which goes to show that it was little more than a positivist projection of the trends inherent in the contemporary world. Marx's ideal society negates each of his basic theses and reveals the "fundamental and flagrant contradictions" of his thought. Arendt observes:

> If labor is the most human and most productive of man's activities, what will happen when, after the revolution, "labor is abolished" in "the realm of freedom," when man has succeeded in emancipating himself from it? What productive and what essentially human activity will be left? If violence is the midwife of history and violent action therefore the most dignified of all forms of human action, what will happen when, after the conclusion of class struggle and the disappearance of the state, no violence will even be possible? How will men be able to act at all in a meaningful, authentic way? Finally, when philosophy has been both realized and abolished in the future society, what kind of thought will be left?[29]

We outlined above most of Arendt's criticisms of Marx. The criticisms are obviously uneven. Some spring from amazing misinterpretations of Marx: some others are plausible on one interpretation of Marx but not on another; some others make points that Marx ignores but which can be incorporated in his thought; and finally, some of her criticism make telling points that seriously impugn the validity of the relevant aspects of Marx's thought. Since we cannot here examine all her criticisms, we shall concentrate on the more important ones.

Most of Arendt's criticisms are based on her view that Marx's is basically a philosophy of labor. For her, Marx took labor, not reason, to be the *differentia specifica* of man, defined labor as the exercise of labor-power or of "life-force," and regarded material abundance as the highest good. Each of these theses rests on a misunderstanding of Marx.

For Marx man differs from the animal in the fact that, unlike the latter, he is capable of *purposive or rational* labor. Marx held this view throughout his life. In his early writings he conceptualized the *differentia specifica* of man in terms of his well-known concept of species-being, which Arendt notes but misunderstands. And although Marx later abandoned the term, he retained the concept.

For Marx, man is a species-being and the animal is not, because man has a capacity to classify objects into relevant species.[30] The ability to classify is ultimately the ability to form concepts, to abstract the shared features of a group of objects, and to make statements of differing degrees of universality. In effect, man is a species-being because he has a capacity for conceptual thinking, for abstraction. Man's capacity for conceptual thinking is the source of further differences between him and the animal. Unlike the latter, man is a self-conscious, free, and universal being. The animal is "directly identical with" or "directly merged" into its life-activity, and is unable to detach itself from its environment and activities. By contrast man is able to distance and distinguish himself from his activities, his environment, and even from himself, and is aware of himself as a subject. Man is not a being-in-himself but a being-for-himself, and is capable of self-consciousness. Further, man is a free being and the animal is not. An animal produces only when compelled by immediate physical needs, whereas man not only anticipates his needs but produces better when no longer under the coercive sway of urgent physical wants. Finally, since man has a capacity for conceptual thinking, his labor, unlike the animal's, is not confined to his "immediate sensible environment" but takes the entire world of nature as its field of action.

Marx's concept of labor then has rationality built into it. Labor to him *means* rational labor. As he puts it, "we presuppose labor in a form that stamps it as exclusively human."[31] Arendt's contrast between Marx's *animal laborans* and the traditional *animal rationale* is therefore mistaken. Marx does not doubt that man is distinguished by his rationality. His point is that the abstract and subjective faculty of reason becomes an effective power in the world only when it is embodied in, and guides, the concrete material activity of production. Marx calls such a rationally planned activity of production, labor. It need hardly be said that he does not view labor as a natural force or an exertion of raw bodily energy, but a purposive and planned activity in which man activates his rational and physical powers to transform nature.

Since Marx understands labor so very differently from Arendt, he invests it with the significance and dignity denied by her. Indeed, for him labor has many of the characteristics of Arendt's three activities. Labor is necessary to ensure the survival of the species. In this sense, and in this sense only, Marx's labor is like Arendt's labor. Labor has many of the characteristics of what Arendt calls work. As we shall presently see, labor for Marx is the activity by which man "works over" nature, produces distinct objects, and acquires a sense of reality and objectivity. By means of labor he interferes with the cyclical processes of nature and creates a habitable world of lasting objects that stand as permanent monuments to his powers and reality. Indeed, *contra* Arendt, Marx's basic concern is not to reduce work to labor but rather the opposite. He aims, somewhat optimistically, to transform all labor into work, into a freely chosen activity that expresses its agent's distinctive powers and results in durable objects.

Labor, finally, has many of the characteristics of Arendt's action. For Marx, labor is a fundamental form of human *praxis*. By means of it man creates not only the world but also himself. He develops his powers of concentration, self-discipline, rational subordination of means to ends, creativity, social cooperation, scientific knowledge, and the like. As he creates the world and himself, he also creates new social and political structures and new modes of perception and thought. Marx's theory is, no doubt, open to criticism, but the point that concerns us here is that, for Marx, labor, like Arendt's action, raises man above the realm of necessity and is a vehicle of human freedom and creativity. Furthermore, since labor is a rational and purposive activity, the objects it creates are not mere use-objects. In the objects he makes and the way he makes them, the worker discloses himself—his capacities, needs, social concerns, and aspirations. The products of human labor are therefore vehicles of meanings and values, and not mute objects upon which meaning is subsequently conferred by some other human activity.

Marx's concept of labor then is far more subtle and complex than Arendt imagines and includes Arendt's three basic activities. The difference between him and Arendt is that while she neatly separates the three activities, Marx views them as three different but interrelated dimensions of a single activity. From Marx's point of view, Arendt's rather rigid trichotomous division leads her to misunderstand the nature of, and the interrelation between, the three activities. In her classificatory schema labor belongs to the realm of necessity, and meaning to that of freedom. Consequently she accepts it as inevitable that labor *must* remain cyclical, repetitive, and monotonous, and can *never* become meaningful and fulfilling. She discusses the realm of necessity almost entirely in terms of the abolition of poverty, and never asks if and how labor can be made satisfying, expressive of the laborer's powers and needs, and a source of self-fulfillment and self-realization.

Arendt's neat separation of the realms of necessity and freedom prevents her from noticing that the realm of necessity allows for considerable freedom, in the sense that men can collectively organize and plan production, devise ways of eliminating or minimizing the detailed division of labor, make working conditions attractive and pleasant, and provide for industrial democracy and collective self-determination.

Even as Arendt misunderstands labor, she misunderstands its opposite, namely action. Arendt's concept of action is so abstract that it does not connect with the world. For her, action represents man's capacity to transcend nature and necessity. Indeed, for her, action is not only a supranatural but a supernatural activity. In action man performs "miracles," creates the "extraordinary" and the "unpredictable," and "reveals" himself. Action appears from "nowhere" and cannot be causally explained. Arendt's detailed discussion of Jesus in the chapter on action, as well as her description of him as the original discoverer of the human capacity for action, reinforce the point. It is also worth noting that she ontologically links the capacity for action to the human condition of natality. She observes: "The miracle that saves the world, the realm of human affairs, from its normal 'natural' ruin is ultimately the fact of natality, in which the faculty of action is ontologically rooted."[32] For her the "glad tidings" announced by the gospels, "A child has been born unto us," provides the "most glorious and most succinct" statement of the human context of action. For Arendt action gives to the mortal man the glimpse of the supernatural within the framework of the natural world. Predictably she conceptualizes action in terms of categories characteristic of the Christian doctrine of revelation. When a man acts, he "reveals" himself and reaffirms the "miracle" inherent in the initial appearance of the human species.

Arendt is led to take such a curious, although fascinating, view of action because of her questionable attempt to separate freedom and necessity. Action must have a content, as otherwise it becomes a self-indulgent pursuit of self-disclosure. And the content can come only from the world, both natural and social. Men act because they want to change the world. Their actions are therefore inevitably subject to the constraints inherent in the structure of the natural and social world. Technological development, the established social structure, the needs and desires it develops, etc., delimit the range of possibility and impose constraints by which action remains bound. Freedom cannot consist in transcending necessity, as Arendt suggests, but in finding its way around in it. Even as the realm of necessity leaves room for freedom, the realm of freedom is profoundly shaped by the realm of necessity.

One can go even further. The way men spend their lives in the realm of necessity profoundly shapes the way they behave in the realm of freedom. As Arendt herself observes, the *animal laborans*, used to the life of necessity, lacks the feel for action. This would seem to suggest to anyone interested in freedom not that the realm of necessity should be kept as it is and freedom confined only to the talented few, as Arendt argues, but rather that the realm of necessity should be radically restructured so as to conduce to freedom as Marx proposed. For Marx when men collectively take all the decisions affecting their lives and are treated with dignity rather than being subject to someone's arbitrary will, that is, when freedom becomes for them a real experience in every area of life, above all work, they develop a desire for freedom and action. Freedom in the realm of necessity is the necessary material basis of freedom in the political and other areas of life.

To be sure, Arendt is not insensitive to Marx's social and economic concerns. She is a political radical who, like Marx, is opposed to the institution of the state and proposes to replace it by a fully fledged system of democratic participation. She is not an economic conservative either. She admires the working-class struggle against the "injustice and hypocrisies" of capitalism, although rather strangely she believes that these evils have now "disappeared."[33] At places she goes even further and her economic thought links up with Marx's. Discussing one of Marx's early articles criticizing the law against the theft of wood, she observes that Marx there shows that the law against the theft of wood views men only as property-owners and worldly objects only as articles of property. She compliments him for emphasizing that "things are denatured when they are used for exchange."[34] Like Marx, Arendt seems to be critical of the very phenomenon of exchange and the implied object-alienation, and therefore of the entire capitalist economy. She is, however, unable to develop these and other radical insights because of her separation of the realms of freedom and necessity in general, and of politics and economics in particular, and the resulting failure to examine the only material and social conditions under which freedom, as she understands it, is possible. Marx would probably say about her what he said about Hegel: She has "prepared and elaborated" her own critique, which strives to "rise far above" her restrictive conceptual framework.

Arendt argues that Marx's obsessive and one-sided preoccupation with labor prevents him from appreciating the objectivity of the world. She even goes so far as to say that Marx is totally opposed to objectification.[35] In the light of our earlier remarks, her criticism is obviously mistaken. The concept of objectification plays a crucial role in Marx's philosophy. For Marx, only what is "objective, observable, visible" is real. An individual acquires a sense of reality when he becomes "objective," that is, objectifies his powers and impulses in concrete objects. "A being that has no object outside itself is not an objective being. . . . A non-objective being is a non-being."[36] An individual's identity is located in and ascertained by means of the objects he creates and values. Marx understands objectification not only in expressivist terms as Hegel did, but also in creative terms. In creating objects, man does not merely express the powers he already possesses but discovers new possibilities and problems, and develops unexpected capacities. For Marx human self-objectification is both a source of human reality and a means of human self-creation.

Since objectification is so crucial to Marx's philosophy of man, it was one of the grounds on which he criticized both idealist philosophers and capitalism. He criticized Hegel for failing to provide for objectification; he criticized the Young Hegelians for their subjectivist "horror of objects"; and he criticized Stirner's

egoism for its tendency to destroy the "objective world." Similarly
Marx criticized capitalism for its "object alienation," its "loss of the
objects," its destruction of the "objective world," and its tendency to
reduce all objects to articles of consumption.[37] Under capitalism
work is not the source of the worker's sense of reality and
self-fulfillment. The worker alienates his labor to another. He has
no control over his activity or its products. Indeed he does not
produce objects but commodities, impermanent and mutually
substitutable articles only produced to be exchanged and
consumed. As a result he lacks a sense of freedom, creative
satisfaction, and objectivity. What is more, under exchange
economy qualitatively distinct human activities and objects are
reduced to an abstract and homogeneous social labor of which they
are so many quantitative determinations. Labor loses its individuality, and the laborer becomes an indistinguishable atom in a vast
social organism. As for the capitalist, he is motivated only by
abstract wealth. Indeed he is nothing but an embodiment of
capital, a human medium through which capital, like Hegel's *Geist,*
realizes its inner *telos.* Even as the worker is reduced to an
objectless subject, the capitalist is reduced to a subjectless object.
In an unplanned society geared only to the accumulation of
wealth, material production becomes, like the processes of nature,
autonomous, self-propelling, cyclical, and coercive.

It would have been noticed that the criticisms Marx makes of
capitalism are substantially similar to those Arendt levels against
Marx. Marx argues that the capitalist society is abstract, nature-
like, destructive of individuality, reduces work to labor and the
products of labor to alienable articles of consumption, and so on.
He does not justify but *condemns* the perversion of labor in the
capitalist society and aims to construct a social order in which labor
can become meaningful work. Strange as it may seem, Arendt's
criticisms of the modern laboring society and of Marx are Marxist
in inspiration and are an unwitting compliment to Marx's
remarkably accurate diagnosis of the world-alienation characteristic of the capitalist society.

Arendt is on stronger grounds in her criticism of Marx's

theories of politics and history, although even here she is guilty of serious misinterpretations. There is no evidence to support her contention that Marx "glorified" violence and considered it the "most dignified" of all forms of political action. As Arendt herself later acknowledged, Marx takes an instrumental view of violence. He never ascribed to violence the ontological properties that Wagner and Bakunin did, nor the epistemological properties that Blanqui and Sorel did, nor the moral properties that Fanon and Sartre do. In his view violence has no creative powers; it can only act as a "midwife" and remove hindrances to the birth of a new social order. Whether even this degree of violence is necessary depends on the behavior of the dominant class. If it chooses to put up resistance, the proletariat has no alternative but to use violence; if it does not, the proletarian violence is unnecessary. Marx did, no doubt, say that organized struggle is necessary to raise proletarian consciousness, but struggle need not be, and Marx did not intend it to be, equated with violence. Struggle refers to agitation, strikes, demonstrations, and the like, in which violence plays a subordinate and essentially defensive role. Marx welcomed universal franchise and thought that the liberal-democratic polity created the possibility, albeit no more than the possibility, of achieving the new social order by peaceful means.[38]

Arendt argues that Marx takes a naturalistic view of politics and ignores the role of speech, individuality, freedom, and principle, which for her are uniquely characteristic of political action. She is only partly right. Arendt argues that Marx's political action is motivated by material interests and not by political principles. Her contention springs from a misinterpretation of Marx and rests on an untenable dichotomy. For Marx, political action aims to create a social order in which every man can freely develop his full human potential and live a rich and meaningful life. Material abundance is a necessary precondition of this, and hence Marx's emphasis on it. However, it is no more than a precondition and derives its importance from the values it exists to facilitate, such as individuality, freedom, absence of domination, collective self-determination, and creative self-realization. Marx's plea for the communist revolution, whether in the *Paris Manuscripts* and *On the Jewish Question* or in the *Grundrisse* and *Capital*, is based on humanist rather than material grounds.

As we observed, Marx would reject Arendt's dichotomy between material interests and political principles. Marx establishes a dialectical relationship between the two. Unlike Arendt, for whom the *animal laborans* is forever confined to the life of consumption, Marx argues that once poverty and wretchedness are eliminated and human life becomes relatively relaxed, men might begin to ask if they must go on consuming like animals or whether they should organize their personal and social lives differently. As they have more time to spend with their family and friends, they begin to rediscover the beauty of love and affection. As they undertake hobbies to fill their free time, they develop creative impulses and interests and wonder why their daily work too cannot offer creative satisfaction. As they read books and take interest in the world, they begin to raise larger questions about the meaning and significance of human life. In short, once the basic needs of the *animal laborans* are satisfied, he might no longer want to remain a mere *animal laborans*. He might develop new impulses and aspirations, which might eventually become the "inner necessity" of his nature, and dialectically generate a new lifestyle, a new set of values. If Marx is guilty of optimism, Arendt is guilty of pessimism—for empirical researches in the lifestyle of the modern affluent society point in both directions.

Arendt is on stronger grounds when she criticizes Marx for ignoring the role of speech in political life. To be sure, speech does play an important role in Marx's political thought. The proletarian consciousness cannot be raised without a constant critique of the dominant ideology, and the political organization of the proletariat needs inspiring words of which Marx's *Communist Manifesto* and his speeches to working-class groups are as good examples as those Arendt admires. However, the fact remains that Marx's theory of language underplays both what Habermas calls the communicative and what Arendt calls the inspirational and symbolic functions of language. Marx takes a rather functional view of language. Political language for him does little more than articulate the political objectives of the working classes and criticize the dominant ideology.

Marx's failure to appreciate the role of language in politics springs from several interrelated sources. Language for him is objective thought, and since, as we shall see, he takes a functional view of thought, he takes a functional view of language also. Further, Marx took an evolutionist and objectivist view of social change. He thought that in the course of its development the capitalist society generates desires and needs which it cannot itself satisfy and which therefore become the sources of revolutionary consciousness. Marx's belief in the absolute immiseration of the proletariat meant that poverty was a sufficient source of revolutionary dynamism. His later emphasis on relative immiseration shifted the source of revolutionary energy from poverty to an equally objective desire for equality and justice. Marx also thought that the constant technological advances in the capitalist society require broadly trained workers and generate in them a desire for "self-activity" that cannot be satisfied within the capitalist society. Since Marx took the view that capitalism by its own inner logic creates revolutionary desires, he did not see the importance of moral and political idealism, and therefore of the inspirational role of language.

Finally, and what is but a converse of the point just discussed, even as Marx thought that the socially generated desires and needs of the proletariat would lead it to undertake revolutionary actions without the assistance of personal moral idealism, he thought that the bourgeoisie, being motivated by such socially generated desires as greed, are not amenable to argument, persuasion, an appeal to their moral idealism or humanity, and the like. The only language they understand is the language of confrontation and struggle. Their ideas are ideological rationalizations of their interests, and while their exposure is necessary to develop proletarian consciousness, it in no way influences bourgeois consciousness nor opens up a dialogue between the two classes. While Arendt grasps the power but not the limitations of argument and discussion, Marx made the opposite mistake.

In criticizing Marx's theory of history Arendt reflects the widespread view that Marx believed in historical laws and necessity. The criticism springs from a mistaken assimilation of Marx's theory of history to Hegel's. It is *assumed* that since the dialectical method implies historical necessity, and since Marx adopted it, he *must* believe in historical necessity. Arendt argues in this way when she observes that Marx "carried the theories of dialectics into action, making political action more theoretical, more dependent upon what we today would call an ideology, than it ever had been before.[39] We cannot here pursue the complex question of the role of the dialectic in Marx's thought, and shall only observe that he drastically modified Hegel's view of it. Marx does not believe that historical epochs necessarily follow one another, and in his letters to his Russian followers disowned all attempts to foist such a view on him. Alfred Schmidt has persuasively argued that Marx generally confines the dialectic to the capitalist society. Marx's analysis of the "laws" of capitalism, no doubt, plays an important part in his political thought, but not the alleged laws of history; and as has been shown by his commentators, Marx used the term "law" rather loosely to mean little more than the tendencies inherent in unrestrained capitalism.

Arendt maintains that Marx anchored proletarian politics in a historicist framework. This is true only of the early Marx. Marx's thought on this question passed through three identifiable stages. In his *Contribution to the Critique of Hegel's Philosophy of Right* and in his Introduction to it, he took it to be the task of philosophy to determine the political imperatives inherent in the objective social being of the proletariat. Relying mainly on Hegel's logic, he looked upon the negative class as the sole vehicle of revolutionary change, and presented the proletariat as the absolute negation of capitalism. On other occasions, principally in the Introduction referred to earlier and some of his journalistic writings, Marx turned from philosophy to history. The philosopher deduces from history its direction of movement, determines the next task on the historical agenda, and turns to the proletariat for its execution. In the *German Ideology* Marx rejected the first view and dismissed philosophy itself as a form of intellectual masturbation; in the same work and in the *Poverty of Philosophy*, he also rejected the second view and dismissed the historicist language as a residue of religious transcendentalism. His view from then onward was that the ends of proletarian political action are derived from the proletariat's own needs and aspirations. Thanks to the development of capitalism, the workers develop needs and powers, such as the need for material prosperity, self-activity, self-determination, cooperative living, and human solidarity, that cannot be satisfied within the capitalist framework. The ends of political action are not superimposed upon the proletariat by an intellectual elite, nor derived from history, but dialectically teased out of their actual hopes, desires, and aspirations.

Arendt's criticisms of Marx's theory of the nature of human thought are vague but suggestive and basically sound. In the absence of a clear statement, it is difficult to see the force of her distinction between thinking, reasoning, cognition, and contemplation. Furthermore, Arendt's epistemology is rather vague. Her view that truth is "given" or "disclosed" by reality and not a product of human endeavor, her hostility to experimental science, her view of contemplation, her view that philosophy is not "of this world," her separation of the pursuit of truth and of human well-being, and her distinction between the *vita activa* and the *vita contemplativa* raise far more awkward questions than she realizes.

Despite these and other inadequacies and ambiguities of her position, Arendt is right to argue that Marx takes an instrumental and ultimately unsatisfactory view of human thought. For Marx consciousness is "consciousness of material existence." It is deeply rooted in the world of *praxis* from which it derives its categories, ends, and problems. It is inherently practical and problem-oriented. Non-practical thinking, imaginative fantasies, playful exploration of ideas, etc. are, in Marx's view, not natural to consciousness and symbols of alienation. It is this assumption that underlies Marx's inquiry into the nature and origin of religion. His analysis of religion rests on the belief that it is not natural to consciousness to fly away from the real world and construct a parallel, "unreal" world. Since the religious consciousness behaves in an "abnormal" and pathological manner, Marx looks for a causal explanation of it in the social structure. Marx likewise treats the Hegelian and the Left-Hegelian philosophy, and indeed, philosophy itself, as a kind of perversion of consciousness. For obvious reasons Marx's somewhat *simpliste* and one-dimensional epistemology has great difficulty explaining such sub-rational, as well as non- and extra-rational, forms of thought as primitive myth and magic, Plato's sense of intellectual wonder, Augustine's feeling of the apparent futility of human existence, the Kierkegaardian "dread," and even religious idealism. No wonder Engels was led to say that such "primitive non-sense" cannot be materialistically and scientifically explained.

The positivist bias of Marx's epistemology, as Arendt rightly points out, limits its critical power. Arendt's view is widely shared and has recently been ably argued, partly under her influence, by Habermas and by Albrecht Wellmer. Marx talks of human needs, but is unable to say which needs are genuinely human, which perverse and alienating, and why. His discussion of the question in the *Paris Manuscripts* is too sketchy to be of much help, and rests on a philosophical anthropology that he later qualified. Marx's inadequacy is strikingly evident in the familiar Marxist perplexity in the face of the proletariat's co-optation in the bourgeois society. When the proletariat is content to fight for higher wages, how can it be persuaded that it *ought* to fight for a new civilization? As this issue has been widely discussed, let us take two examples from the rather mundane but nevertheless important area of human sexuality which demonstrate Marx's limitations equally well.

The Marxist New Left sees nothing wrong in homosexuality, whereas Engels and the Communists condemn it. For the latter it is a product of man's alienation from woman in the class-divided society, and will disappear in the communist society. The alienation argument is, obviously, shaky. If homosexuality is a product of the class-divided society's degradation of woman, it could also be argued that this is no less true of heterosexuality. A class-divided society values only productive labor, and therefore both idealizes heterosexuality, which is productive, and condemns homosexuality, which is not. The communist society takes a different view of labor and must therefore approve of homosexuality as well. The only argument Marx and Engels advance in support of heterosexuality is that it is necessary for the reproduction of the species. In an age when test-tube babies are within the realm of possibility, the development of reproductive forces no longer requires old relations of reproduction. Heterosexuality is no longer as important as it once was. *Should* we then accept all forms of sexual gratification as legitimate? One looks to Marx in vain for guidance on this question.

Marxist thought offers equally little guidance on the question of incest, a hotly debated issue among feminists. For both Marx and Engels the taboo on incest was made necessary by the need to preserve the integrity of the family, which in turn was necessary for the preservation of the institution of property. It follows that with the disappearance of private property in the communist society, the taboo *need* not continue. However this does not tell us whether it *should* continue. For some Marxists it should; for others, incest should become a legitimate practice in the communist society. Since Marx did not develop a critical theory of men, he is unable to offer a criterion for resolving the debate.

Although philosophers aim to be comprehensive and to do full justice to all aspects of reality, their systems of thought are almost invariably partial and imbalanced. For a variety of reasons they are struck by some particular aspect or aspects of reality that absorb most of their attention and energy. They analyze these aspects with great subtlety and skill and offer new and brilliant insights. Their strength, however, is also their limitation.

The intensity of their concentration on some aspects of reality leads them to ignore, misunderstand, or underplay the importance of others, They see some things so very clearly that those they do not see so clearly fall out of their vision.

Arendt and Marx are no exceptions. Arendt is fascinated by the phenomenon of action and offers a brilliant and original analysis of it. No other political philosopher has articulated the nature, mechanism, complexity, pathos, and significance of action as well as she has. However, because she places so much importance on and is so very preoccupied with action, and views the *vita activa* from its standpoint, she misses some crucial aspects of work and, especially, of labor and betrays a lack of imagination in her discussion of them. She overlooks the wide range of diverse activities that each includes. Labor involved in giving birth to a child is different from labor in a factory, and the production of a tool is a different kind of work from producing a work of art. Further, she overlooks and underplays the importance of the several crucial aspects of both labor and work. She does not appreciate that labor is not merely concerned with survival but is also a mode of human self-expression. And similarly she fails to notice that work is itself a source of meaning. Composing a poem or painting a picture can be as fulfilling and meaningful as political action, if not more so. Again, while she is right to highlight the distinctive nature of action and its close links with freedom, she is wrong to disjoin freedom and necessity as neatly as she does.

In contrast to Arendt, Marx is the philosopher of what Arendt calls work. The nature and significance of the phenomenon of work absorbs his attention. He offered a brilliant analysis of it whose originality is widely recognized. He saw its world-creating power and offered a powerful critique of its degrading and wasteful use in the class-divided society. Marx's emphasis on work, or material production, led him to develop a most stimulating theory of historical materialism and class struggle. However, his strength was also his limitation. As we saw he underemphasized or failed to appreciate the complexity of human society, the mutidimensionality of human thought, the role of speech, the significance of human individuality, and so on. Indeed, unable to appreciate the complexity of political life and the need for philosophical thought, Marx was unable to develop a political philosophy. Since his failure was not a personal deficiency but sprang from the basic limitations of his thought, his followers have never really been able to provide a viable alternative to, or a powerful critique of, the mainstream tradition of political philosophy.

Since Arendt's political philosophy is brilliant and valid in some areas but pedestrian and even invalid in others, her criticisms of Marx are necessarily uneven. Her criticisms of his cavalier attitude to philosophy and of his epistemology are persuasive, and so are her criticisms of his neglect of the role of language and individuality in politics. By contrast her criticisms of Marx's theories of work, history, revolution, historical materialism, etc., fail to carry conviction. A philosopher's limitations are closely tied up with his strength. And therefore no philosopher can be effectively criticized unless the critic fully appreciates his strength. One cannot go beyond a philosopher without first getting as far as he has got. Arendt generally fails to appreciate the magnitude of Marx's achievements, and consequently, while some of her criticisms are valid and deserve close attention, her overall critique remains unpersuasive.

NOTES

1. Hannah Arendt, *The Human Condition* (Chicago: University of Chicago Press, 1971), p. 14.

2. Ibid., pp. 136*ff.*

3. Ibid., p. 177.

4. Ibid., pp. 59, 70, 71, 135.

5. Ibid., pp. 176, 236.

6. Ibid., pp. 109, 207, 208.

7. Hannah Arendt, *Between Past and Future: Six Exercises in Political Thought* (London: Faber and Faber, 1961), pp. 24*ff.*

8. Arendt, *The Human Condition,* p. 100.

9. Ibid., p. 108.

10. Hannah Arendt, *The Origins of Totalitarianism* (London: Allen and Unwin, 1962), p. 464 and *The Human Condition*, p. 111*ff.*

11. Arendt, *The Human Condition*, p. 321.

12. Ibid., p. 116.

13. Ibid., p. 108.

14. Ibid., p. 256.

15. Ibid., pp. 117*ff.*, 128.

16. Arendt, *Between Past and Future*, pp. 22*ff.*

17. Hannah Arendt, *On Revolution* (New York: The Viking Press, 1963), p. 108.

18. Ibid., pp. 55*ff.*

19. Ibid., p. 58.

20. Arendt, *Origins of Totalitarianism*, p. 34.

21. Arendt, *The Human Condition*, p. 71.

22. Ibid., p. 133.

23. Arendt, *Between Past and Future*, p. 89.

24. Ibid., pp. 76*ff.* and *On Revolution*, pp. 45*ff.*

25. Arendt, *Between Past and Future*, p. 80.

26. Ibid., p. 32.

27. Ibid., p. 30.

28. Arendt, *The Human Condition*, p. 133.

29. Arendt, *Between Past and Future*, p. 24.

30. For a detailed discussion of Marx's concept of species-being see my *The Concept of Socialism* (New York: Holmes and Meier, 1975), pp. 46*ff.*

31. Karl Marx, *Capital* (London: Lawrence and Wishart, 1970), Vol. 1, pp. 42*ff.*

32. Arendt, *The Human Condition*, p. 247.

33. Ibid., p. 219.

34. Ibid.. p. 254.

35. Ibid., pp. 89, 102.

36. Karl Marx, *Economic and Philosophic Manuscripts* (Moscow: Progress Publishers, 1961), p. 157.

37. Ibid., p. 69.

38. See, for example, Shlomo Avineri, *The Social and Political Thought of Karl Marx* (London: Cambridge University Press, 1970), pp. 186*ff.*, 202*ff.*

39. Arendt, *Between Past and Future*, p. 30.

Kenneth Frampton

THE STATUS OF MAN AND THE STATUS OF HIS OBJECTS: A READING OF *THE HUMAN CONDITION*

> *The only philosophy which can be responsibly practised in the face of despair is the attempt to contemplate all things as they would present themselves from the stand-point of redemption; all else is reconstruction, mere technique. Perspectives must be fashioned that displace and estrange the world, reveal it to be, with its rifts and crevices, as indigent and distorted as it will appear one day in the messianic light.*
>
> Theodor Adorno
> Minima Moralia, 1947

The Architectural Corollaries of Labor and Work

In her book *The Human Condition*, significantly subtitled "a study of the central dilemmas facing modern man," Arendt designated three activities—*labor, work,* and *action*—as being fundamental to the *vita activa*. She established at the beginning of her argument the particular meaning that she would consistently assign to each of these terms. Of *labor* she wrote: "Labor is the activity which corresponds to the biological process of the human body, whose spontaneous growth, metabolism, and eventual decay are bound to the vital necessities produced and fed into the life process by labor. The human condition of labor is life itself."[1]

Of *work* she wrote: "Work is the activity which corresponds to the un-naturalness of human existence, which is not embedded in, and whose mortality is not compensated by the species' ever-recurring life-cycle. Work provides an artificial world of things distinctly different from all natural surroundings. Within its borders each individual life is housed while this world itself is meant to outlast and transcend them all. The human condition of work is worldliness."[2]

In her definition of the public and private attributes of the *vita activa*—the former having a dependency on the latter— Arendt amplified further her unusual distinction between *work* and *labor*. She argued that labor by being a constantly transforming but repetitive procedure—akin to the cycle of biological survival—is inherently *processal, private,* and *impermanent,* whereas work, by virtue of being the precondition for the reification of the world as the space of human appearance, is by definition *static, public,* and *permanent.*

An architect could hardly fail to remark on the correspondence between these distinctions and the fundamental ambiguity of the term "architecture"; an ambiguity that finds reflection in the *Oxford English Dictionary* in two significantly different definitions—first, "the art or science of constructing edifices for human use" and second, "the action and process of building."[3] These definitions with their potential hierarchy latent even in the etymology of the Greek term *architektōn*—meaning chief constructor—proffer themselves as paralleling the distinction that Arendt draws between work and labor.[4]

The designation "for human use" imparts a specifically human, if not humanist, connotation to the whole of the first definition, alluding to the creation of a specifically human world, whereas the phrase "the action and process of building" in the second definition clearly implies a continuous act of building forever incomplete, comparable to the unending process of biological labor. The fact that the dictionary asserts that the word "edifice" may be used to refer to "a large and stately building such as a church, a palace, or a fortress" serves to support the work connotation of the first definition, since these building types, as the "representations" of spiritual and temporal power, have always been, at least until recent times, both public and permanent. Furthermore, the word "edifice" relates directly to the verb "to edify," which not only carries within itself the meaning "to build" but also "to educate," "to strengthen," and "to instruct"—connotations that allude directly to the political restraint of the public realm. Again the Latin root of this verb—*aedificare*, from *aedes*, a "building," or, even more originally, a "hearth," and *ficare*, "to make," has latent within it the public connotation of the hearth as the aboriginal "public" space of appearance. This aspect persists even today in the domestic realm, where surely no place is more of a forum in the contemporary home than the hearth or its surrogate, the television set, which as an illusory public substitute tends to inhibit or usurp the spontaneous emergence of "public" discourse within the private domain.

Within the corpus of modern architectural theory, no text is more aware of the respective *stati* of architecture and building than Adolf Loos's essay "Architecture 1910," wherein he characterizes the eminently biological, innate, and repetitive nature of vernacular construction in the following terms:

> The peasant cuts out the spot on the green grass where the house is to be built and digs out the earth for the foundation walls. Then the mason appears. If there is loamy soil in the vicinity, then there will also be a brickworks to provide the bricks. If not, then stone from the riverbanks can be used for the same purpose. And while the mason places brick upon brick and stone upon stone, the carpenter has established himself nearby. The strokes of the axe ring out merrily. He makes the roof. What kind of roof? One that is beautiful or ugly? He does not know. The roof. . . . His aim was to build a house for himself, his family and his livestock and in this he has succeeded. Just as his neighbours and ancestors

succeeded. As every animal which allows itself to be led by its instincts, succeeds.[5]

Loos was aware that, like the pure instrumentality of engineering, this rooted vernacular had nothing whatsoever to do with the traditionally representative role of architecture. Later in the same text he wrote:

> Only a very small part of architecture belongs to art: the tomb and the monument. Everything else, everything which serves a purpose should be excluded from the realms of art. . . . If we find a mound in the forest, six foot long and three foot wide, formed into a pyramid, shaped by a shovel, we become serious and something within us says, someone lies buried here. This is architecture.

The Public Realm and the Human Artifice

While the representative scope of architecture had already become severely curtailed by the turn of the century, the space of public appearance could still serve not only to house the public realm, but also to represent its reality. Where in the nineteenth century the public institution was exploited as an occasion on which to reify the permanent values of the society, the disintegration of such values in the twentieth century has had the effect of atomizing the public building into a network of abstract institutions. This dissipation of the *agora* reflects that mass society whose alienating force stems not from the number of people but from "the fact that the world between has lost its power to gather them together, to relate and to separate them."[6]

While the political life of the Greek *polis* did not directly stem from the physical presence and representation of the city-state, Arendt emphasizes, in contrast to our present proliferation of urban sprawl, the spontaneous "cantonal" attributes of concentration:

The only indispensable material factor in the generation of power is the living together of people. Only where men live so close together that the potentialities for action are always present will power remain with them and the foundation of cities, which as city states have remained paradigmatic for all Western political organization, is therefore indeed the most important material prerequisite for power.[7]

Nothing could be further from this than our present generation of motopia and our evident incapacity to create new cities that are physically and politically identifiable as such. By the same token, nothing could be more removed from the political essence of the city-state than the exclusively economic categories of rationalistic planning theory; that theory espoused by planners such as Melvin Webber, whose ideological conceptions of *community without propinquity* and the *non-place urban realm* are nothing if not slogans devised to rationalize the absence of any adequate realm of public appearance within modern suburbia.[8] The manipulative and "apolitical" bias of such ideologies has never been more openly expressed than in Robert Venturi's *Complexity and Contradiction in Architecture*, wherein the author asserts that the Americans don't need piazzas, since they should be at home watching television.[9] These and similar reactionary modes of beholding seem to emphasize the impotence of an urbanized populace who have paradoxically lost the object of their urbanization. That their power grew initially out of the city finds corroboration in Arendt's conception of the relations obtaining between politics and built form:

> Power preserves the public realm and the space of appearance, and as such it is also the life blood of the human artifice, which, unless it is the scene of action and speech, of the web of human affairs and relationships and the stories engendered by them, lacks its ultimate *raison d'être*. Without being talked about by men and without housing them, the

world would not be a human artifice but a heap of unrelated things to which each isolated individual was at liberty to add one more object; without the human artifice to house them, human affairs would be as floating, as futile and vain as the wandering of nomadic tribes.[10]

It was a similar realization that the monuments of the Ringstrasse, built around Vienna during the second half of the nineteenth century, were nothing but a sequence of "unrelated things," that caused Camillo Sitte to demonstrate that each of these isolated public structures could be restored to being a *res publica* in itself. In his *City Planning According to Artistic Principles* (1889), he revealed how the fabric of the medieval town had had the capacity of enclosing as a single "political" entity both the monument and its civic piazza.[11]

The Private Realm and the Rise of the Social

While Arendt acknowledges that the rise of modern intimacy and individualism has largely eliminated the aspect of privation from the term "privacy," she nonetheless remains aware that a life excluded from the public realm is still "deprived" by virtue of its being confined to the shadowy domestic interior of the *megaron*— that traditional single-cell volume of the Greek peninsular, whose very etymology reveals the household as the domain of darkness.[12] Unlike the Greeks, who despised the individual domain or *idion* as the province of idiocy,[13] but like the Romans, who valued the interdependence of both realms, Arendt conceives of the private as the essential "darker" ground that not only nourishes the public realm but also establishes its experiential depth. At the same time she recognizes that the rise of the social—to which the intimate is of course related—has had the ultimate effect of impoverishing both the public and private spheres and with this the mediatory capacity of built form to articulate one from the other. Arendt argues that the flowering of the social art form, the novel, after

1750 effectively coincided with the progressive decline of all the public arts, especially architecture.[14] The ultimate triumph of the social in collectivized life has, as Arendt puts it, given rise to a ". . . mass society [that] not only destroys the public realm but the private as well, [and] deprives men not only of their place in the world but of their private home, where they once felt sheltered against the world and where, at any rate, even those excluded from the world could find a substitute in the warmth of the hearth and the limited reality of family life."[15]

This thesis, as to the loss of the private realm at the hands of the social, finds some corroboration in the fragmentary writings of the Mexican architect, Luis Barragan, who has criticized the overexposed landscape of the contemporary suburb in the following terms: "Everyday life is becoming much too public. Radio, TV, the telephone all invade privacy. Gardens should therefore be enclosed, not open to public gaze." Elsewhere, Barragan continues: "Architects are forgetting the need of human beings for half-light, the sort of light that imposes a tranquility, in their living rooms as well as in their bedrooms. About half the glass that is used in so many buildings—homes as well as offices—would have to be removed in order to obtain the quality of light that enables one to live and work in a more concentrated manner. . . ."[16]

Arendt's insight that the triumph of laboring society has condemned man to perpetual movement[17] finds a further echo in Barragan texts wherein he asserts:

Before the machine age, even in the middle of cities, Nature was everybody's trusted companion. . . . Nowadays, the situation is reversed. Man does not meet with Nature, even when he leaves the city to commune with her. Enclosed in his shiny automobile, his spirit stamped with the mark of the world whence the automobile emerged, he is, within Nature, a foreign body. A billboard is sufficient to stifle the voice of Nature. Nature becomes a scrap of Nature and man a scrap of man. . . .[18]

This tendency towards global reduction, not to say of a total fusion, between man. machine. and Nature—latent in the processal triumph of industrial production—finds its ideological corollary in the behavioral sciences of which Arendt has written:

> To gauge the extent of society's victory in the modern age, its early substitution of behavior for action and its eventual substitution of bureaucracy, the rule of nobody, for personal rulership, it may be as well to recall that its initial science of economics, which substitutes patterns of behavior only in this rather limited field of human activity, was finally followed by the all-comprehensive pretension of the social sciences, which as 'behavioral sciences,' aim to reduce man as a whole, in all his activities, to the level of a conditioned and behavioral animal.[19]

The Duality of the Homo Faber: *Artifice* versus *Instrumentality*

The dependency of the human artifice on the work of *homo faber* stems from the intrinsic durability of objects and their capacity to withstand (*Gegenstand*) both the erosions of nature and the processes of use. As Arendt has written:

> The man-made world of things, the human artifice erected by *homo faber*, becomes a home for mortal men, whose stability will endure and outlast the ever-changing movement of their lives and actions, only insomuch as it transcends both the sheer functionalism of things produced for consumption and the sheer utility of objects produced for use. Life in its non-biological sense, the span of time each man has between birth and death, manifests itself in action and speech, both of which share with life its essential futility. . . . If the *animal laborans* needs the help of *homo faber* to ease his labor and to remove his pain, and if mortals need the help of *homo faber*

in his highest capacity that is the help of the artists, of poets and historiographers, the monument builders or writers, because without them, the only product of their activity, the story that they enact and tell would not survive at all. In order to be what the world is meant to be, a home for men during their life on earth, the human artifice must be a place fit for action and speech, for activities not entirely useless for the necessities of life but of an entirely different nature from the manifold activities of fabrication by which itself and all things in it are produced.[20]

No other passage in *The Human Condition* formulates the essential duality of the *homo faber* so succinctly as this—man as the maker split between the fabrication of useless things, such as works of art, which are ends in themselves, and the invention and production of useful objects, which serve as various predetermined means to a given set of ends. For Arendt, *homo faber* is at once both artificer and tool-maker; the builder of the world and the maker of the instruments with which it is built. Where the one addresses itself to the "what" of representation and reification— that is to say, to that object of commemoration which Loos was to consign to the province of art—the other concerns itself with the "how" of utility and process, in which tools tend, at least in the modern world, to be the sole things to survive the occasion of their use. Nothing reveals this second condition of production more than the machine fabrication of goods for consumption, nor the first than the cyclical history of built monuments which, from inception to demolition, testify to a continual transference of value from the past into the future.

The ambiguity of architecture—its status as "edification" or as "building" and often as different aspects within the same physical entity—reflects the parallel ambiguity of the *homo faber*, who is neither pure artist nor pure technician. In a similar manner, representation and commemoration can never be entirely prized apart and the present embodiment of past value already assures its availability for the future. All signification in built form

thus embodies a sense of immortality. This much Arendt attempts
to make clear in her discussion of art:

> In this permanence, the very stability of the human artifice
> which being inhabited and used by mortals can never be
> absolute, achieves a representation of its own. Nowhere else
> does the sheer durability of the world of things appear in such
> purity and clarity, nowhere else therefore does this thing-
> world reveal itself so spectacularly as the non-mortal home
> for mortal beings. It is as though worldly stability had become
> transparent in the permanence of art, so that a premonition
> of immortality, not the immortality of the soul or life but of
> something immortal achieved by mortal hands, has become
> tangibly present to shine and be seen, to sound and be heard,
> to speak and to be read.[21]

While fabrication invariably terminated in the ancient world
in either an instrument of use or an art object, it came with the
emergence of empirical science to insinuate its process into the
methodology of research and, with this deviation, to remove itself
from the traditional teleology of artifice in favor of achieving the
abstract instruments of cognition. The Renaissance, split between
the liberal and the mechanical arts—already anticipatory of the
industrial division of labor—led to the rise of the *homo faber* as a
man of invention and speculation; of which the architect and
uomo universale, Filippo Brunelleschi, was one of the earliest
examples. As G. C. Argan has shown, this rise of the *homo faber* as
architect resulted in widening the incipient division between
invention and fabrication and led to the degradation of the
traditional craftsmen into the status of the *animal laborans*.

> Brunelleschi thought that a new technique could not be
> derived from the past, but must come from a different
> cultural experience, from history. In this way he refuted the
> old "mechanical" technique and created a new "liberal"
> technique based on those typically individualistic actions

which are historical research and inventiveness. He abolished the traditional hierarchical form of the mason's lodge where the head was the co-ordinator of the specialized work of the various groups of skilled workers who made up the lodge of the masters. Now, there was only one planner or inventor; the others were merely manual laborers. When the master mason rose to the status of sole planner, whose activity was on a par with the other humanistic disciplines, the other members of the team of masons fell from the rank of *maestri* in charge of various aspects of the job to that of simple working men. This explains the impatience of the masons and their rebellion against the master mason who had become "architect" or "engineer."[22]

This willful creation of distance between conceiving and building pervades the entire Renaissance. It was as much present in Brunelleschi's invention of perspective or in his machines for the building of the cupola over Sante Maria dei Fiori in Florence in 1420, as it was in Galileo Galilei's invention of the telescope in 1610, with which men first established the proof of the Copernican universe. The effective split of appearance and being that was the consequence of this proof, served to institute Cartesian doubt as the fundamental basis of the new scientific perspective. As Arendt has written:

. . . the Cartesian method of securing certainty against doubt corresponded most precisely with the most obvious conclusion to be drawn from the new physical science; though one cannot know the truth man can at least know what he makes himself. This indeed became the most general and the most generally accepted attitude of the modern age and it is this conviction, rather than the doubt underlying it that propelled one generation after another for more than three hundred years, into an ever quickening pace of discovery and development.[23]

Just as the shift to a heliocentric model of the universe was developed with the aid of an optical tool—the telescope—so the *homo faber* came to his place in the modern world through a reevaluation of his traditional role. From Galileo on, he was not so much valued for his product as an end result but for his process as a means to an end. As Arendt shows, fabrication, which had hitherto disappeared into the product, now became an end in itself since pure science was not interested in the appearance of objects, but in the capacity of objects to reveal the intrinsic structure lying behind all appearance. It abandoned the passive contemplation of objects *per se* for the instrumental penetration of the laws of nature. This effectively reversed the traditional hierarchy of contemplation and action—a shift which, as Arendt shows, had profound consequences for the object of architecture.

As far as *homo faber* was concerned this modern shift of emphasis from the "what" to the "how," from the thing itself to its fabrication process, was by no means an unmixed blessing. It deprived man as maker and builder of those fixed and permanent standards and measurements which prior to the modern age have always served as his guides for doing and criteria for his judgment. It is not only and perhaps not even primarily the development of the commercial society, that with the triumphal victory of exchange value over use value, first introduced the principle of interchangeability, then the relativization, and finally the devaluation of all values. . . . it was at least as decisive that man began to consider himself part and parcel of two super-human, all encompassing processes of nature and history, both of which seemed doomed to an infinite progress without ever reaching any inherent *telos* or approaching any preordained idea.[24]

This shift from the "what" to the "how" found its reflection in the division of engineering from architecture during the Enlightenment; first in Colbert's categorically anti-guild creation of the various royal academies for the arts and sciences including the

Academie Royale d'Architecture (1677), whose "architectural" graduates were to dedicate themselves solely to the "what," that is, to the reification of public structures commissioned by the State; and then in 1747, with Perronet's creation of the *École des Ponts et Chaussées*, whose "engineering" graduates were to concern themselves largely with the "how," namely, with the processal means of gaining permanent access to the realm. That these two aspects of the *homo faber* had already become professionally divided over the defense and siege of the walled city may be gauged from the fact that according to Michel Parent and Jacques Verroust: "In the sixteenth century the defense of towns and castles was the work of *architects*. The word *engineer* remained reserved for those who not only built the siege machines but also handled them."[25] The progressive invasion of the city of artifice by the machine —first the siege engine and later the locomotive, and then of course the electric tram and the automobile—accompanied the ultimate dissolution of the walled city in the middle of the nineteenth century. Aside from its monumental rhetoric and its simultaneous reduction of honorific built-form to the status of being a rentable commodity, the Ringstrasse that came to replace Vienna's fortification in the second half of the century was coincidentally the initial proving ground for the horse-drawn tram.[26]

Deprived by Cartesian doubt of its faith in the received culture of the Renaissance, architectural theory was compelled to search for its authority in the knowledge of an objective archaeology. At the same time it began to look for its creative principle in the all-encompassing processes of nature. Thus while architects began to record and emulate the surviving models of antiquity, natural law came to be asserted as the prime universal principle. Our modern concepts of archaeology and history were both the outcomes of developments such as these. Stripped by science of its magical coalescence, the modern world began to fragment. Since appearance now belied truth, it became necessary to regard form as being separate from content and to this end the modern science of esthetics came into being with Baumgarten's *Aesthetica* (1750). At the same time architectural theoreticians, such as the Abbé Laugier in his *Essai sur l'Architecture* (1753), began to advocate "natural" primitive structures of self-evident lucidity. Pure reduced structure became the paradigm of architecture and light came to be regarded as a metaphor for the illumination of reason itself.

The ascendance of the bourgeoisie, the rise of the social and the intimate, the rediscovery of antiquity, the duality of light and nature as the sublime emanence of the Supreme Being, and above all the influence of Rousseau and Newton combined to distract architecture from the task of realization and to project it into either an archaeologically remote past or an unattainable utopian future. This ideological distraction is prominently displayed in the works of Etienne Boullée, who imagined spectacular masses of masonry, at the scale of natural escarpments—vast megaliths of prohibitive size, penetrated by endless galleries of often inaccessible space. Is it not just such a figure that Arendt had in mind when she wrote of the *homo faber* renouncing his traditional calling in favor of the *vita contemplativa?* "All he had to do was let his arms drop and prolong indefinitely the act of beholding the *eidos,* the eternal shape and model he had formerly wanted to imitate and whose excellence and beauty he now knew he could only spoil through any attempt at reification."[27]

While architectural theory tended toward total dematerialization, as in the writings of Laugier, or toward the surreality of sublime, unrealizable form, as in the images of Boullée, engineering proceeded to work upon nature and to subject its untamed wastes to a measured infrastructure of metalled roads and embanked canals. Its province was now no longer the bastions and counterscarps of the fortified city, but the viaducts, bridges, and dams of a universal system of distribution. Its technique not only outstripped the performance of traditional materials and methods but also afforded a more explicit form of structural expression—one in which structure was transparently penetrated by process. From now on architecture looked to such structure for much of its symbolic substance and we find a late neo-classical architect, such as Karl Friedrich Schinkel, totally ignoring contemporary architecture on his first visit to England in 1826 and recording instead the distributive and productive achievements of the time; the Menai Straits suspension bridge and the "processal" mill buildings of Manchester.

The Animal Laborans *and the Fungibility of the World*

The brute concentration of natural labor-power, as though it were akin to water power, preceded, as Robin Evans has attempted to show, the late-eighteenth-century development of industrial production as it is now generally understood. The workhouse as a place of production, secrecy, and moral improvement (this last being nothing more than forcibly obtaining "desirable" behavior from the human animal) was fully instituted long before the invention of such important productive instruments as Newcomen's engine or Arkwright's spinning jenny. That this workplace was invariably a closed world only served to emphasize the essential *worldlessness* of labor for all that the privacy arose primarily out of a need for industrial secrecy. It was in any event a hermetic domain, where deprivation in the original sense was coupled with the work ethic and placed at the disposal of the machine. In the earliest workhouse the imprisoned vagrants, who had hitherto only been subjected to pillory, were punished for their nomadic idleness, after the mid-sixteenth century, by being forced to engage in both useful and useless production. Useful in the sense that Jeremy Bentham's Panopticon project of 1797—to cite a highly developed workhouse type—was a machine for the extraction of improving labor from those ". . . on whose part neither dexterity nor good will were to be depended."[28] Useless, in the sense that William Cubitt's treadmill installed in the Brixton House of Correction in 1821 powered a rotating windsail on top of the mill house that indicated only too well the inutility of the prisoner's efforts.

The fundamental worldlessness of the *animal laborans* that manifested itself in the eighteenth century with the "blind" mechanical production of the workhouse and the mill was paralleled in the twentieth century by the equally blind processes of mass consumption. As Arendt has written:

> In our need for more and more replacement of the worldly things around us, we can no longer afford to use them, to respect and preserve their inherent durability; we must consume, as it were, our houses and furniture and cars as though they were the "good things" of nature which spoil uselessly if they are not drawn swiftly into the never-ending cycle of man's metabolism with nature. It is as though we had forced open the distinguishing boundaries which protected the world, the human artifice, from nature, the biological process which goes on in its very midst, as well as the natural cyclical processes which surround it, delivering to them the always threatened stability of a human world.[29]

Arendt goes on to argue that the modern age has increasingly sacrificed the ideas of permanence and durability to the abundance ideal of the *animal laborans* and that we live in a society of laborers inasmuch as the labor-power has been divided in order to eliminate from the thrust of its natural metabolism the "unnatural" and conscious obstacle of the human artifice—the original object of the *homo faber*.

That the *animal laborans* cannot construct a human world out of its own values is borne out by the accelerating tendency of mass production and consumption to undermine not only the durability of the world but also the possibility of establishing a permanent place within it. The science fiction forms projected by the utopian urbanists of the twentieth century have arisen out of either elitist or populist attempts to reify industrial process as though it were some "ideal" manifestation of a new nature. From the futurist architect Antonio Sant 'Elia's *Cittá Nuova* (1914), of which, to quote from the *Manifesto of Futurist Architecture*, he stated that "our houses will last less time than we do and every generation will have to make its own,"[30] to Constant Nieuwenhuys' spontaneously dynamic "New Babylon" (1960),

where urban change would be so accelerated as to render it
pointless to return home—in each instance we are presented with
equally kinetic images that project through prophetic exaggera-
tion the fundamental placeless tendency of our present urban
reality. Nieuwenhuys wrote: "There would be no question of any
fixed life pattern since life itself would be as creative material. . . .
In New Babylon people would be constantly travelling. There
would be no need for them to return to their point of departure as
this in any case would be transformed. Therefore each sector
would contain private rooms (a hotel) where people would spend
the night and rest for a while."[31]

From the point of view of machine or rationalized production,
architecture has been as much affected as urbanism by the
substitution of productive or processal norms, for the more
traditional criteria of worldliness and use. Increasingly buildings
come to be designed in response to the mechanics of their erection
or, alternatively, processal elements such as tower cranes,
elevators, escalators, stairs, refuse chutes, gangways, service cores,
and automobiles determine the configuration of built form to a far
greater extent than the hierarchic and more public criteria of
place. And while the space of public appearance comes to be
increasingly over-run by circulation or inundated at the urban
scale by restricted high-speed access, the free-standing, high-rise
megaliths of the modern city maintain their potential status as
"consumer goods" by virtue of their isolated form. At the same
time the prefabricated elements from which such forms are
increasingly assembled guarantee the optimization of their
production and consumption within the overall industrial
economy. Their potential for rapid amortization, convenient
demolition, and replacement begins to invalidate the traditional
distinction of *meubles* from *immeubles*, a diffusion of meaning
that was first announced in the nineteenth century, with the
wholesale "removal" of structures intact.[32] In a related but more
immediate way automation imposes equally processal conditions
on all industrial design, for it tends towards the servo-mechaniza-
tion of consumption, wherein machine rhythms amplify the

fundamental tendency of life to destroy the durability of the world.[33] In this manner even the worldly category of use is to be absorbed by consumption inasmuch as use objects—in this instance, tools—become transformed by abundance into disposable "throwaway" goods; a subtle shift whose real significance resides in the intrinsic destructiveness of consumption as opposed to use.

The consequence of all this for contemporary architecture is as distressing as it is universal. Elevated on freeways or pedestrian decks or alternatively sequestered behind security fences, we are caused to traverse large areas of abstract, inaccessible urban space that can be neither appropriated nor adequately maintained. In a similar way we are confronted by piazzas whose hypothetical public status is vitiated by the vacuousness of the context or alternatively we are conducted down streets evacuated of all public life by the circulatory demands of traffic. We pass across thresholds whose public-representative nature has been suppressed or we enter foyers which have been arranged or lit in such a manner as to defeat the act of public promenade. Alternatively we are caused to depart from airports whose processal function defies the ritual of leave-taking. In each instance our value-free commodity culture engenders an equivalency wherein museums are rendered as oil refineries and laboratories acquire a monumental form. By a similar token public restaurants come to be rudely incarcerated in basements, while schools find themselves arbitrarily encased within the perimeters of windowless warehouses. In each case a ruthless cultural reduction masks itself by the rhetoric of *kitsch* or by the celebration of technique as an end in itself.[34]

The Identity of Consumption and the Worldlessness of Play

The earliest concentrations of labor-power, beginning first with the workhouse and then with the mill, brought about the uprooting of agrarian populations who then became as alienated from their traditional culture as they were from the objects of industrial production. This loss of "vernacular" was to return to haunt the descendants of these populations as soon as they became the "emancipated" consumers of their own output. While the specific form of "worldlessness" that resulted from this induced consumption varied with successive generations and from class to class, the initial loss of identity enforced by the conditions of industrial production was eventually sublimated, irrespective of class, by an identity to be instantly acquired through consumption. The phenomena of *kitsch*—from *Verkitschen*, "to fake"—appears with the advent of the department store, around the middle of the nineteenth century, when bourgeois civilization achieves for the first time an excessive productive capacity and is brought to create a widespread culture of its own—a culture that was to remain strangely suspended between the useful and the useless, between the sheer utility of its own puritan work ethic and a compulsive desire to mimic the licentiousness of aristocratic taste.[35]

While Marx, writing just before mass consumption began in earnest, projected the eventual liberation of all mankind from the necessity of remorseless labor, he failed to account for the latent potential of machine production to promote a voracious consumer society wherein, to quote Arendt " . . . nearly all human labor-power will be spent in consuming, with concomitant serious consequences for leisure."[36] In such a society the basic problem is no longer production but rather the creation of sufficient daily waste to sustain the inexhaustible capacity for consumption. Arendt's subsequent observation that this supposedly painless consumption only augments the devouring capacity of life, finds its corroboration in a world where shorter working hours, suburbanization, and the mass ownership of the automobile have together secured for the realm of consumption the ever-accelerating rate of daily commutation within the megalopolis, a situation in which the hours saved from production are precisely "compensated" by the hours wasted in the consumptive journey to work.

The victory of the *animal laborans* with which Arendt

concludes her study of the dilemmas facing modern man turns not only on the reduction of art to the problematic "worldlessness" of free play, but also on the substitution of social gratification for the fabricating standards of function and use. For, as Arendt has argued:

> Nothing perhaps indicates clearer the ultimate failure of *homo faber* to assert himself than the rapidity with which the principle of utility, the very quintessence of his world view, was found wanting and was superseded by the principle of the "greatest happiness for the greatest number."[37]

While utility originally presupposed a world of use objects by which man was significantly surrounded, this world began to disintegrate with the "tool-making" tendency of each object not to be an end in itself but rather a means of other objects and other ends. At this juncture, where, as Arendt has put it, "The 'in order to' has become the content of the 'for the sake of,' utility established as meaning generates meaninglessness."[38]

Art, on the other hand, as the essence of inutility—and this of course includes the non-functional aspect of architecture—is rendered worldless in such a society, insofar as it is reduced to introspective abstraction or vulgarized in the idiosyncratic vagaries of *kitsch*. In the first instance it cannot be easily shared and in the second it is reduced to an illusory commodity. If, as Arendt insists, the world must be constructed with thought rather than cognition[39] then insomuch as it is not essential to the life processes of a laboring society, art loses its original worldliness and comes to be subsumed under play. This, of course, raises the problematic question as to the conditions under which play may be considered to be worldly. Be this as it may, freedom in laboring society is perceived solely as release from labor, namely, as play, and it is Arendt's recognition of this fact that makes her text such a perceptive, if partial, critique of Marx.

> Marx predicted correctly, though with an unjustifiable glee, "the withering away" of the public realm under conditions of

unhampered development of the "productive forces of society," and he was equally right, that is consistent with his conception of man as an *animal laborans*, when he foresaw that "socialized men" would spend their freedom from laboring in those strictly private and essentially worldless activities that we now call "hobbies."[40]

The Human Condition *and Critical Theory: A Postscript*

Given Hannah Arendt's skepticism as to the redemption promised by the Marxist prognosis it will no doubt appear extraneous to compare her discourse to the critical theory of the Frankfurt School.[41] The reserve which Arendt publicly exercised in respect to this school of Marxist criticism should be sufficient caution against making such a comparison. Yet despite the disdain she seems to have felt for those whom she regarded as renegade Marxists, a common concern and even method may be found to relate the arguments developed in *The Human Condition* to the socio-cultural analyses of the Frankfurt School. It is clear that both Arendt and the Frankfurt School were equally obsessed with the interaction of structure and superstructure in advanced industrial society, even if such terms were entirely foreign to her thought.

These qualifications accepted, one may argue that the succession of the Frankfurt School, specifically the theoretical progression that links the later thought of Herbert Marcuse to the writings of Jürgen Habermas—takes up a number of themes that were either suppressed or suspended at the conclusion of the *The Human Condition*. Amongst these issues one may arguably posit two. First, the problematic cultural status of play and pleasure in a future laboring society after its hypothetical liberation from the compulsion of consumption (Marcuse) and, second, the problematic possibility for mediating the autonomous rationality of science and technique through the reconstitution of the space of public appearance as an effective political realm (Habermas).

If one derives from *The Human Condition* the implication

that a highly secular, laboring, and industrialized order must inevitably prevail in either state-capitalist, capitalist, or socialist societies, and if one posits some future state in which the "fatality" of an ever-accelerating consumption is, in some measure, redeemed, then the question arises as to what are the minimum environmental priorities that such a transformed state could realistically envisage?

While the *vita activa* in the ancient sense would no doubt initially remain in abeyance, some upgrading of the private habitat, essential to the quality of domestic life, would surely assert itself as a priority once this life was no longer subject to either rapacious consumption or optimized production. For while it is true, as Arendt asserts, that from the point of view of nature, it is *work* rather than *labor* that is destructive, this observation overlooks that qualitative dimension of consumption beyond which "man's metabolism with nature" becomes even more destructive of nature than *work,* beyond that frontier that we have already crossed, where non-renewable resources such as water and oxygen begin to become permanently contaminated or destroyed.[42] At this juncture, labor, as optimized consumption, stands opposed to its own Benthamite cult of life as the highest good, just as privacy *per se,* as the quintessence of labor and life, is undermined by the productive reduction of all built objects to the status of "consumer goods"; a threshold that has again been reached in the mobile-home industry of the United States.

Human adaptability notwithstanding, the basic criterion of privacy asserted by Barragan, posits itself not only as the necessary "figure" to the public ground, but also as the only standard by which a *balanced and rhythmic* life for the species could eventually be maintained. The urban consequences of applying such criteria as economic densities would be to spontaneously create the boundaries of a "negative" urban form—namely, some kind of public realm, even if this would not immediately constitute a "world" in the Arendtian sense. That the public space of the medieval city was the physical counterform of the private fabric Arendt herself has recognized in her assertion that it is the exterior perimeter of the private realm that effectively shapes the space of the city.

As to art, that is to say, as to the symbolization of common values and the manner in which they might be represented, this immediately introduces the cultural dilemma of "play" and the extent to which communal expression may or may not be reified. Permanence is not the absolute pre-condition for reification, music being an obvious exception, as Arendt herself acknowledges: "In music and poetry, the least materialistic of the arts, because their material consists of sounds and words, reification and the workmanship it demands are kept to the minimum."[43]

Twentieth-century *avant-garde* art has frequently resorted to collective play or at least to aleatory forms of art as the necessary expression of an essentially "social" and dynamic future, although in many instances innate "laboring" values have assured that nothing could be achieved save the tautology of production itself.[44] While this strategy may capitalize on the indisputable authority of instrumentality, the parallel tendency of art to survive through the reductive assertion of its own autonomy is yet a further illustration of the general tendency of a laboring society to move toward privatization. It is hardly an accident that both these *avant-garde* strategies first emerged in the early years of the Soviet Union; the former, the *productivist sensibility*, being typified at its most extreme in the self-referential films of Dziga Vertov where the production of films about production exemplified production itself;[45] and the latter, the cult of *autonomous structure*, being reflected in the general artistic formalism of the period. The failure of this *avant-garde* to find its ostensible public led to the familiar withdrawal of the Soviet state into the *kitsch* of social realism. Only the repressed *Proletcult* with its political theater and its program for the "theatricalization of everyday life" retained some lucid potential for a collective realization of an alternative culture.

Whether architecture, as opposed to building, will ever be able to return to the representation of collective value is a moot point. At all events its representative role would have to be contingent on the establishment of a public realm in the political sense. Otherwise limited by definition to the act of commemoration it would remain exactly where Adolf Loos left it in 1910. That this commemorative impulse would remain alive even in a laboring society became manifest after the First World War in the numerous memorials to the "unknown soldier"; those testaments to an unidentifiable somebody whom four years of mass slaughter should have revealed.[46]

Nothing less is outlined in *The Human Condition* than the teleological abyss that has progressively opened up before the path of industrialized man. That Arendt and the Frankfurt School perceived the same void but drew different conclusions from it, may be sensed in the following passage from Herbert Marcuse's *Eros and Civilization:*

> The argument that makes liberation conditional upon an ever higher standard of living all too easily serves to justify the perpetuation of repression. The definition of the standard of living in terms of automobiles, television sets, airplanes, and tractors is that of the performance principle itself. Beyond the rule of this principle, the level of living would be measured by other criteria: the universal gratification of the basic human needs and the freedom from guilt and fear—internalized as well as external, instinctual as well as "rational." . . . Under optimum conditions, the prevalence, in mature civilization, of material and intellectual wealth would be such as to allow the painless gratification of needs, while domination would no longer systematically forestall such gratification. In this case, the quantum of instinctual energy still to be diverted into necessary labor . . . would be so small that a large area of repressive constraints and modifications no longer sustained by external forces would collapse. Consequently the antagonistic relation between pleasure principle and reality principle would be altered in favor of the former. Eros, the life instincts, would be released to an unprecedented degree.[47]

While this utopian projection of a future where "the elimination of surplus repression would *per se* eliminate if not labor, then the organization of human existence into an instrument of labor" does nothing if not stress the life-bound values of the *animal laborans*, Marcuse's recognition that the cult of *productivity* as an end in itself is the primary impasse of industrial society brings him surprisingly close to Arendt.

> Efficiency and repression converge: raising the productivity of labor is the sacrosanct ideal of both capitalist and Stalinist Stakhanovism. The notion of productivity has its historical limits: they are those of the performance principle. Beyond its domain, productivity has another content and another relation to the pleasure principle: they are anticipated in the processes of imagination which preserve freedom from the performance principle while maintaining the claim of a *new* reality principle.[48]

That one day such a reality might still be achieved seems to be anticpated to an equal degree by Arendt's appraisal of the earliest Russian soviets and Jürgen Habermas' prognostications for the future of the *vita activa*. The two relevant passages are given below, the former from Arendt's study of revolutionary politics entitled *On Revolution* and the latter from Habermas' essay, dedicated to Marcuse on his seventieth birthday, bearing the title "Technology and Science as Ideology." Of the soviets, Arendt was to write:

> The councils, obviously, were spaces of freedom. As such, they invariably refused to regard themselves as temporary organs of revolution and, on the contrary, made all attempts at establishing themselves as permanent organs of government. Far from wishing to make the revolution permanent, their explicitly expressed goal was "to lay the foundations of a republic acclaimed in all its consequences, the only government

which will close forever the era of invasions and civil wars";
no paradise on earth, no classless society, no dream of socialist
or communist fraternity, but the establishment of "the true
Republic": was the "reward" hoped for as the end of the
struggle. And what had been true in Paris in 1871 remained
true for Russia in 1905, when the "not merely destructive but
constructive" intentions of the first *soviets* were so manifest
that contemporary witnesses "could sense the emergence and
the formation of a force which one day might be able to effect
the transformation of the State."[49]

And was it not just such a transformation that Habermas had in
mind when he attempted to establish the following necessary
limits for the emergence of a truly scientific rationality?

Above all, it becomes clear against this background that two
concepts of rationalization must be distinguished. At the
level of subsystems of purposive-rational action, scientific-
technical progress has already compelled the reorganization
of social institutions and sectors, and necessitates it on an
even larger scale than heretofore. But this process of the
development of the productive forces can be a potential for
liberation if and only if it does not replace rationalization on
another level.

Rationalization at the level of the institutional framework can only occur in the medium of symbolic interaction
itself, that is through removing restrictions on all communication. Public, unrestricted discussion, free from domination,
of the suitability and desirability of action-orienting principles
and norms in the light of the socio-cultural repercussions of
developing subsystems of purposive-rational action—such as
communication at all levels of political and repoliticized
decision-making processes—is the only medium in which
anything like "rationalization" is possible.[50]

We are confronted in this complex passage with an
existential political perspective that for Arendt and Habermas

alike is the only possible vehicle for the rational determination of human ends. Such a decentralized "cantonal" conception, tends, I would submit, to return us to the dependency of political power on its social and physical constitution, that is to say, on its derivation from the living proximity of men and from the physical manifestation of their public being in built form. For architecture at least, the relevance of *The Human Condition* resides in this—in its formulation of that political reciprocity that must of necessity obtain, for good or ill, between the status of men and the status of their objects.

NOTES

1. Hannah Arendt, *The Human Condition* (Chicago: University of Chicago Press, 1958), p. 7.

2. Ibid.

3. *The Shorter Oxford English Dictionary*, 3rd ed., rev. (Oxford: The Clarendon Press, 1947).

4. Arendt provides the following etymological footnote on p. 136 of *The Human Condition* (the comment is referential to Chapter IV, footnote 1). The Latin word *faber*, probably related to *facere* ("to make something" in the sense of production), originally designated the fabricator and artist who works upon hard material, such as stone and wood; it also was used as translation for the Greek work *tekton*, which has the same connotations.

5. Adolf Loos, "Architecture 1910," in Tim and Charlotte Benton, eds., *An International Anthology of Original Articles in Architecture and Design, 1890–1939* (New York: Watson Gupthill, 1975), pp. 41–45. In her essay "Thinking and Moral Considerations" Arendt directly relates representation with thought in her footnote on Augustine: "The image, the representation of something absent, is stored in memory and becomes a thought object, a 'vision of thought' as soon as it is willfully remembered." See *Social Research*, Vol. xxxviii, no. 3 (Autumn 1971), p. 424.

6. Arendt, *The Human Condition*, p. 53.

7. Ibid., p. 201.

8. See Melvin Webber, *Explorations into Urban Structure* (Philadelphia: University of Pennsylvania, 1964). See also his article in Wingo Lowdon, Jr., ed., *Cities and Space* (Baltimore: Johns Hopkins Press, 1963).

9. Robert Venturi, *Complexity and Contradiction in Architecture,* MOMA Papers no. 7 (New York: Museum of Modern Art, 1966), p. 133.

10. Arendt, *The Human Condition,* p. 204. See also her "Thinking and Moral Considerations," pp. 430, 341. In this text Arendt opposes the house to the nomadic tent. "We can use the word *house* for a great number of objects —for the mud hut of a tribe, the palace of a king, the country home of a city dweller, the cottage in the village, or the apartment house in town—but we can hardly use it for the tents of some nomads. The house, in and by itself, *auto kath'auto,* that which makes us use the word for all these particular and very different buildings, is never seen, neither by the eyes of the body, nor by the eyes of the mind; . . . the point here is that it implies something considerably less tangible than the structure perceived by our eyes. It implies "housing somebody" and being "dwelt in" as no tent could house or serve as a dwelling place which is put up today and taken down tomorrow." This recognition of the house as a *place of dwelling* is fundamentally Heideggerian and as such relates to the "darkness" of the *megaron.* As in Martin Heidegger's *Building, Dwelling, and Thinking* the argument implicitly links "housebuilding" to agriculture and to rootedness.

11. Camillo Sitte, *City Planning According to Artistic Principles,* George R. Collins and Christiane Craseman Collins, trs., Columbia University Studies in Art History and Archaeology No. 2 (New York: Random House, 1965). As the translators point out, Sitte made pointed use of the term *platz* ("place") rather than the word "square" which has geometrical connotations antipathetic to Sitte's urban principles. Sitte's work was polemically against the normative gridded city as advocated by Reinhard Baumeister.

12. Arendt provides the following etymological footnote on p. 71 of *The Human Condition*: "The Greek and Latin words for the interior of the house, *megaron* and *atrium,* have a strong connotation of darkness and blackness." She cites Mommsen, *Romische Geschichte,* 5th ed., Book 1, pp. 22, 236.

13. Ibid., p. 38.

14. Ibid., p. 39.

15. Ibid., p. 59.

16. Clive Bamford-Smith, *Builders in the Sun: Five Mexican Architects* (New York: Architectural Book Publishing Co., 1967), p. 74.

17. Arendt, *The Human Condition,* p. 122.

18. Bamford-Smith, *Builders in the Sun,* p. 77.

19. Arendt, *The Human Condition,* p. 45.

20. Ibid., pp. 173, 174.

21. Ibid., pp. 167, 168.

22. G. C. Argan, *The Renaissance City* (New York: Braziller, 1969), pp. 25–26.

23. Arendt, *The Human Condition,* pp. 282, 283.

24. Ibid., p. 307.

25. Michel Parent and Jacques Verroust, *Vauban* (Paris: Éditions Jacques Freal, 1971), p. 60.

26. The horse-drawn tram of the Ringstrasse gave way to the electric tram in the early 1890s. In his *Teoria General de Urbanización* (1867), Ildefonso Cerda, the planner of modern Barcelona and inventor of the term *urbanización,* argues that "the form of the city is, or must be, derived from the necessities of locomotion." From this date onwards the city becomes inundated by mechanized movement.

27. Arendt, *The Human Condition,* p. 304.

28. See Robin Evans, "Regulation and Production," *Lotus 12,* Rivista trimestrale di architettura (Milan: September 1976).

29. Arendt, *The Human Condition,* pp. 125, 126.

30. See Reyner Banham, *Theory and Design in the First Machine Age* (New York: Praeger, 1960), p. 135.

31. For the complete text see Constant Nieuwenhuys, "New Babylon," *Architectural Design* (June 1964), pp. 304, 305.

32. See Stanley Buder, *Pullman: An Experiment in Industrial Order and Community Planning, 1880–1930* (London: Oxford University Press, 1967). George Pullman, founder of the Pullman Palace Car Company, had, in fact, made his start in Chicago in 1855 raising buildings above the then-existing ground level.

33. Arendt, *The Human Condition,* p. 132.

34. Innumerable examples exist of the specific displacement of the public realm in contemporary building. Among the more recent instances, one might cite the following: The Ford Foundation Building, New York, for its provision of a false "public" foyer which is programmed in such a way as to assure that no public realm may be allowed to come into existence. The Centre Pompidou, Paris, for its reduction of its "users" to the same status as the "services"—the users being piped-in, so to speak, on one side, and the services fed into the structure on the other. In short, the reduction of a museum to the status and the model expressiveness of an oil refinery! The Richards Laboratories at the University of Pennsylvania where service towers are rendered as monumental elements and where the whole structure is pervaded by a sense of "religiosity" inappropriate to the processal nature of a laboratory building. In this last example a misplaced monumentality fails to transcend the manifest absence of an appropriately "representative" or "commemorative" program, whereas in the first case the presence of a "representative" program is rendered null and void by the rhetoric of the machine. Consciously designed as a cultural supermarket, art in the name of populism is reduced to a commodity.

35. See Herman Broch, "Notes on the Problem of Kitsch," in Gillo Dorfles,

ed., *Kitsch: The World of Bad Taste* (New York: Universe Books, 1969), p. 54.

36. Arendt, *The Human Condition*, p. 131.

37. Ibid., p. 101. See also footnote pp. 307, 308.

38. Ibid., p. 154.

39. Ibid., p. 171. Arendt's distinction between "thought" and "cognition" is worth repeating here: "Thought and cognition are not the same. Thought, the source of art works, is manifest without transformation or transfiguration in all great philosophy, whereas the chief manifestation of the cognitive processes, by which we acquire and store up knowledge is the sciences."

40. Ibid., pp. 117, 118.

41. For a historical account of the Frankfurt School and Institute of Social Research see Martin Jay, *The Dialectical Imagination* (Boston: Little, Brown, 1973).

42. Earl F. Murphy, *Governing Nature* (Chicago: Quadrangle Books, 1967), p. 31. See also p. 118 for an interesting comment on the nature of industrial consumption: "Men have assumed that there was a direct line from production to consumption to disappearance. Now it is evident that man, whether as producer or consumer, is part of a cycle. The residue streaming from his production and consumption do *not* disappear. . . ."

43. Arendt, *The Human Condition*, p. 169. See also p. 127 and Johan Huizinga, *Homo Ludens: A Study of the Play Element in Culture* (Boston: The Beacon Press, 1950). As to the limits of play in respect of art we find Huizinga writing: "The 'music' arts live and thrive in an atmosphere of common rejoicing; the plastic arts do not" (p. 167).

44. The history of the *Proletcult* movement in the Soviet Union and its cult of production has yet to be written. For an introduction to the founding principles of the movement and work of Alexander Malinowsky, otherwise known as Bogdanov, see J. B. Billington, *The Icon and the Axe* (New York: Knopf, 1968), p. 489.

45. See Annette Michelson, "The Man with the Movie-Camera: From Magician to Epistemologist," *Art Forum* (March 1972).

46. Arendt, *The Human Condition*, p. 181.

47. Herbert Marcuse, *Eros and Civilization* (New York: Vintage Books, 1962), p. 139.

48. Ibid., p. 141.

49. Hannah Arendt, *On Revolution* (New York: The Viking Press, 1965), p. 268.

50. Jürgen Habermas, *Towards a Rational Society* translated by Jeremy Shapiro (Boston: The Beacon Press, 1970), pp. 118–19.

Robert W. Major

A READING OF HANNAH ARENDT'S "UNUSUAL" DISTINCTION BETWEEN LABOR AND WORK

The distinction between labor and work which I pro-
pose is unusual. The phenomenal evidence in its favor
is too striking to be ignored, and yet historically it is a
fact that apart from a few scattered remarks, which
moreover were never developed even in the theories of
authors, there is hardly anything in either the pre-
modern theories or in the large body of modern labor
theories to support it. Against this scarcity of historical
evidence, however, stands one very articulate and ob-
stinate testimony, namely, the simple fact that every
European language, ancient and modern, contains two
etymologically unrelated words for what we have come
to think of as the same activity, and retains them in the
face of their persistent synonymous usage.

> Hannah Arendt
> The Human Condition[1]

Historically, the difficulty with discoveries of this sort
[uncovering unusual distinctions hidden in the Western
tradition as that between labor and work, thinking and
knowing] is that they give rise to new misunderstand-
ings. During her lifetime Hannah Arendt's books oc-
casioned a great deal of misunderstanding, some of it

> *perverse. Though her students did not usually misunder-*
> *stand her . . . her readers did, particularly political*
> *scientists and philosophers. To what extent these mis-*
> *interpretations were due to the originality of her*
> *thought or to her manner of expressing it I do not*
> *know, conceivably in part to both. In any event I fear*
> *that her distinction between thinking and knowing*
> *will suffer a similar fate.*
>
> J. Glenn Gray
> "The Winds of Thought"[2]

This essay is a reading of Hannah Arendt's fundamental distinction in the *vita activa* between work and labor. To read this distinction requires that one confront its "unusual" position with respect to Western theory, i.e., its virtual neglect by ancient and modern theories despite its sedimentation in the ancient and modern languages. This, in turn, requires that one confront Arendt's way of thinking, which is at the same time a meditation upon "language and the fundamental human experiences underlying it" and upon Western theory, and a reading of the language and the texts of Western theory. But to confront Arendt's thinking is to confront the fate of the "reifications" of her thought (her texts) in the modern world. And that fate has been either not to be read or to be misread.

TEXT
A Reading of Arendt's Text on Labor and Work

The "objective" distinction between labor and work which Arendt articulates in the *vita activa* is accomplished by recovering the etymological differences sedimented in the ancient and modern verbs for labor and work.

The Greek language distinguishes between *ponein* and *ergazesthai*, the Latin between *laborare* and *facere* or *fabricare*, which have the same etymological root, the French between *travailler* and *ouvrer*, the German between *arbeiten* and *werken*.[3]

The English language also distinguishes between "labor" and "work." In ancient and modern usage, however, "labor" and "work" have been, for the most part, treated as synonymous, as signifying what was considered to be the same activity, namely, labor. In spite of this persistent reduction in use, each of these languages retained the two words in question. Moreover, in ancient and modern usage only the verb forms of "work" and "labor" are truly synonymous, i.e., as referring to the process dimensions of the activity. Where the result of the activity has been at issue, i.e., where a noun form is required to designate the result, ancient and modern usage did not form a corresponding noun for labor.

> The word "labor," understood as a noun, never designates the finished product, the result of laboring, but remains a verbal noun to be classed with the gerund whereas the product itself is invariably derived from the word for work, even when current usage has followed the actual modern development so closely that the verb form of the word "work" has become rather obsolete.[4]

For Arendt a reconsideration of the human condition in our time is a question of thinking "what we are doing."[5] Such an attempt to rethink the human condition, i.e., to recover its fundamental distinctions with their corresponding activities, transcends a hermeneutics of language to a philosophical anthropology. But, at the same time, these distinctions can only be thought out through language, since it is in language that the testimony to that which has been lost to memory and neglected by theory has been preserved and can be recovered. Being "objective" and "world-oriented," language is a repository of sedimented facts, i.e., of "testaments" about the "human condition" and *vita activa.* Language not only reveals itself, but also points beyond itself—teaches about the world, its things, and the activities which produced them.[6]

In proposing the "unusual" distinction between labor and work[7] Arendt has recovered not just a linguistic distinction, but also, and most importantly, a fundamental anthropological distinction in the *vita activa*. Work and labor are fundamental because they correspond to basic human conditions, i.e., "conditions under which life on earth is given to man,"[8] and because they are connected to the most general human conditions, namely, natality (birth) and mortality (death). However, for Arendt, fundamental does not designate "essential." Her philosophical anthropology neither attempts nor pretends to identify essential characteristics of human existence. It is not a philosophical anthropology of human nature: ". . . the human condition is not the same as human nature, and the sum total of human activities and capabilities which corresponds to the human condition do not constitute anything like human nature."[9] For Arendt, the problem of human nature is one which cannot be answered from either an individual psychological or a philosophical perspective, but only from a theological one. An anthropology that attempts to answer the question about human nature, i.e., "what am I" as opposed to "who am I," must be a theological anthropology grounded in a divinely revealed answer. The answer to the question "who are we" is, for Arendt, given only in action and speech.[10]

In the course of the modern age, the sciences have also attempted to provide the answer to the question of human nature. But instead of answering the question from a theological perspective, science answers it from the Archimedean perspective; and instead of providing a divinely revealed answer, it provides an explanation based on logic and experiment. The divine "watcher" is replaced by the scientific "watcher" in whose perspective man becomes a biological organism.[11] From the perspective of Arendt's philosophical anthropology, however, man is not "watched," but is "thought." And it is in this thinking "man" that he is comprehended as someone other than an *imago dei* or a biological organism and that the fundamental distinction between labor and work is recovered and their respective characteristics unfolded.[12]

Arendt's distinction between labor and work is "unusual" in the context of ancient and modern theories which have neglected it because their approach, essentially subjective and man-oriented, blinds them to it. It is characteristic of her thinking to recover "unusual" distinctions that have been neglected in the tradition of Western theory—such as those between power and violence, private and public, story and history, thinking and knowing. Out of her extraordinary knowledge of the Western tradition, but grounded in the "incidents of living experience," Arendt thinks through the conceptual language of the tradition to uncover distinctions sedimented in its language, but neglected by it and by contemporary theorists. In words closer to her own, she rummages through the linguistic attic of the tradition and "hits upon" those "unusual" distinctions that have been neglected. This rummaging type of thinking, thinking that uncovers neglected and thus "unusual" distinctions, is thus "eccentric" with respect to both the tradition and those theorists who have never ventured into that attic.

One consequence of this relation is that her own thought and its recovered distinctions have been neglected by many contemporary theorists; though recognized, they have not been to any significant extent appropriated. Book-length, English-language texts devoted entirely to her work are currently limited to the not entirely satisfactory effort of Margaret Canovan, *The Political Thought of Hannah Arendt*. Another consequence is that when her work and her thought-distinctions have been appropriated, they have been for the most part misunderstood.

This "fate" of Arendt's work poses not just specific and unique questions of interpretation and scholarship, but also more general questions about texts and their reception by different reading publics; or even more fundamentally, about "texts," the "act of reading," and the possibility of "misunderstanding." By their being written down, the unusual distinctions have become "thought things," "thought texts." As such, they are of the world and separated from their original home, her thinking activity. And being of the world they can be read or not, understood or not. Not to be read is to be neglected and ultimately to be forgotten. To be read is to be recognized and ultimately to be remembered. To be read also involves the possibility of misunderstanding. The relationship between the act of reading and the text is not a transparent and simple one, but rather a complex and problematical one. That it is becomes immediately clear when the question of misunderstanding a text is raised: Is the misunderstanding "in the text or in the act of reading?"[13]

As documented by Arendt's text, this problematic of text, reading, and the possibility of misunderstanding is involved in the tradition's reading of itself and Arendt's reading of the tradition. As evidenced by the reception of her work, it is involved in contemporary readings, particularly in specialist readings such as those by political scientists and philosophers. And, at the same time, it is involved in my reading of Arendt's text and the specialist readings.

TEXT-WORK
Part I: On Textual Neglect and Text Reading

In the course of this text's reading of Arendt's unusual distinction between labor and work, it has "hit upon" the question of textual reception and the problematic of textual reading. Any serious attempt at reading a text must confront such issues. It is therefore requisite that this reading take up these issues for reflection. In the context of reading Arendt's text, this requirement is even more critical, for her texts have suffered neglect and "a great deal of misunderstanding, some of it perverse."[14] Part I is the response to this requirement. It takes up the question of textual neglect and the problematic of textual reading in terms of different specialist readings of Arendt which involve these textual issues.

The Reading of Textual Neglect

Glenn Gray, in his memorial essay on Arendt and her distinction between knowing and thinking, recognized the salience of the phenomenon of "neglect." He addressed it in this way:

The simplicity of this crucial distinction [between knowing and thinking] is equalled only by the extraordinary knowledge of the western tradition that is its source. When stated simply, as I have tried to do, it seems astonishing that we have not discovered it long ago. Socrates, the thinker *par excellence*, always insisted that he *knew* nothing. And Kant made very clear that reason did not, indeed could not, *know* even that which is presumably closest to us, the essential self. Why have we had to wait so long to draw the consequences of these age-old convictions? Surely Aristotle was right in suggesting that we human beings suffer from a peculiar blindness: the difficulty lies in us and not in the facts. "For as the eyes of bats are to the blaze of day, so is reason in our soul to the things which are by nature most evident of all."[15]

The distinction between knowing and thinking has been sedimented in but also neglected by the tradition, while we who think and are summoned to think by virtue of living in a traditionless age have failed to think this distinction. This neglect now resides *in us*, not in the facts. This "in us" points to what Arendt identifies as the man-oriented and subjective theories we use in our attempts at understanding. For our commitment to subjectivity blinds us to the testimony of the facts as they have been covered over in the tradition, but preserved in language. The neglect of Arendt's text on labor and work can be read in the same terms: it indicates the subjectivistic pre-understanding that characterizes modern theories about labor and work.

A Reading of Misreading

In many instances the specialist readers of Arendt's text on labor and work indicate a misreading of that text. A representative example of such a specialist misreading is inscribed in Walter Weisskopf's *Alienation and Economy*. At an integral moment in his argument to link "alienation and economy," Weisskopf introduces Marx's concept of labor. To explicate that concept he appropriates Arendt's text on Marx and labor:

The best formulation of what Marx meant by labor can be found by a non-economist, Hannah Arendt in her book, *The*

Human Condition. Labor is the activity which corresponds to the biological process of the human body, whose spontaneous growth, metabolism and eventual decay are bound to the vital necessities produced and fed into the life process by labor. The human condition of labor is life itself. For the young Marx, labor was the essential human process by which man produces, and thereby separates himself from an object. In consuming the objects man himself has created, he negates this separation and reunites subject and object. Here, the Hegelian split between subject and object and the striving for union is translated into the economic language of production and consumption, and is understood as a physiological process of metabolism, creating and supporting life itself, by consuming whatever it produced. The process is disturbed when production is not fully "negated" by consumption. This disturbance is caused by capital and the capitalist who retains part of the product for capital accumulation and his own enrichment. The unequal distribution of the result of production—poverty caused by exploitation—disturbs the metabolic circle. . . . Before private property, the individual can freely dispose of, and consume his product. Private property and the division of labor destroy this freedom and thereby cause alienation. Finally, in the classless society, the collective ownership of the means of production leads to the negation of alienation: Man is again reunited with the products of his labor.[16]

This appropriation of Arendt's text reveals Weisskopf's misappropriation of it. The argument of his text moves seamlessly from Arendt to Hegel, but his continuity is made possible by displacing her critique of Marx with his own Hegelian interpretation. He neutralizes the critical dimensions of her analysis. Arendt is concerned not only to comprehend Marx's concept of labor, but also to identify its consequences for the world. For example, she writes, "Within a completely 'socialized mankind,' whose sole purpose would be the entertaining of the life process—and this unfortunately is the quite unutopian ideal that guides Marxist theory—the distinction between labor and work would have completely disappeared; all work would have become labor because all things would be understood, not in their worldly, objective quality, but as results of living labor power and function of the life process."[17]

Weisskopf's misappropriation of Arendt's text, in fact, undermines his own argument. His concern is to comprehend the "basic scheme of alienation" in the early as well as the later texts of Marx. "What matters here is the basic scheme of alienation, not the substance of these ideas. . . . the earlier state, without alienation, the later state with alienation, and the restoration of a non-alienating state on a higher plain of development, and present . . . in the ideas of the young and old Marx."[18] However, to comprehend Arendt's argument would be to reject the basis of such a concern, since for her, Marx's theory of labor expresses the *"principle of world alienation"* that informs the modern age. Accordingly Weisskopf's concern to comprehend the basic scheme of alienation reflects "the modern age's extreme subjectivism, i.e., *world-alienation* interpreted as *self-alienation*. As such, it could not provide, as Weisskopf argues, the basis for a critique of contemporary industrial society.

The judgment that "Marx's criticism in his early writings is still valid, and applies equally well to socialist and communist countries"[19] cannot be sustained in terms of Arendt's understanding of Marx. This judgment, and his concluding remark that "it is no accident that these earlier ideas about alienation have been recently revived, especially under the influence of existentialist thought, [in] the critique of industrial and technological society, either in its capitalist or its communist form,"[20] reveal the extent of his failure to comprehend Arendt's thinking about work and labor and about Marx's theory of labor. The existentialists' revival of the young Marx is consistent with their "worry and care for the self," with their concern for *self-alienation* in the technological society that, for Arendt, reflects *world-alienation*.

Weisskopf also uses Arendt's text to explicate the differences between two historical types of consumption—the puritan and the modern. He introduces her philosophical and historical analysis to ground this typology:

> The old type of consumption corresponding to the Puritan ethos, and the value orientation of classical and neoclassical economics was related to work and aimed at the acquisition of durable goods. Work creates durable goods which become durable property. The end of production and consumption was then the creation of an artificial durable world, composed of private property, as an extension and support of the individual personality. The modern consumerism for which formalism and value-relativity open the way, is related to labor and to the metabolic process.[21]

His appropriation of Arendt's text to support this typology once again reveals that he has comprehended neither her philosophical anthropology nor her historical anaysis. The production consumption cycle belongs, not to the world-making activity of work, but to labor. The artificial world created by work is never entirely a world of private property. It is also a public world. Work creates a world of things, "a world which is common to all of us and distinguished from our privately-owned place in it."[22] The artificial objective world cannot be reduced to expressions of the individual personality. Historically, both the puritan ethic and the classical and neo-classical economics reflected not a concern for the artificial durable world, but for the self—whether it be in the form of the soul or labor. Classical and neo-classical economics were theories of labor and wealth, not of work and durable property. The puritan ethos expressed a concern for the soul, not a concern for the world of things produced by work. It expressed world-alienation: "The greatness of Max Weber's discovery about the origins of capitalism lay precisely in his demonstration that an enormous, strictly mundane activity is possible without any care for, or enjoyment of the world whatever, an activity whose deepest motivation, on the contrary, is worry and care about self. *World alienation, and not self-alienation, as Marx thought, has been the hallmark of the modern age."*[23]

Thus, both Weisskopf's philosophical and historical appropriation of Arendt's text reveal his misreading of it—a misreading grounded in his theoretic pre-commitment to the priority of the subjectivity of the self over the objectivity of the world and to self-alienation over world-alienation as the hallmark of the modern age.

A Reading of Reading

An exceptional instance of reading Arendt's unusual distinction between labor and work by a specialist is Kenneth Frampton's set of essays, "Work, Labor and Architecture" and "Industrialization and the Crises of Architecture," which show themselves to be built upon the "work of Hannah Arendt,"[24] i.e., grounded in her distinction between the activities of work and labor, in her distinction between the public and private realms as they relate to these activities, and in her understanding of the work of art. The work of Hannah Arendt is the "model" Frampton has followed in his construction of a theory of architectural activity and meaning:

> As yet no contemporary theory even attempts to discriminate between the word-concepts "architecture" and "building." Yet the dictionary continues to proffer two significantly different definitions. . . . The word "architecture," from the Greek word *architekton* meaning constructor, is defined firstly as "the art or science of constructing edifices for human use" and secondly as the "action and process of building."
>
> These two definitions, at once, suggest themselves as parallels to the distinction Hannah Arendt draws between "work" and "labor." The phrase "for human use" imports a specifically human or anthropomorphic connotation to the whole of the first definition, alluding to the creation of the "human world." Conversely, it may be argued that, in the second definition, the use of the words "action" and "process"

in the phrase "the action and process of building" clearly implies a continuous act of building, forever incomplete, comparable to the continual process of biological labor.[25]

Frampton's appropriation of Arendt's text is not limited to its philosophical anthropology of work and labor.[26] He has also appropriated her historical analysis of the fate of these fundamental activities in the modern age, as the crisis of world alienation, for his comprehension of the crises that have characterized the fate of modern architecture; Cartesianism, instrumentalism, privatism, functionalism, and consumerism punctuate and structure his historical interpretation of the crises of modern architecture. It is clear that in his appropriation of Arendt's text on the modern world he has properly understood world-alienation. For it is within the context of world-alienation that Frampton comprehends the erosion of the traditional object of architecture and the triumph of architectural functionalism.

The critical question thus poses itself: what permits Frampton to "read" Arendt's text? The answer is given in his architectural concerns and commitment. His essays reveal a concern to comprehend architecture both theoretically and historically and a commitment to worldly architecture, i.e., to an architecture that erects a world of built-objects informed by and transparent to human meanings.[27]

The architectural historian and theorist encounters the modern city as no longer constituting a world of built-objects that show themselves to be transparently durable and memorable, i.e., to be materializations of human and most importantly, public meanings. He encounters it rather as an environment of consumptibles, i.e., a network of units designed and built to fulfill certain "basic functions"—the functions of the human life process.[28]

Compelled to comprehend this modern crisis of architecture, Frampton surveys the archive of architectural theory for "readings" with which to understand it and finds no adequate theory. He continues his search elsewhere and "hits upon" the work of

Hannah Arendt. In her text he encounters the unusual distinction between labor and work, the articulation of the private and public realms, the "objective" world of work, the world of durable objects, and the "memorable" work—the work of art. Here, in other words, he finds a model that permits him to formulate a theory of architectural activity and architectural objects that at the same time provides the standards for a critique of architectural functionalism.

Her analysis, in conjunction with his assimilation of her model, allows Frampton to situate the predicaments of modern architecture within the larger modern phenomenon in industrialization and the ideology of waste. Frampton's encounter with Arendt's text is thus an encounter of reading because it is inscribed by a pre-understanding of the worldly "objectivity" of work, i.e., by his architectural concern for and commitment to the world of built objects.

This encounter between Frampton's specialist reading and Arendt's text on labor and work is revealing when set against other specialist readings of that text. As was the case with Weisskopf's specialist reading, they have for the most part misread that text—misread it because their readings are inscribed by a pre-understanding which reflects a commitment to the self, i.e., "subjectivity," and to self-actualization, i.e., overcoming "self-alienation." And historically they are concerned to comprehend the crisis of the modern age as the crisis of self-alienation rather than as the crisis of world-alienation.

TEXT-WORK
Part II: A Re-reading of Arendt's Text on Labor and Work or Arendt's Text Misreads Itself

What has been worked out in the text-work of Part I are two specialist readings of Arendt's text on labor and work. What is indicated by these readings is the possibility for the understanding and misunderstanding of that text as well as its neglect. However, this does not preclude the possibility that Arendt's text inscribes its own form of misreading and of neglect.

Arendt recovers the labor-work distinction by thinking ordinary language and the conceptual language of the Western tradition; and this thinking involves her reading of texts. Since this reading uncovers a distinction that has been neglected by the tradition, i.e., neglected in its reading of itself, and which is thereby unusual, it posed the problematic of textual understanding-misunderstanding that is inscribed in her understanding of the it has understood what the tradition has misread in reading itself.

Another, but not unrelated, possibility is given in Arendt's text on the human body. This text is as critical to her distinction between labor and work as that on the objectivity of work. While apparently transparent and unambiguous, it is, in fact, at odds with itself. The first section of Arendt's text on labor is headed with a quotation from Locke: "The Labour of our Body and the Work of our Hands." This quotation reappears throughout texts on labor and work. It is, for Arendt, one of those illuminating "gems" that are buried in the tradition and that can be uncovered by rummaging through it. In her text it illuminates the distinction between work and labor. But in this context, it illuminates the misunderstanding that is inscribed in her understanding of the human body.

This illumination is concealed in the subtitle of the English text, but is revealed in the German translation of *The Human Condition: "Die Arbeit unseres Körpers und das Werk unserer Hände."*[29] What is illuminated in the German text is her rendering of the English word for human body. The English language has only one word for designating the phenomenon "body." German, however, has two words: *"der Körper"* and *"das Leib."* These words reflect different conceptions of the human body. *"Der Körper"* refers to the human body as "just a 'body,' 'a physical body,' 'the body as object,' a physio-chemical system, understandable through established laws of physics; the object of investigation of the positive sciences and biomedical sciences."[30] *"Der Leib"* refers to the human body in two senses—as "living," i.e., as animate organism, and as "lived," i.e., the experienced center of acting, perceiving, and opportunities.[31] In the context of her presenting her understanding of labor, Arendt has rendered "human body" as "*der Körper.*" Her understanding of the human body thus reveals itself—the human body is understood as "physical body." This understanding is consistent and unvarying throughout the text of *The Human Condition;* the human body is always rendered as "*der Körper.*"

Her linguistic substitutions for and textual elaboration of this representation of the human body indicate, however, that she understands the human body to be more than a mere physical object. It is represented in biological terms: ". . . 'laboring' always moves in the same circle, which is prescribed by the biological process of the *living organism* and the end of its 'toil and trouble' comes only with the death of this organism."[32] In her text on labor, the human body is thus also represented as *living body,* as a phenomena constituted by a physio-chemical system and by a metabolic system—as animal body. But this representation does not supplant the other in the movement of the text. Both representations of the human body, "*der Körper*" and "living organism," are inscribed in the text without differentiation and are, in fact, treated synonymously. By treating them synonymously, the text misreads itself; and by misreading itself, it blinds itself to an alternative understanding which is indicated by the designations of "*der Körper*" and "living organism." Such an understanding would read these designations, not in their separateness, but in their relatedness—"lived body in a physical body (*als Leib in Körper*)."[33] Every animal, including man, "is" and "has" a body: "Both *is* a body, that is a physical system, and *has* a body, that is, it lives a center of perceiving and acting, in and out of its given biological endowment and into and out of its given biological environment.[34]

Arendt's blindness to this alternative understanding is at the same time reinscribed in her reading of the Western tradition. Her understanding of the human body is worked out primarily on the basis of her reading of Marx's text on labor. This reading of Marx is supplemented by references to the texts of other modern labor theorists, particularly nineteenth-century political economists. Her reading of the tradition, however, omits those texts that recognize the human body "*als Leib in Körper.*" The texts of philosophical anthropologists and biologists[35] are not read, but neglected. And this neglect reinscribes Arendt's blindness to an alternative understanding of the human body.

In the context of Arendt's understanding of work, the human body is not represented as such. It disappears from her text on work. And it must disappear because it is absorbed into her understanding of labor as living body. However, at the same time that the human body has disappeared from this text, it makes its reappearance, but in a different form, and against the will of the text. In the first sentence of her text on work, Arendt reintroduces John Locke's aphorism: "*The work of our hands as distinguished from the labour of our bodies* . . . fabricates the sheer unending variety of things whose sum total constitutes the human artifice."[36] Appropriated in its own terms, "the work of our hands" designates a reference to the human body. Hands presuppose the human body. They belong to the human body; they are bodily limbs and instruments of the human body. In this relation of hand and body there is indicated another understanding of the human body, namely that which understands the human bodily existence as "instrumentality":

> [Man] experiences himself as a thing and in a thing: but a thing which differs from all other things because he himself is that thing, because it obeys his intentions or at least responds to them . . . yet at the same time it forms a resistance never to be wholly overcome. In this unity . . . which he must constantly renew, man's living body is disclosed to him as a means, i.e., as something he can utilize to move about, carry loads, sit, grasp, strike, and so on. This adaptability, together with its independent objective thinghood, makes the living body an instrument.[37]

The instrumental character of living body reveals the *mediated* character of man's bodily existence, but at the same time a certain immediacy attaches to this mediation: When my body is mastered as instrument, it is embodied in that instrumentality. However, the tension between mediacy and immediacy is never overcome, but must constantly be confronted. Man's capacity for reflexivity is what Helmuth Plessner calls man's "eccentric position." The living human body that exhibits this structural capacity remains tied to its existence, yet is detached from it. This same relationship holds with respect to the human body's relation to its environment. It is tied to its earthly environment, but it is not bound to it.

In the context of her discussion of "the work of the hands," Arendt, however, passes over the textual references to the human body in this aphorism from Locke and to the understanding inscribed in it. This blindness to the textual presence of the human body and of an alternative understanding reveals once again the problematic of reading and misreading in her text. Arendt reads the text of Locke in such a way that her understanding of it is at the same time a misunderstanding. She understands it as a fundamental insight into work; it testifies to the objectivity of work and to its instrumentality. But this insight recovered by her reading is bought at the price of blindness to a fundamental insight into the human body. In other words, her reading is at the same time a misreading because it does not recover the insight into the human body inscribed in this text, namely its instrumental character, its mediated-immediate relationship to itself as well as to its environment and world, and its "eccentric position." What remains in the last analysis, then, as Arendt's reading of the human body is that which is given in her text *"Die Arbeit unseres Körpers."* And this is a reading which inscribes within itself the possibility of misunderstanding.

T E X T - W O R K
Part III: Arendt Re-reads Her Text on the Human Body

In her last work, *The Life of the Mind*, Arendt once again confronts the phenomena of the living organism, life processes, and the body. This re-engagement of the bodily phenomenon is not worked out within the context of labor and work, but rather within the context of the thinking experience and the world of appearance. What is worked out in this context indicates a re-reading of her text on the human body.

The re-reading is accomplished primarily through the reading of texts by Adolf Portmann and Maurice Merleau-Ponty. While both these texts were neglected in her reading of bodily phenomena in *The Human Condition*, they are here integral to her "phenomenological reading of the world of appearance and of the living organism as an 'appearing being.'" Her reading of Portmann's texts is of critical importance to this effort.

In a number of publications on the various shapes and forms in animal life, the Swiss zoologist and biologist Adolf Portmann has shown that the facts themselves speak a very different language from the simplistic functional hypothesis that holds that appearances in living beings serve merely the two-fold purpose of self-preservation and preservation of the species. From a different and, as it were, more innocent viewpoint, it rather looks as though, on the contrary, the inner, non-appearing organs might exist only in order to bring forth and maintain the appearances. Portmann writes, "Prior to all functions for the purpose of preservation of the individual and the species . . . we find the simple fact of appearing as self-display *that makes these functions meaningful.*"[38]

According to [the functionalist] interpretation, "the external shape of the animal serves to conserve the essential, the inside apparatus, through movement and intake of food, avoidance of enemies, and finding sexual partners." Against this approach Portmann proposes his "morphology," a new science that would reverse the priorities: "*Not what something is, but how it 'appears' is the research problem.*"[39]

What Arendt's appropriation of Portmann's text indicates is a revisioning, a revising, of her text on the living organism. What, in effect, it accomplishes is a translation of *der Körper* into *das Leib*—that is, of the body as a metabolic body whose home is nature into the body as a lived body whose home is the world of appearances. Living organisms are no longer presented as mere creatures of cyclical life processes, but are represented as pre-eminently creatures of self-display:

> [Portmann's] findings suggest that the predominance of outside appearance implies, in addition to the sheer receptivity of our senses, a spontaneous activity: *whatever can see wants to be seen, whatever can hear calls out to be heard, whatever can touch presents itself to be touched.* It seems, indeed, that everything that is alive—in addition to the fact that its surface is made for appearance, fit to be seen and meant to appear to others—has *an urge to appear*, to fit itself into the world of appearances by showing and displaying not its "inner self" but itself as an individual.[40]

And since the human body belongs to everything that is alive, it too is a creature of self-display. In fact it is the creature of self-display *par excellence:* "It is precisely this self-display, quite prominent already in the higher forms of animal life, that reaches its climax in the human species.[41] The human body is thus recovered from its consignment to the invisible body of *animal laborans*. With outward appearance restored to the human body, it is now fit to appear and to make its appearance.

As evident from *The Human Condition* and other writings, Arendt's concern for and thinking about the world of appearances is not novel. In these texts, she provides an incisive and sensitive phenomenological analysis of the structure of the world of appearance. And what is more, there is much in common between this analysis and the language in which it is presented and the analysis and its linguistic representation found in this text.

However, what crucially distinguishes the former from the present analysis is the status of the living organism and the human body. In her former analysis, Arendt does not admit the living organism and the human body into the world of appearances. The analysis is accomplished without reference to them, even though their absence haunts that accomplishment and makes it vulnerable. In the present analysis, Arendt re-admits, through Portmann's text, the living organism and the human body into the world of appearance and thereby effects a significant accomplishment in her thinking career.

NOTES

1. Hannah Arendt, *The Human Condition* (Chicago: University of Chicago Press, 1970), p. 94.
2. J. Glenn Gray, "The Winds of Thought," *Social Research* Vol. XLIV, No. 1 (Spring 1977), p. 53. This article was originally given as a memorial address at Bard College, May, 1976.
3. Arendt, *The Human Condition*, p. 80.
4. Ibid., p. 80–81.
Arendt's footnote to her discussion of this point is illuminating:

This is the case [that the verb form of "work" has become rather obsolete] for the French *ouvrer* and the German *werken*. In both languages, as distinguished from the current usage of the word "labor," the words *travailler* and *arbeiten* have almost lost the original significance of pain and trouble. . . . It is also interesting that the nouns "work," *oeuvre*, *werk*, show an increasing tendency to be used for works of art in all three languages. (Ibid., p. 81.)

In American English it remains more or less the case that the verbal form of "work" is still "in play." It is still used more or less synonymously with "labor." However, contrary to Arendt's claim, it too has shed much of its "original" significance of pain and labor. Technical developments in the manufacturing and agricultural sectors of the economy as well as the transformation of the economy into a "service economy" have been critical factors in modifying labor, i.e., in the lightening of the "burdens of labor," in post-industrial America; and usage has reflected this development. Finally, even though the English noun "work" is still currently used to talk about "works of art," some legitimate doubt can be raised about its appropriateness in the context of current developments in the field of American art. In other words, have not such current developments as conceptual art, environmental art, and self-consuming art rendered its use obsolete?

5. Ibid., p. 5. Emphasis is mine. Since this paper is concerned solely with understanding Arendt's "unusual" distinction between labor and work, no direct consideration is given to her discussion of action, moreover, since it is concerned with understanding her articulation of her historical treatment of them—her tracing of the "various constellations within the hierarchy of activities as we know them from Western history." (Ibid., p. 6.) Her historical treatment does, however, make its appearance in the context of the analysis of texts which have appropriated her re-thinking of labor and work. In representing what is involved in Arendt's re-thinking the human condition, a critical characteristic of thinking as she understands it has been underemphasized. For her thinking, though done in solitude, is neither initiated nor done abstractly. That is, it is always inspired by and oriented by concrete events and actual experiences: ". . . my assumption is that thought itself arises out of incidents of living experience and must remain bound to them as the only guideposts by which to take its bearings." (Hannah Arendt, *Between Past and Future* (New York: Viking Press, 1968), p. 14.) The "incidents of living experience" which inspired and provided the guideposts of her re-thinking of *The Human Condition* were the decisive events of the launching of the first space satellite in 1957 and the advent of automation.

6. Ibid., p. 94.

7. The language which Arendt thinks in making this distinction between labor and work and in articulating their characteristics is that of "ordinary language," ancient and modern, and the languages of theories, ancient, particularly Plato's and Aristotle's, and modern, particularly Locke's and Marx's. Presupposed, but not textually present, is her thinking of the language of Martin Heidegger, particularly his language of "earth," "world," "tool," and "work of art."

8. The earth, for Arendt, is the "quintessence of the human condition." (Ibid., p. 9.) It provides man with that environment (*Umwelt*) in which he can live, i.e., move and breathe, without the mediation of the world (*Welt*), i.e., without "the artificial world of things."

9. Ibid., p. 10.

10. Ibid., p. 179.

11. Ibid., pp. 322–23.

12. For Arendt's unfolding of the characteristics of labor and work, the reader is referred to Part II, "Labor" (pp. 79–135), and Part IV, "Work" (pp. 136–74), of *The Human Condition*. For her story of their fate in the modern

age, see specifically the following sections in Part VI, "The *Vita Activa* and the Modern Age": 42. "The Reversal within the *Vita Activa* and the Victory of *Homo Faber*" (pp. 274–305); 43. "The Defeat of *Homo Faber* and the Principle of Happiness" (pp. 305–313); 44. "Life as the Highest Good" (pp. 313–320); and 45. "The Victory of the *Animal Laborans*" (pp. 320–325).

13. Some textual critics argue that every reading is in fact a misreading. Others argue, in addition, that the text itself involves its own misreading and therefore that every reading of the text will be a misreading of a misreading.

14. J. Glenn Gray, "The Winds of Thought," p. 53.

15. Ibid., pp. 52–53.

16. Walter Weisskopf, *Alienation and Economy* (New York: E. P. Dutton, 1971), pp. 68–69.

17. Arendt, *The Human Condition*, p. 89. The neutralization of Arendt's critique is effected again in a footnote which Weisskopf appends to his text on Marx. In it, he introduces Arendt's distinction between labor and work as well as her argument that Marx does not make such a sharp distinction between the two "concepts." However, nothing follows from this footnote; he makes nothing of her distinction or of her argument. In effect, he has neutralized them by merely noting them, i.e., by not comprehending their significance for his analysis and argument.

18. Weisskopf, *Alienation and Economy*, p. 69.

19. Ibid., p. 70.

20. Ibid., p. 70–71. The use of the early Marx critique as the source of a program for a critical theory of advanced industrial society, which Weisskopf attributes to Jürgen Habermas in a footnote, cannot be dealt with so summarily. To confront Habermas with Arendt raises too many important issues, questions, and problems to be adequately considered in this context. Nevertheless, it is necessary to indicate at this point that Arendt would find Habermas's reformulation of Marx's "forces of production" as "work" or "instrumental action" as reflecting the same confusion that plagued Marx. It fails to understand the distinction between labor and work, a distinction grounded in the "objectivity" of work. In embracing both Arendt and Habermas in his text on Marx's concept of labor, Weisskopf has thus left himself vulnerable to criticism from both perspectives. And ultimately this is to argue that he cannot embrace both Arendt's and Marx's texts in the context that he has. For Arendt's text deconstructs that of Marx and thereby his own text. If he had not misread her text, he would never have introduced it.

21. Ibid., p. 110.

22. Arendt, *The Human Condition*, p. 52.

23. Ibid., p. 65. Emphasis is mine.

24. These two essays by Frampton were composed at different times,

but are internally linked. The first was written for a collection of essays entitled *Meaning in Architecture*, published in 1970. The second was read before the Arendt conference "The Work of Hannah Arendt," held at York University, Toronto, in 1972. The latter was one of the two architectural presentations upon which I commented at that conference. As part of that commentary, I used my textual reading of the conference title as a way of (as a pretext for) commenting upon his Arendtian comprehension of the human activity and meaning of architecture. That is, I attempted to show that what made the title of the conference so correct and fitting is precisely what for Frampton is so correct and fitting for a theory of architectural activity and meaning—namely, her understanding of the distinction between work and labor and of the work of art.

25. Kenneth Frampton, "Labor, Work and Architecture," in *Meaning and Architecture*. Charles Jencks and George Baird, eds. (New York: Braziller, 1970), p. 152.

26. Three qualifying comments are in order with respect to Frampton's appropriation of Arendt's text as revealed in this essay. First, his reading of Arendt's activity concept of "action" is ambiguous. On the one hand, "action" appears to be assimilated to "labor," i.e., to process, but on the other hand it is related, at an earlier point in his essay, to the "existential preliminary of every building act." (Ibid., p. 151.) This ambiguity is not resolved in the course of the essay's analysis and argument. In fact, "action" drops out as a central concern of his presentation—a situation, however, which is reversed in his other essay. Secondly, Frampton fails to identify what is at stake in the introduction of "anthropomorphic" connotation into his discussion of "human use." He introduces it in order to assimulate "human use" to Arendt's "human world." From an Arendtian perspective "use" is a human capacity and is related both to the production of objects and to their appropriation. It is to be distinguished from "consumption," a capacity that men share with animals, and is related to the appropriate "products" generated by labor. "Use" is tied to the world whereas consumption is tied to nature. At the same time, however, "use" within the Arendtian perspective is related to the private realm and to experience, of use itself, both with respect to the production of made objects and to their appropriation. And this relation to the experience of use itself carries within it the project of "instrumentalization which generates meaninglessness": "The issue at stake is, of course, not instrumentality, the use of means to achieve an end, as such, but rather the generalization of the fabrication in which usefulness and utility are established as the ultimate standards for life and the world of men (whereby the world and nature became meaningless). This generalization is inherent in the activity of *homo faber* because the experience of means and end . . . is extended to its ultimate end, which is to serve as a use object." (Arendt, *The Human Condition*, p.

157.) And the only possible response to this situation of meaninglessness created by the instrumentalization of the world and the earth is anthropocentrism: "Only in a strictly anthropocentric world, where the user, that is, man himself, becomes the ultimate end which puts a stop to the unending chain of ends and means, can utility as such acquire the dignity of meaningfulness. Yet the tragedy is that in the moment *homo faber* seems to have found fulfillment in terms of his own activity, he begins to degrade the world of things . . ." (Ibid., p. 155). Anthropocentrism is thus not a real solution to the dilemma of *homo faber*—the meaningfulness and worth of the world. Frampton's "anthropomorphic connotation" when viewed in this context thus reveals connections and significations which belie his attempt at assimilating "human use" to Arendt's human world. Thirdly, Frampton does not preserve Arendt's disjunctive distinction between public and private in the construction of his architectural theory. He argues that "a construction, as opposed to a work of fine art, is almost invariably erected to serve or house a function of the society, hence it is of essence in some respect public, save on these increasingly numerous occasions when it comprises the single family unit or isolated private house . . . [which] remains essentially ephemeral and private, dedicated as it inevitably is to the process of biological survival." (Frampton, "Labor, Work and Architecture," p. 151.) A construction is not a work of art *per se,* for it serves a purpose beyond itself. However, since that purpose is a public one, construction's proper destination is the public realm and to that extent approximates the work of art. A construction can also be functional in character, i.e., shelters for housing the family. And since such a function is a biological one, its proper destination is the private realm. However, as Frampton argues, the private realm "reveals the presence of an 'operational' public aspect contained within it." (Ibid., p. 153.) This he identifies in terms of the "hearth" and the television set. For Frampton, the discrimination between public and private, work and labor, cannot be made abstractly, but must be made concretely in every particular case.

27. Kenneth Frampton, "Industralization and the Crises of Architecture," *Oppositions,* 1 (September 1973).

28. Frampton, it could be argued, again follows Arendt in situating his thinking within "living experience." His essays testify to Arendt's assumption about thinking that was quoted earlier that "thought itself arises out of incidents of living experience and must remain bound to them as the only guideposts by which to take its bearings." (Arendt, *Between Past and Future,* p. 14.)

29. Hannah Arendt, *Vita Activa oder von tätigen Leben.* (Stuttgart: W. Kohlhammer Verlag, 1960), p. 76.

30. Stuart F. Spicker, "The Lived-Body as Catalytic Agent," in *Evaluation and Explanation in the Biomedical Sciences.* H. T. Englehardt and S. F. Spicker, eds. (Dordrecht, Holland: D. Reidel Publishing Co., 1975), p. 184.

31. This conception of the body as "lived" has its "origins" in the philosophical/anthropological "branch" of modern European philosophy. "Origins" designate in this context not "discovery," but "recovery," i.e., "recovery" of a dimension of the human body that had been concealed by the Western tradition of theology and philosophy, but which is given in human experience. Among the most important philosophical anthropologists and biologists associated with this movement are: Jacob von Uexküll, Helmuth Plessner, Erwin Straus, Herbert Plügge, Victor von Gebsattel, F. J. J. Buytendijk, J. H. Van Den Berg, Gabriel Marcel, M. Merleau-Ponty, Adolf Portmann, and Hans Jonas.

32. Arendt, *The Human Condition*, p. 98. Emphasis is mine. The German rendering of this passage does not reveal anything different: ". . . ist das Arbeiten niemal fertig: sondern dreht sich in unendlichen Wiederholung in den immer wiederkehrenden Kreise, den der biologische Lebensprozess ihm vorschreibt und dessen 'Mühe und Plage' erst mit dem Tod des jeweiligin organismus Endet Findet." (Arendt, p. 90.)

33. Helmuth Plessner, *Laughing and Crying*. J. S. Churchill and M. Grene trans. (Evanston: Northwestern University Press, 1970), p. 34.

34. Marjorie Grene, "People and Other Animals," *Philosophical Forum*, III, 2 (Winter 1972), p. 169. Emphasis is hers. Her text is based on Plessner's philosophical anthropology of the "lived body."

35. Cf. Footnote 31 for names of recognized philosophical anthropologists/biologists.

36. Arendt, *The Human Condition*, p. 136. Emphasis is mine.

37. Plessner, *Laughing and Crying*, p. 41.

38. Hannah Arendt, *The Life of the Mind: Thinking* (New York: Harcourt Brace Jovanovich, 1978), Part 1, p. 27. Emphasis is mine.

39. Ibid., p. 28. Emphasis is mine.

40. Ibid., p. 29. Emphasis is mine.

41. Ibid., p. 30.

Peter Fuss

HANNAH ARENDT'S CONCEPTION OF POLITICAL COMMUNITY[1]

The observation that men reveal their distinctive identities as human beings in what they do and say seems neither very original nor very controversial. But consider the following set of implications: that men disclose their uniqueness as individuals more fully and surely when they act and speak spontaneously than when they labor to maintain biological subsistence or work to produce a tangible world of human artifacts; that action and speech together make up a "web of human relationships" that forms the more or less intangible, but at the same time most vital, dimension of human community; that, paradoxically, when they act and speak in human community men are most truly free and yet least in control of their own destinies; that when deprived, as they can be, of human community men quickly lose the sense of their own reality as well as that of a world experienced in common; that the Athenian citizenry of Pericles' time, apparently well aware of all this, constituted the greatest and possibly the last authentically "political" community in Western history; and that Pericles' faith in the power of the Athenian *polis* to actualize and to sustain human greatness was, for understandable reasons, so short-lived that political thought and political decision from Plato to the present day might well be regarded as an escape from "politics" altogether.

These contentions are the guiding themes of Hannah

Arendt's *The Human Condition*. Richly textured, astonishingly erudite, and difficult to read, this book is to my mind one of the most profound and provocative exercises in political thinking in recent times. Prompted by this conviction, I have chosen to present and to elaborate, mostly in her terms but occasionally in my own, her conception of political community. My method in what follows will be, like Arendt's, "phenomenological" in a loose and somewhat stretched sense of the term. I shall simply equate, as did Aristotle, what appears to all to be so with what is. The reasons for this equation of appearance with reality, doubtless shocking in a post-Cartesian age, will, I hope, become clear in the sequel. Even then, certain quite legitimate metaphysical and epistemological questions will have to be "bracketed" here, as perforce they are in *The Human Condition*.

Action and Speech

The basis of the human condition is human plurality, a plurality that differs from that of inorganic as well as of organic entities. Unlike the sheer otherness of a multiplicity of inorganic objects, unlike even the variations and distinctions between specimens of the same organic species, human plurality is the paradoxical plurality of unique beings. Man alone has the capacity to distinguish himself and to express this distinction—to communicate *himself* and not merely some shared attribute or drive or feeling-state. He shares sheer numerical otherness with everything that is, and qualitative distinctness with everything alive; but the ability to reveal who he uniquely and unrepeatedly is, is a power that he alone has.

Men reveal their uniqueness by acting within[2] the human community, the world of their fellow men. Whereas *labor* for biological survival is under the sway of necessity and involves an endlessly repeated cyclical process of production and consumption in metabolism with the world of nature; whereas *work* directed toward the production of more or less durable human artifacts for use and enjoyment is governed by standards of utility and involves a process of harnessing known means to predictable ends; *action* manifests itself in the initiation of unprecedented processes whose outcome is uncertain and unpredictable and whose meaningfulness lies in the disclosure of the identities of the agents themselves.[3]

Intimately related to and inseparable from the power of action is the power of speech. Speech is the distinctive way in which men identify themselves as actors, announcing what they do, have done, and intend doing. It is also the distinctive way in which men answer, respond, and measure up to what happens and what is done by others in the human world. Because many, perhaps most, actions are performed in the mode of speech, speech has an even closer affinity with revelation than does action, just as action has a closer affinity with beginning or initiation than does speech. In any event, action without speech would lose its power to reveal a human agent; and, dependent as it is upon the power of speech to illuminate its meaningfulness, action without speech has a tendency to degenerate into violence.

The non-utilitarian character of action pertains to speech as well. No doubt man's power to act is highly useful in the pursuit of his sundry interests, just as his power to act in concert is indispensable at times for self-defense. But behavior, especially organized behavior, is considerably more effective in the pursuit of definite ends than is initiatory action with all of its inherent spontaneity, uncontrollability, and unpredictability. Similarly, speech is highly useful in the communication of information; but from the point of view of sheer utility, it is a poor substitute for the efficiency and precision of sign language.

Action and speech require initiative, but the failure to take such initiative is tantamount to the failure to be human. Men may live lives that are human, however unjust, without laboring by compelling others to toil for their own physical survival. They may live lives that are human, however parasitical, by merely using and enjoying the things that make up the realm of human artifacts—without themselves contributing anything to that realm. But a life without action and speech never comes alive, as it were, within the human community directly; it falls short of being a human life because it fails to disclose what is uniquely and unrepeatably individual about this life.

Who and What

Our distinctive physical identities—the particular shape of our bodies and the peculiar sound of our voices—appear in the world by the mere fact that we are there, without any special effort on our part. In addition to our physical identities, we possess certain qualities, character traits, talents, gifts, virtues, shortcomings, and the like, and we maintain certain positions and play certain roles in society—father, factory worker, taxpayer, etc. Over these characteristics and roles we have a considerable degree of control: we may cultivate or waste, display or hide, overcome or succumb to, enhance, modify, or change them as we choose. Together with our physical attributes, they constitute *what* we are. But *who* we are, i.e., our unique identities as persons (our "personhood," as it is sometimes expressed) is revealed only in acting and speaking, although to be sure it is implicit in everything we do and say. It can be hidden only in utter passivity and silence, in the radical privacy that is, for example, forced upon men under the rule of tyrannical or totalitarian regimes (whose first order of business is to destroy the community of action and speech by depriving it of all public visibility and significance). On the other hand, the disclosure of who we are is rarely if ever achieved with purposeful deliberateness: we do not possess and cannot therefore dispose of *who* we are in the way that we possess and control the characteristics that make up *what* we are. In fact, it is rather the case that who we are, while it may appear clearly and unmistakably to those who know us, remains relatively hidden from ourselves.

By a somewhat different strategy of analysis, we might pursue the distinction previously suggested between human behavior and human action. Behavior is in principle precedent-laden and stereotyped, imitable if not fully copiable, conditioned if not determined, and to a great extent predictable, controllable, and manipulable. Action (and speech), on the other hand, is by nature original and originative, spontaneous and inimitable, stimulatable by the presence of others whose company we may seek but never determined by them, and radically unpredictable and uncontrollable. Thus if men always behaved and never acted, we would require no distinction between what they are and who they are. Moreover, we would encounter none of the difficulties that we do in fact meet in attempting to define "human nature." As matters stand, there probably is no such thing as a definable human nature; even if there were, only a god could know and define it—provided, we must add, that he chose to regard a "who" as though it were a "what." A man's pattern of behavior, then, does not tend to single him out as a unique individual, whereas the exercise of his capacity to act (and to speak) does just that.

Having said that much about the "who," however, it might be best to say no more. It is one thing to adumbrate this singular dimension of human experience by way of negation, i.e., by focusing attention on what it is not. It is quite another matter to aim at direct conceptual articulation.

> The manifestation of who the speaker and doer unexchangeably is, though it is plainly visible, retains a curious intangibility that confounds all efforts toward unequivocal verbal expression. The moment we want to say *who* somebody is, our very vocabulary leads us astray into saying *what* he is; we get entangled in a description of qualities he necessarily shares with others like him; we begin to describe a type or a "character" in the old meaning of the word, with the result that his specific uniqueness escapes us.[4]

The notorious intangibility of the "who," the frustrating unreliability of its revelation, is perhaps the main reason why the world of human affairs in general, and the public, political realm in particular, is so beset with uncertainty. Our inability to name, that is, to fix in words the distinctive essence of the person as it manifests itself in the living flow of action and speech appears to be closely interrelated with the fact that we cannot handle the realm of human affairs (in which after all we exist primarily as actors and speakers) in the way we can handle things whose nature is so much at our disposal—just because we are able to name (to specify, to classify, in the end to have done with) them. Most action and speech does, of course, have an "objective" content or reference. It is largely *about* a tangible world of things in which men are interested—a world which exists, so to speak, "in-between" them, relating, separating, and binding them together. But no matter how energetically one's deeds and words concentrate on this tangible world of objects, they continue to reveal a "who" as their subject; because no matter what one's action and speech is about, its significance is still a matter of direct address *to* other men. Thus there arises a second, "subjective" in-between, appropriately called the "web of human relationships" because of its intangibility. For all of its intangibility, however, it is no less real than is the tangible in-between of a commonly experienced world of things.

But it is, as its name suggests, dismayingly fragile. The remainder of this essay will focus on some reasons for, and some consequences of, the fragility of the realm of speech and action.

Freedom and Sovereignty

Initiatory action and revelatory speech are the forms in which men most fully manifest their freedom and disclose their unique identities. But men do not act and speak by the mere fact that they are men, no more than they are free merely by virtue of their being men. Action and speech specifically, and freedom generally, are potentialities of men, potentialities whose actualization cannot be taken for granted. What Kant said of human freedom—namely, that it is a task and not a given—is true *a fortiori* of human self-revelation. Acting and speaking within the human community, allowing oneself to become part of the larger web of human relationships, requires courage, a willingness to take risks, and faith. Courage is needed to expose and disclose one's self in public; risk is involved in that one is not master of what he thus reveals; and one must have sufficient faith in the community of one's fellow men to entrust to its care this precious self—a self which, it should be noted, is not in fact "mine" in the sense of something that I can cultivate and bring to fulfillment in isolation. The risk had better be taken, then—unless the faith is totally unwarranted.

We do not possess and control the "who" we reveal. Our deeds and words fall into a pre-existing web of human relationships within which, indeed, they begin new processes; but these processes immediately are affected by, as they affect, the innumerable conflicting wills and intentions of other actors and speakers. Because of this web, action rarely achieves its purpose. On the other hand, since action is meaningful and real only within this web, it issues in "life stories" with a remarkable naturalness and inevitability. The difficulty is that we are neither singly and unequivocally responsible for the consequences of what we do and say, nor are we in fact the authors of our own life stories. When we act and speak, we reveal at best an identifiable initiator of a process. But the processes we initiate are inherently boundless, irreversible, and unpredictable. Moreover, we disclose ourselves piecemeal during the entire course of our lives, outliving what we do and say even while these deeds and words in turn outlive us. Thus the full meaning of what we initiate can be known, if at all—and the full story of who we are can be told, if at all—only in retrospect, after we are dead, by the historian and the storyteller. For the agent himself, the meaningfulness of what he does and says clearly cannot lie in the story that follows him. In short, it quickly becomes apparent

that he who acts never quite knows what he is doing, that he always becomes "guilty" of consequences he never intended or even foresaw, that however disastrous or unexpected the consequences of his deed he can never undo it, that the process he starts is never consummated unequivocally in one single deed or event, and that its very meaning never discloses itself to the actor but only to the backward glance of the historian who himself does not act.[5]

To the contemplative eye, what inescapably manifests itself here is the baffling paradox that men are most free when they are least sovereign. Exercising their capacity for initiative, the essence of their freedom, they help create a web of human relationships that so thoroughly entangles them that they seem more the helpless victims than the masters of what they have done. When it appears that men forfeit their freedom at the very instant they avail themselves of it, that human freedom exists only to lure men into necessity, the temptation to condemn action—and thereby to retreat from or even to destroy the web of human relationships altogether—becomes almost irresistible. One readily concludes that the burden of action and speech, of revealing and witnessing who men are, under the haphazard and chaos-ridden conditions of human plurality, is simply too great.

Reality and Appearance

Nevertheless, it must be emphasized that whereas a life of acting and speaking in human community is perilous and to a great extent frustrating, the abandonment of life in community in favor of a life of supposed self-sufficiency and self-mastery in isolation proves to be little short of suicidal. For apart from the web of human relationships, action and speech, initiation and self-revelation are utterly futile. They lose their capacity for endurance as they lose their very meaning. They fail to *appear*—and, from a human point of view, what does not appear is not real. In fact, intersubjective confirmation is the ground of our assurance that anything whatever—ourselves, our fellow men, the world of natural objects and the world of man-made things—is real.

This reality is certified, as it were, in and through our relationships with other human beings who are like us in that they are all human, but who are all human in that each is unique. In the human world, which may fittingly be called the "space of appearances," each individual, apart from being an actor and speaker, is a witness, testifying to what takes place from the vantage point of his own irreducibly unique perspective. Yet because each individual shares a common humanity with every other, he is able to communicate his perspectives to others. This power to communicate makes possible a continuity of perspectives. When perspectives are multiple yet continuous, they illumine more or less fully, "from all sides," as it were, a single person or object perceived in common.

As a dramatic depiction of the plight of the individual isolated from human community, Dostoevski's *Notes from the Underground* is probably still without peer.[6] Unwitnessed and unconfirmed by others, Dostoevski's anti-hero acts and speaks almost exclusively within the confines of his own ego—"into" and to himself alone. In this endless, and in the end tedious, narcissistic drama, he almost succeeds in becoming what he cannot be: the manipulator of his own identity and the author of his own life story. But of course he is not actually an actor and speaker; he is much more like a puppet-master. At the ends of his strings are hallucinatory internalizations of "others" who, he keeps trying to pretend, are as he would have them be, not as they really are. "They" do not stand over against him; against "them" he does not have to measure up, since he has created them in the first place and can annihilate them at his pleasure. Similarly, when he does emerge from the Underground into the "light of day," he is not, as Plato would have it, blinded by the radiance of what appears. Instead, he sees perfectly well. But what he sees is not what is there; he sees nothing but the fantastic projections of his own inner states. To borrow a phrase from Martin Buber, he "gives the lie to being" wherever he goes. But such power, kept "underground," is a hollow self-mockery, and our protagonist is anything but content with the fact that he is forced to try to manufacture, rather than being free to be able to disclose, his self. He comes dangerously close to bringing to life in his own suffering person what was traditionally supposed to stay safely put in philosophy textbooks as a mere hypothetical extreme—namely, solipsism. But lived solipsism does not in fact conform to its traditional philosophic definition. When solipsism is experienced, rather than speculated on, it is not the case that only one's self is real. Nothing is real, one's self included.

However, the loss of reality does not occur only when men are radically isolated from one another. It occurs just as readily when men become massified, when they behave as though they were all but numerically indistinguishable, when each merely multiplies and prolongs his neighbor's perspective.

In both instances, men have become entirely private, that is, they have been deprived of seeing and hearing others, of being seen and being heard by them. They are all imprisoned in the subjectivity of their own singular experience, which does not cease to be singular if the same experience is multiplied innumerable times. The end of the common world has come when it is seen only under one aspect and is permitted to present itself in only one perspective.[7]

When men are together without being distinct, just as much as when they are distinct without being together, they lose their "common sense," their sense of reality. A brief additional comment may be helpful here. Our familiar expression "common sense" harbors a rich ambiguity. On the one hand, it refers to our sense of sharing something in common, our conviction that, perhaps as much because of as in spite of our distinctive plurality as human individuals, we live in one and the same world, a world stable enough to hold the diversity of our perspectives together in a continuous and coherent dialogue. On the other hand, when we appeal to an individual's "common sense," we are frequently trying to recall him away from some private idiosyncrasy of his and back to "what everybody knows," to what has again and again been intersubjectively experienced and confirmed. As Arendt has taken great pains to make clear throughout her writings, nothing can be taken for granted here. Our sense of sharing something in common may erode or be deliberately destroyed, and the wisdom of common sense may at any time be unmasked as the folly of unexamined stereotypes or all too long-standing bad habits. Yet the fact remains that our sense of reality is intact only when "what is" can be confirmed by many in a diversity of aspects without changing its essential identity, so that those who surround it know that they see sameness in diversity.

The Polis *and the Meaning of Politics*

Western history preserves the clear memory of at least one community of men who, for a brief moment, prized the web of human relationships—frail, frustrating, and paradox-ridden as it is—so highly that it can almost be said they lived for it alone. The ideal Athenian citizen during the "Golden Age" of Pericles was, to our understanding, a strange sort. Leaving the administration of his household to his wife, the cultivation of his fields to hirelings or slaves,[8] and the conduct of his commercial affairs to foreigners, he sailed forth into the *polis* to act and to speak in the company of his true peers. Here alone could he breathe the air of freedom, because he had left behind everything that had to do with his merely "private" concerns—those governed by the standards of utility as well as those under the sway of necessity. Here alone he found himself released from the need both to rule and to be ruled. Here alone did the opportunity to reveal his individuality, to distinguish himself from all others, fully present itself.

If we judge by the sheer "quantity" of greatness that manifested itself in that small and relatively isolated Greek city during so short a period of time, he did not waste his opportunities. But more to the point, and still stranger to our ways of thinking, was his understanding of what political life means. For him, the public revelation of men's unique identities through action and speech was the very content of politics. Mistrusting expertise and holding professionalism in somewhat low esteem, he took upon himself the burden of legislation, adjudication, and the administration of public affairs in general. But it never occurred to him that these exercises of civic responsibility were anything but pre-political activities. He regarded them at best as necessary procedures in the creation and maintenance of the "space," so to speak, in which the authentically political activities of acting and speaking were to appear. When Pericles, in his Funeral Oration, assured the Athenian citizens that "wherever you go, you will be a *polis*," he was merely reminding them of something they already knew: the substance of politics is the space of appearances that distinguishes yet binds men together and that in its living essence is independent of time, place, and physical circumstances.

In the Athenian conception the *polis*, as the space of appearance, was understood to have a double political function. In the first place, it was to multiply the occasions of action and speech, thereby affording every citizen repeated opportunity to distinguish himself in the eyes of his fellows.[9] In the second place, it was to overcome the futility of action and speech through communal remembrance, thus ensuring that those deeds deserving of "immortal fame" would never be forgotten. Together, the two functions of the *polis* would assure mortal actors that their passing existence and their fleeting greatness would be accorded the reality that comes from being seen and heard by their contemporaries, and remembered by those who came after them.

If this conception of the meaning of politics seems astonishing to us, we may well be aghast when we read that Pericles (or Thucydides) claimed the glory of the Athenians to lie in their legacy of "good and evil deeds," as though these were fully on a par. In point of fact, the Athenians apparently did regard conventional moral and utilitarian standards as being to a large extent inappropriate in the domain of action and speech. These standards legitimately apply only to ordinary human behavior, whereas it is in the very nature of action and speech to be extraordinary, unprecedented, and *sui generis*. Conventional morality's double focus—on motives and aims on the one hand and on consequences and achievements on the other—is of limited relevance in the political realm just because the former are non-unique and the latter are generally beyond the power of the agent to predict and to control. The specific meaning of each deed lies exclusively in the performance itself, and can be assessed in terms of one criterion alone: greatness.

The supreme Periclean confidence in the power of the *polis* to enact and, at the same time, to preserve greatness was short-lived indeed. Yet it sufficed to elevate action and speech to the highest rank in the hierarchy of human activities and to confer upon politics a dignity that has still not been entirely lost. Nevertheless, the tradition of Western political theory, already beginning with, and never entirely free from, the enormous influence of Plato, may well be regarded as a more or less ongoing repudiation of the Athenian political experience and its articulation. How, according to Arendt, did this come about?

The Escape from Politics

There is nothing self-evident about the conviction that man's greatness consists of his own disclosure, for its own sake, in action and in speech. Nor has this conviction ever been universally shared. Opposed to it stand both the craftsman's conviction that what he makes may be greater than what he is, as well as the laborer's (and lately the consumer's) belief that life itself is the greatest of all values. Both are naturally inclined to view action and speech as vain idleness, and to evaluate public activities on the basis of their subservience to allegedly higher ends: the utility and beauty of the world in the eyes of the former, the ease and length of life as such in the eyes of the latter. Both, therefore, are un-politically and even anti-politically oriented. Yet it is the gradual accession of the attitudes and activities, first of the former and then of the latter, to preeminence in the hierarchy of human values that has marked the course of Western political history.

It would be an understatement to say that, in the meantime, political thought has not kept the Periclean faith. Exasperated with the perplexities inherent in action—the irreversibility of its processes, the unpredictability of its consequences, and the relative anonymity (and hence inevitably the moral irresponsibility) of its authors, to name only the most salient—thinker after thinker has proposed solutions that would replace the life of action and speech with something else. The usual pattern has been to urge that the content of politics be entrusted to one or a few men, relatively isolated from the rest, who would be and remain masters of what they did. Conceptually underlying these proposals has been the replacement of categories pertaining to action and speech by categories appropriate to fabrication or work. The result throughout has been a degradation of politics from the position of being the substance, or at least the arena, of what men do and say for their own sakes, to a mere means of securing some other and supposedly loftier end. From the Periclean point of view, the organization of the political realm, in late antiquity, to protect the best (especially the philosophers) from the tyranny of the mob; in the Middle Ages, to further the salvation of souls; and, in the modern age, to guarantee a productive, progressive "society"[10] —would each and all be regarded as forms of escape from politics as such.

On the conceptual level, the figure of Plato looms so large in the post-Periclean tradition because he may have been the first, and probably was the greatest, philosopher to introduce the categories of fabrication and making into the political realm. In the web of human relationships, action has validity and meaning only so long as it is inseparably united with thought. But in the experience of fabrication, knowing and doing are separate "moments," as it were, in a process divisible into parts. As Plato understood the fabrication process, the craftsman first apprehends the model or form of his "end-product"; only then does he begin the actual work of carrying out his design by organizing the appropriate means. The first stage of this process requires knowledge, and it is the knowledge that accounts at once for the craftsman's dignity and for his claim to exercise sovereign mastery over a reliable process which he alone could begin and should oversee, but which others, with a modicum of instruction, could then carry through to its predetermined end. Plato, a post-Periclean deeply disenchanted with what had become of the isonomic community of action and speech, saw in the master craftsman the model of a ruler-expert fit to govern an orderly, function-oriented state.

> By sheer force of conceptualization and philosophical clarification, the Platonic identification of knowledge with command and rulership, and of action with obedience and execution, overruled all earlier experiences and articulations in the political realm and became authoritative for the whole tradition of political thought, even after the roots of the experience from which Plato derived his concepts had long been forgotten. [I have inserted an extra set of commas in order to make this sentence a little easier to read.][11]
>
> Within this frame of reference, the emergence of a utopian political system which could be construed in accordance with a model by somebody who has mastered the techniques of human affairs becomes almost a matter of course; Plato, who was the first to design a blueprint for the making of political bodies, has remained the inspiration for all later utopias.[12]

According to Arendt, then, our very conception of politics has been almost definitively shaped by the peculiar wedge Plato saw fit to drive in this domain between thought and action—a wedge that helped legitimate for two millennia the notion that there should be rulers who think for subjects who "act" (execute orders). Hence the well-entrenched notions that politics need not be everyone's concern, and that it is a necessary evil or even a dirty business.

An Inconclusive Comment

It is no doubt clear from the preceding that I find Hannah Arendt's rearticulation of the ideals of the Periclean political community a refreshing departure from "politics as usual," and more importantly from political thought as usual. But I must add that I have found it difficult to reconcile her "agonal" conception of politics with one that is not merely more familiar to us, but that is at least as attractive: politics as the institutionalization of the arts of persuasion and accommodation. Interestingly enough, Arendt herself has tended, since *The Human Condition*, to accentuate the latter conception. Her laudatory assessment of the roots of the American political experience in *On Revolution* is, in the final analysis, a tribute to a politics of persuasion and mutual accommodation rather than to a *polis* dedicated to the manifestation of individual excellence. This, it seems to me, is much more than a gracious gesture toward the country that has adopted her. Good phenomenologist that she is, Arendt would be the last to become fixated in a conceptual model whose experiential ground has all but vanished. Ironically, among the very few men in recent Western history to come anywhere close to constituting a Periclean *polis* have been the American Founding Fathers; and the form that their action took was essentially that of legislation (for the Pericleans, a *pre*-political craft). The Founding Fathers were, as Arendt insists, authentic revolutionaries who really did act insofar as they founded a new body politic. Yet she is equally careful to point out how lucky these revolutionaries were in being able to build on models of constituted liberty already available in the several colonies, and how this, along with the remoteness of all these happenings from a mother country whose attitude toward keeping her North American colonies under her thumb was, in any case, quite ambivalent, enabled the American Revolution, in contrast with the French and the Russian, to take so relatively non-violent a course.

Now as Arendt herself conceives of it, power is distinguished from both (individual) strength and (collective) force in that it is generated by men acting in concert, who in doing so actually augment their power in the very process of "dividing" it among themselves. Thus understood, power is a distinctively political, indeed *Periclean* political concept. But at the same time, the prior step of bringing men together to act in concert and thus to generate the power they share is itself an act, one whose success relies heavily upon the arts of persuasion and mutual accommodation.[13] It becomes apparent, I think, that we are actually dealing here with two kinds (or better, perhaps, two "moments") of power, even if to a certain extent they overlap: *viz.*, the founder-legislator's power to establish and secure a "space of appearances" in which, once this space has been formed, others can in turn exercise freely and confidently their power to act and to speak individually and in concert. Bearing in mind the distinction as well as the overlap, we might attempt to reconcile the agonal thrust of *The Human Condition* with the accommodational emphasis of *On Revolution* in a schema something like the following:

> Politics, the range of activities pertinent to the public realm (the space of appearances which concerns all of us in common), may be understood as having two distinct but ultimately inseparable dimensions:
>
> 1) *Substantively*, the content of politics is the realm of personal initiatives individually enacted and plurally responded to. (A variant formulation: the content of politics is human distinctiveness expressed through the witnessed deed and the communicated word.)
>
> 2) *Procedurally*, politics is the realm of (ideally isonomic) decision-making with respect to the best way to promote and preserve (1). The procedural stuff of politics is opinions, whereas the procedural style consists in the classic forms of non-violent confrontation: persuasion and accommodation.
>
> In both of its dimensions, politics is a domain of the relative in the double sense of that term: interpersonally relating and non-absolute. There are no absolutes in politics. Every attempt to introduce them dooms the *polis* to violence and terror.[14]

And yet I doubt that this will wash. Agonal and accommodational politics are probably antithetical, especially so from the perspective at which Hannah Arendt so often achieves her most arresting insights—the psychological. There is, it seems to me, something inevitably and unregenerately absolutistic in the "psychological set" of the agonal type. He tends to be ruthless in his urgency to achieve and express individual excellence, especially when he is forced to pause in behalf of the needs and wishes of others. The one who is ideally suited first to help create, and then to care for, the "space of appearance" itself, on the other hand, must cultivate what Arendt calls "representative thinking," *viz.*, the ability to view any given situation from as many different points of view as possible in order to arrive at the most informed opinion. Arendt is quite right to insist that this is a distinctively *political* virtue, an attitude of mind that is indispensable for anyone who has genuine concern for the world. But this virtue is seldom to be found among those who act spontaneously and originatively "into" the space of appearances—those agonal personalities without whom the world would never be revitalized, yet whose deeds might well destroy the world were it not for the caretakers of the *polis,* those whose boundless capacity for empathetic projection makes them unfit for action in its more dramatic and decisive forms.

On more than one occasion Hannah Arendt has taught us to follow the paths of unresolved tension and contradiction in the mind of a great thinker if we wish to arrive at the true significance of his thought. Tempting as it is to use this fruitful method of approach to Arendt's own work, I think we would do well to forbear. After all, her writings subsequent to *The Human Condition* are fairly consistently weighted on the side of politics as persuasion, accommodation, and care. Thus, as we go from the earlier to the later writings, it may be less a matter of tension than transition: transition to a point of view that somewhat de-emphasizes spontaneous action precisely because of the terrible price it, and above all its counterfeits, can exact. Indeed, in the wake of the perplexities into which our age has been thrown by an awesome legacy of unbridled "doings," it is not surprising to find it stated already in the foreword to *The Human Condition* that thought, the least worldly and most solitary of man's capacities, is in fact the highest and quite possibly the purest of his activities. If this serves only to uncover a paradox at the very center of her thought—*viz.*, that thinking, which must never be confused with acting, is nonetheless the only decent thing that remains for most of us to do—so be it. For were we once to carry out what she proposes there, "to think what we are doing," the air of paradox might well be dissipated by a most creative tension.

NOTES

1. An earlier version of this essay appeared in *Idealistic Studies,* Vol. III, no. 3 (September 1973). The present, somewhat expanded version owes much to the insightful and encouraging suggestions of the editor.

2. Arendt's locution "acting into," although it is more suggestive (and indeed, given her Periclean conception of action, more felicitous), grates on one's sense of proper English usage.

3. Clearly, it is not that simple. In our experience the conceptual distinctions between labor, work, and action easily become blurred. There has always been overlap, and technological developments may before long require a reformulation, perhaps even an abandonment, of Arendt's historically quite well-founded distinction between labor and work.

4. Hannah Arendt, *The Human Condition* (Chicago: University of Chicago Press, 1958), p. 181. The reader might try for himself the experiment of describing a "who"—say, that of his best friend—to, say, his second-best friend.

5. Ibid., p. 233.

6. This paragraph is my first "sustained" departure from a fairly close rendition of Arendtian material.

7. Arendt, *The Human Condition*, p. 58.

8. It should be noted that Arendt makes no attempt to gloss over the appalling injustice—indeed moral blindness and profound philosophical inconsistency—inherent in Greek slavery. And, although she herself makes no special point of it, I would add that much the same needs to be said concerning Greek male chauvinism.

9. "One, if not the chief, reason for the incredible development of gift and genius in Athens, as well as for the hardly less surprising swift decline of the city-state, was precisely that from beginning to end its foremost aim was to make the extraordinary an ordinary occurrence of everyday life" (Ibid., p. 197).

10. "Society is the form in which the fact of mutual dependence for the sake of life and nothing else assumes public significance and where the activities connected with sheer survival are permitted to appear in public" (Ibid., p. 46). Society "normalizes" its members, requires that they behave, and either discourages, deflects, or finds harmless, non-disruptive outlets for initiative and spontaneity.—The reason for the quotes should now be obvious.

11. Arendt, *The Human Condition*, p. 225.

12. Ibid., p. 227.

13. One might say here compromise, provided it is understood that compromises are urged in this context not with an eye to furthering private ends but to adjust personal eccentricities to the exigencies of a common cause.

14. In this connection, see in particular the fascinating interpretation of Melville's *Billy Budd* in *On Revolution*.

James Miller

THE PATHOS OF NOVELTY: HANNAH ARENDT'S IMAGE OF FREEDOM IN THE MODERN WORLD[1]

To breed an animal with the right to make promises—
is not this the paradoxical task that nature has set itself
in the case of man? Is it not the real problem regarding
man?

—*Nietzsche*
On the Genealogy of Morals
Second Essay, §1

On Revolution occupies a special place in the work of Hannah Arendt. Her principal inquiry into the possibilities of politics today, it commemorates those institutions, events, and people that helped make manifest, for however brief a span, the experience of freedom in the modern world.[2] And yet it commences obliquely, with a meditation on war and the crime of violence that accompanies virtually any new political venture. A book of paradoxes, the text itself is marked by violent jolts, startling vistas. Shock mingles with surprise, doubt with assent, in a tangled web of response that eludes any comfortable characterization, even the reassurance of recognition. We encounter praise for participation, self-government, and the soviets, as well as the American constitution; and we are faced with critiques of the nation-state, political parties, and national elections, as well as workers' control. In what is perhaps the strangest paradox of all, her banishment of the "social question" and violence from the realm of politics "proper" climaxes in a veritable hierology of revolutionary institutions of self-government; to this extent, student leftists in the sixties were not mistaken to find in Arendt's thinking a confirmation of their own.

Perplexities nevertheless abound. For example, how to explain Arendt's articulation of history, so perversely selective, if not downright misleading? How to take her penchant for ordaining, often by fiat, important conceptual distinctions? How to account for her choice and treatment of models among political theorists, which often seems equally arbitrary? Finally, what precisely is Arendt's vision? What promise of political existence does she hold out for us?

In what follows, I will entertain such queries, and advance some criticisms. But my ultimate aim is constructive. Through an analysis of *On Revolution,* I hope to uncover what matters in the philosophy of Hannah Arendt to those still concerned with the prospects for freedom in our world today.

*O**n Revolution* is a book about what happens—and what ought to happen—when "the course of history suddenly begins anew." A distinctively modern phenomenon, revolution involves the emergence of freedom: "Only where change occurs in the sense of a new beginning, where violence is used to constitute an altogether different form of government, to bring about the formation of a new body politic, where the liberation from oppression aims at least at the constitution of freedom can we speak of revolution."[3] In an inversion of the classic socialist understanding, the criteria of a "real" revolution becomes not social and economic transformation, but the more strictly "political" act of constituting principles that promote "freedom."

Since we will be using the concept a great deal, it will help to recall what Arendt means by freedom. In the first place, she intends to describe the ability of a human being, through action, to reach out and attain, in deed, gesture, and word, realms, feelings, and thoughts heretofore unimagined; the ability, so to speak, to establish the world anew. To borrow Machiavelli's terminology, freedom in this sense inheres in an act of *virtù*, in "the excellence with which man answers the opportunities the world opens up before him in the guise of *fortuna*." The arena within which such action can unfold must be public; for action to stand out as free, it needs to appear and be recognized as such. Thus, the second aspect of Arendt's understanding: freedom requires a public realm, defined by principles that enable human beings to appear together, to act in common, and to be valued for their deeds; within such a realm, human beings are able to establish, through action, "a reality of their own."[4]

While the tone of Arendt's discussion clashes with the optimistic enthusiasm generated by much of the socialist literature on revolution, it collides just as sharply with the self-serving note of paranoid gloom sounded by many conservative accounts. Her tone is somber, her prose elegiac: her object is to arouse a kind of thinking passion in response to the events she recalls, to elicit a sense of *pathos*.

The quality of pathos is inherent in the very act of beginning anew. For at the heart of the revolutionary act lies a fundamental contradiction between the novelty of the deed and the permanence required of a lasting "constitution of freedom." Permanence in novelty: constituting freedom in this fashion is like trying to create an organic tradition *ex nihilo,* which helps to explain the quest for absolutes to justify revolutionary deeds and sanctify the new institutions. For the eighteenth-century revolutionaries, that meant creating civic religions; for their twentieth-century descendants, it has more often meant having recourse to the religion of history.

So we arrive at a second paradox, that this most free of political acts—beginning again—masquerades as a god-given or historically compelled inevitability. The sense of inevitability infects the participants as well as observers; choices are rendered nugatory and any unanticipated development—novelty itself, the very stuff of revolution—comes to appear fearsome, even to the most radical of revolutionary actors.[5] Finally the realm of public liberty is itself consumed by the very process of beginning again: for in conditions of mass poverty, the social forces set in motion by the novel experience of liberation cannot help but overwhelm attempts to constitute a durable framework for freedom. Where survival is at stake, the demand for freedom must be deferred: "Liberation from necessity, because of its urgency, will always take precedence over the building of freedom."

In a cruel reversal, the experience of freedom at the outset of each genuine revolution is thus systematically repressed. The aim of revolution comes to be seen as mere survival rather than freedom, and the constitution of liberty, where it is undertaken at all, becomes a mechanical manipulation of empty devices, a routinized invocation of "civil liberties," social welfare, and the sanctity of "public opinion," terms that effectively make such equally important concerns as "public freedom," "public happiness," and "public spirit" sound hopelessly archaic.

The pathos in all this is clear; its significance for thinking about politics today, less so. Rather than resolving the tension implicit in the lamentable antinomies she articulates, Arendt relentlessly draws it out with each new concept. Revolution, this greatest of modern political phenomena, will not be surrendered to the pious slogans of any party—the stakes are too high.

If Hannah Arendt's aim in *On Revolution* is contentious, her method of proceeding is at first just plain baffling. On one level, the book can be read simply as an application of certain categories and themes developed in *The Human Condition* to a body of historical materials on modern revolutions. But if this is all Arendt is doing, her concepts are of dubious value, her history shoddy. These events—the American and French revolutions, the council and soviet tradition in European labor history—have been far more plausibly examined elsewhere. From this perspective, her concepts function only as a distorting lens. Furthermore, if she is out to apply her concepts plausibly to modern political history, why does she take such liberties with her material?

To take an obvious example: the American Revolution is rendered in deceptively pure tones. There is nothing in Arendt's book on the subterfuge and manipulation used by the Federalists to win ratification for the Constitution of 1787; instead we are presented with a sharp contrast between the violence of the French revolutionaries and the legal fairness of the Americans, for whom "nothing was permitted that would have been outside the range of civil law."[6] She similarly portrays the Constitution as a document rooted in confidence in the people—a characterization that manages to neatly miss the whole point.[7]

Her treatment of the council tradition is no less misleading. Neglecting the fact that revolutionary organs of self-government are almost always established and defended by an armed populace, she marvels at "the amazing formation of a new power structure which owed its existence to nothing [*sic*] but the organizational impulses of the people themselves."[8] The soviets are similarly endorsed as institutions where "party membership played no role whatsoever"—a comment comical to anyone versed in the history of the Russian soviets in 1917.[9] Indeed, the very way she construes the council "tradition" minimizes important differences in institutional structure and political program between, say, the Parisian popular societies of 1793 and the Petrograd soviet of 1905, the former directly democratic in procedure and terrorist in aim, the latter hierarchically organized but calling for a national constituent assembly. To the wary reader, her gloss on revolutionary history begins to sound like so much wishful thinking.

But this reading of Arendt's method cannot be right. For one thing, it is scarcely credible that she simply suppresses contrary evidence, since such evidence occasionally figures in her own text.

For example, early in the book she details the "Rights of the Sans-Culottes," remarking that their demands for clothing, food, and the "reproduction of their species" promoted the terror and helped change the goal of the French Revolution from freedom to the "happiness of the people." Yet by the last chapter, the clubs and societies of the very same sans-culottes are esteemed as the true "pillars of the constitution," comprising the very "foundations of freedom."[10] Either claim in isolation is deceptive; juxtaposing them at least makes it clear that Arendt herself is well aware of the ambiguities surrounding the political beliefs and behavior of the sans-culottes. She must obviously not see herself as a historian in any conventional sense. On the other hand, *On Revolution* is hardly an orthodox essay on political concepts. What precisely then *is* she doing?

Some hints are provided by Walter Benjamin's "Theses on the Philosophy of History," a work that Arendt certainly knew and admired.[11] Benjamin, arguing against historicism, asserts that "to articulate the past historically does not mean to recognize it 'the way it really was' (Ranke). It means to seize hold of a memory as it flashes up at a moment of danger." The danger, for Benjamin, is that the memory will either disappear or become "a tool of the ruling classes." For Arendt, by contrast, the ruling class is scarcely the major problem; far more alarming is the tendency of the actors themselves to repress or misunderstand the true meaning of their own deeds in the past. But that possibility only adds urgency to Benjamin's principal point: "For every image of the past that is not recognized by the present as one of its own concerns threatens to disappear irretrievably."

If it is a question of retrieval, not just any chronicle will do. Major and minor events must be distinguished. Major events crystallize the tensions within a situation, and present us with a kind of historical monad, the congealed essence of an entire era. Revolutions, for Benjamin and Arendt alike, are just such major events, "the sign of a Messianic cessation of happening," as Benjamin put it. By focusing on such an essential phenomenon, the narrator can "blast open the continuum of history."[12]

When Benjamin's account here is supplemented by his remarks on storytelling, we move even closer to Arendt's own method. Arendt herself seized on the image of the storyteller in *The Human Condition,* where she called history "the storybook of mankind." Arendt finds the image of the storyteller congenial because it evokes the frailty of even the most heroic action, which can live on only in the remembrance of those who come after. For Benjamin, the storyteller preserves in a secularized form the "eschatological orientation" of the medieval chronicler. The contrast between "the writer of history, the historian, and the teller of it, the chronicler," could hardly be sharper, according to Benjamin. "The historian is bound to explain in one way or another the happenings with which he deals; under no circumstances can he content himself with displaying them as models of the course of the world."[13]

In *On Revolution,* Arendt retrieves historical monads as "models of the course of the world," a course thrown into relief only by brushing "history against the grain," as Benjamin put it. History in fact occupies her attention, not as the narrative of a coherent, causally connected chain of events, nor indeed as the reconstruction of a process with a secret teleology. She does not perceive history as a concatenation of events requiring explanation or demanding justification. Rather, she follows Benjamin in constructing revolutionary history as an episodic set of stories needing to be remembered and told again, lest the true revolutionary spirit, with its redeeming commitment to freedom, be lost "through the failure of thought and remembrance."

Her conceptual apparatus is only a tool to this end. The distinctions she insists upon are only meant to draw out the pathos of the story, and render it fit to serve as a model. "For if it is true that all thought begins with remembrance, it is also true that no remembrance remains secure unless it is condensed and distilled into a framework of conceptual notions within which it can further exercise itself." Moreover, if Arendt's definitions sometimes seem almost magical, both in their power to conjure up a world and to dissolve difficult problems, that may be intentional as well. I am reminded of the note Franz Kafka wrote in his diaries, on what amounts to a "reenchantment of the world" through naming: "It is entirely conceivable," he remarks, "that life's splendor forever lies in wait about each one of us in all its fullness, but veiled from view, deep down, invisible, far off. It *is* there, though, not hostile, not reluctant, not deaf. If you summon it by the right word, by its right name, it will come. This is the essence of magic, which does not create but summons."[14]

From this perspective, *On Revolution* itself can be viewed as a "new beginning," concerned with "the Word," and hence with a salvation that might point the way beyond the cycle of futile crime that has scarred modern political history. At a juncture where political thought has irrevocably lost its original ground in religion, tradition, and authority, only a commemoration that marks out the major events and figures of our past remains feasible. By telling her stories and drawing her distinctions, Arendt is thus engaged in nothing less than attempting to "summon" a tradition, "which selects and names, which hands down and preserves, which indicates where the treasures are and what their worth is." Even more: this new tradition will be a tradition *of the new,* a reassertion of the continuity in human affairs that, no longer bound by previous tradition, confronts a past which "only now will open to us with unexpected freshness and tell us things no one has yet had ears to hear."[15] Hence the title of the last chapter in *On Revolution:* "The Revolutionary Tradition and Its Lost Treasure"— as if to anticipate her own description of Benjamin's procedure:

> Like a pearl diver who descends to the bottom of the sea, not to excavate the bottom and bring it to light but to pry loose the rich and the strange, the pearls and the coral in the depths, and to carry them to the surface, this thinking delves into the depths of the past—but not in order to resuscitate it the way it was and to contribute to the renewal of extinct ages. What guides this thinking is the conviction that although the living is subject to the ruin of time, the process of decay is at the same time a process of crystallization, that

in the depths of the sea, into which sinks and dissolves what once was alive, some things "suffer a sea-change" and survive in new crystallized forms and shapes that remain immune to the elements, as though they waited only for the pearl diver who will come down to them and bring them up into the world of the living—as "thought fragments," as something "rich and strange," and perhaps even as everlasting *Urphänomene*.[16]

One puzzle remains. On first glance, the story told in *On Revolution* seems contradictory. But our initial confusion is dispelled once we realize that the book comprises not one, but at least three stories. Each concerns a revolutionary moment, but in each instance the treasure hunter has cast her net in a different direction. She thus retrieves, in succession, three "historical monads," each of them crystallizing a different aspect of the revolutionary phenomenon.

To oversimplify, the first story tells a tale of necessity—the French revolutionaries and their doomed attempt to solve the social question. The second story tells a tale of freedom promised but never quite redeemed—the American revolutionaries and their failure to establish organs of public freedom. Finally, the third story, the most pathetic of all, concerns those who have lost, and thus those who most need to be remembered: namely, the revolutionary advocates of councils and soviets. And as her attention shifts from the mainstream of history to these subterranean currents, we may well feel as if the pearl diver has finally found her *Urphänomene*—forms of public freedom waiting to be rescued from the continuum of the past.

However, before attempting to distill the moral of these stories, it would be good to consider Arendt's choice of models to emulate among philosophers and political theorists. Approaching her thought from this angle will help clarify the aims of her own political theory, and the form taken in *On Revolution* by her political ideal—an ideal that, oddly enough, represents an "existential" variant on modern contract theory. Which predecessors does Arendt use to arrive at and think through this ideal? I will begin with an obvious but puzzling case: her treatment of Jean-Jacques Rousseau.

For many years I was perplexed by Arendt's disdain in *On Revolution* for the author of *The Social Contract*. Here, after all, was the preeminent modern exponent of public liberty and participation, ideals Arendt cherished; here also was a political thinker eager, like Arendt herself, to preserve images of freedom from antiquity. Yet instead of extolling Rousseau's virtues, Arendt rarely misses an opportunity to attack him. In *On Revolution*, she finds her heroes elsewhere, among the Founding Fathers of the American Revolution. Why?

Clues are strewn throughout the book. Examining them, I believe, will lead us to the heart of Arendt's political thought: an utterly modern thought that defines itself by rejecting the era's idols.

At the outset, Arendt accuses Rousseau of promoting "compassion" as a public virtue, "an innate repugnance at seeing a fellow creature suffer." She implies that such compassion issues in "the new assumption of social scientists that those who belong to the lower classes of society have, as it were, a right to burst with resentment, greed and envy." Such rancor merely masks Arendt's graver objections, however, even as it faithfully conveys the temper of her attack; the stubborn single-mindedness of her misreading even confirms the suspicion that something more is at stake.

Elsewhere in *On Revolution*, she elaborates her objections to Rousseau. His insistence on honesty and transparent personal relations triggered a politically disastrous quest for absolute good; his distrust of masks and social convention sanctioned a search for motives and a suspicion of other political actors; finally, his proclivity to paranoia, issuing in the urge to unmask opponents, "abolishes the distance, the worldly space between men," a distance similarly violated by compassion. In this context, Rousseau's notorious remark in *The Social Contract* about citizens being "forced to be free" assumes an unambiguously sinister significance.[17]

Thus far, Arendt's interpretation hardly distinguishes itself from dozens of other postwar diatribes, casting Rousseau as a protototalitarian. But she is animated by a far more subtle and provocative fear than that. It concerns the centrality of "will" to Rousseau's philosophy.

She distrusts his concept of the general will, and for three interesting reasons. First, since there is nothing in principle to keep it from constantly changing, this will cannot provide a suitable foundation for freedom: any institutions built upon this basis would be "built on quicksand." Second, Rousseau's insistence that it is "absurd for the will to bind itself for the future" anticipates, she believes, the faithlessness and opportunism of later revolutionaries. In *Between Past and Future*, she adds a third and equally telling objection: Rousseau's ideal is far too individualistic. He improperly held that in an ideal republic the people come to a resolution "without any communication among the citizens"; he thus made the mistake of believing that in order to avoid factions "each citizen should think only his own thoughts."[18] And it is *these* objections that motive her rejection of Rousseau:

> All political business is, and always has been, transacted within an elaborate framework of ties and bonds for the future—such as laws and constitutions, treaties and alliances —all of which derive in the last instance from the faculty to promise and to keep promises in the face of the essential uncertainties of the future. A state, moreover, in which there is no communication between the citizens and where each man thinks only his own thoughts is by definition a tyranny. That *the faculty of will and will-power in and by itself, unconnected with any other faculties, is an essentially nonpolitical and even anti-political capacity* is perhaps

nowhere else so manifest as in the absurdities to which Rousseau was driven and in the curious cheerfulness with which he accepted them.[19]

Arendt's attitude toward the modern "philosophy of will" is critical for understanding not only her stance toward Rousseau, but indeed her approach to the entire tradition of Western thought. It is also crucial for understanding the distance she carefully establishes between her political thinking and the philosophy of such mentors as Karl Jaspers, Martin Heidegger, and, more indirectly, Friedrich Nietzsche.

Her modernity consists in her willingness to work through the inversions accomplished by nineteenth- and twentieth-century thought, rather than merely condemning that thought as a record of immoral mistakes.[20] When "the thread of tradition finally broke," after the revolutions had exposed "the dubious nature of government in the modern age," thinking about politics had to adjust itself accordingly. The conservatives "who clung to tradition and the past as to fetishes" failed to understand the elementary fact the revolutions had rendered obvious: the Western tradition "had lost its anchorage, its beginning and principle, and was cut adrift." Similarly, most radicals who hailed the revolutions sought to justify their tragic course of substituting the continuity of historical necessity and the cult of progress for the lost tradition.[21] Few of them, it turned out, could face the real situation of uncertainty, any more than they could appreciate the genuinely new political institutions that had sprung up before them.

However, if Arendt seems willing to confront modern thought, the extent to which she is ready to appropriate that thought seems considerably more obscure. She has often been mistaken for a kind of conservative, anxious to restore "the tradition," eager to exalt the prudence embodied in America's constitution. How has Arendt's "modernity" informed her own thinking? In particular, how does she define her political ideal in relation to those "philosophies of will" she believes characteristic of the modern era?

In *Between Past and Future*, Arendt evaluates the three nineteenth-century figures who performed the great inversions on Western thought: Kierkegaard, Marx, and Nietzsche. Of these three, she clearly prefers Nietzsche; it was he who came closest to grasping the enormity of what had happened, and the promise as well as risk in what lay ahead. At the same time, of course, it was Nietzsche who, with Rousseau, apotheosized the individual faculty of will, exalting it as the supreme power in life.

Let us pause with Nietzsche for a moment. Consider the following passage in *The Twilight of the Idols*, from the section entitled "How the 'True World' Finally Became a Fable," a passage that Arendt herself cites:

> The true world—an idea which is no longer good for anything, not even obligating—an idea which has become useless and superfluous—*consequently*, a refuted idea: let us abolish it!
>
> (Bright day; breakfast; return of *bon sens* and cheerfulness; Plato's embarrassed blush; pandemonium of all free spirits.)
>
> The true world—we have abolished. What world has remained? The apparent one perhaps? But no! *With the true world we have also abolished the apparent one.*[22]

Nietzsche's fable is instructive. Like Nietzsche, Arendt greets the collapse of transcendent authority—of the belief in a realm of true Being as the measure of human action—with cheerfulness; she has no interest in restoring the dogma of a "True World." She also fears for the outcome of this collapse. Does his inversion of values in effect entail the abolition of the apparent world, too? Does it thus hasten a devaluation of everything human, through an obliteration of our shared world of appearances, that fragile "web of human affairs and relationships and the stories engendered by them"?

Or has the meaning of the true world's disappearance perhaps been radically misunderstood? Might it not open the way, as well as force the issue, of creating, by human artifice empowered through joint effort, a public realm where human beings could express in speech and action who they distinctively were? And what can Nietzsche's aphorism mean, then, if not that the task ahead involves securing such an apparent world against the storm of uncertainty unleashed by the collapse of the "true" one?[23]

If Nietzsche poses the issue sharply, Arendt will have nothing to do with his final resolution of it. She believes that the modern philosophy of will fatally misunderstands the work of beginning anew that might secure the world of appearances. For one thing, the inversion of values that esteems action over thought blurs important "distinctions and articulations within the *vita activa* itself." By the very nature of inversion as an operation, "the conceptual framework is left more or less intact," rather than being enriched.[24] It is primarily this task of conceptual enrichment that Arendt addresses in *The Human Condition*.

More importantly for our present purposes, the modern philosophy of will, in its individualistic voluntarism, issues in a political philosophy that is strangely apolitical, a thinking that lauds lonely rulers, these "violent men" unafraid to use "power to become preeminent in historical being as creators, as men of action. Preeminent in the historical place, they become at the same time *apolis*, without city and place, lonely, strange and alien, without issue amid the existent as a whole, and at the same time without statute and limit, without structure and order, because they themselves *as* creators must first create all this."[25] In these terrifying words of Martin Heidegger, which condense the essential outcome of a politics of individual will, Hannah Arendt might have observed the immolation of Western political thought.

She defines her own political thinking against that thought which single-mindedly praises the noble individual, the will to power and authenticity—a thinking that issues, Arendt suggests, in

French existentialism, which she castigates as "an escape from the perplexities of modern philosophy into the unquestioning commitment of action."[26]

In opposition to any such doctrine, she argues that the distinction of the individual, for example, can only be defined publicly, in a forum where ideas can be exchanged, persuasion exercised, works exhibited, and deeds performed; it is here that individuality—and indeed nobility—genuinely appears. Only here can the individual be identified and remembered; only here can men show "who they really and inexchangeably are." The "will to power," on the other hand—this empty "I will"—is superseded for Arendt by the "We can"—by the conviction, instilled by the very recollection of freedom in the modern revolutions, that "action, though it may be started in isolation and decided upon by single individuals for very different motives, can only be accomplished by some joint effort." The demand for authenticity, finally, and the obsession to unmask human actors, are to be replaced by the frank acknowledgment that the only human world is the world of appearances, and that "to men, the reality of the world is guaranteed by the presence of others, by its appearing to all."[27]

Instead of a stormy transvaluation of value by lonely heroes, Arendt proposes a collective effort to establish an abiding structure of shared public principles, principles that to the extent they embody the "We can" and the will to coexist, rule out arbitrariness and the caprice of a political creator "without statute or limit." At the core of this artificial "human power" would lie that most precious of human faculties, which Arendt believes enables men to fabricate principles and institutions that will endure the passage of time: the ability to make promises. Indeed, the greatest application of this faculty comes precisely in the act of beginning, when pledges and promises are exchanged. Thanks to this reciprocal transaction, a space for human freedom can be secured.[28]

For Arendt, "what saves the act of beginning from its own arbitrariness is that it carries its own principle within itself." But what can this possibly mean? Elsewhere she suggests that morality cut loose from its moorings in custom and tradition has "at least politically, no more to support itself than the good will to counter the enormous risks of action by readiness to forgive and to be forgiven, to make promises and to keep them. These moral precepts . . . arise . . . directly out of *the will to live together* with others in the mode of acting and speaking, and thus they are like control mechanisms built into the very faculty to start new and thus unending processes."29

Arendt, in short, poses the possibility of the joint exercise of the will to coexist that, liberated from such external constraints as poverty, violence, and tradition, can through mutual promises contract to create an abiding objective framework of public principles—a constitution—that founds authority anew, by defining a space where human power may become manifest and where freedom can appear, precisely in the free play of appearances. Such a constitution would establish isonomy, that state of no-rule which abolishes the division between rulers and ruled and guarantees equality: for freedom and equality are scarcely natural attributes, to be divined by reference to some natural law or right, but instead "conventional and artificial, the products of human effort and qualities of the man-made world."30 This is Arendt's utopia.

To flesh out this ideal, which is indeed a kind of contract theory, let us return to an analysis of Arendt the storyteller. How does her utopia appear in *On Revolution*?

We have already seen the pathos of revolution evoked in the popular demands for survival engendered by conditions of poverty: in the cautionary tale of necessity that opens *On Revolution*, we are warned of how the freedom promised by the French revolutionaries of 1792 was displaced by the urgent need to feed, clothe, and deliver from obscurity an overwhelming majority of the French people. But if this story tempers any subsequent sense of optimism, it scarcely accounts for the sense of fragile hope sustained by Arendt's finale.

In reconstituting Arendt's utopia in *On Revolution*, her two final stories matter much more. The first is the story of American constitutionalism, which establishes the preconditions for freedom, and introduces Arendt's ideal of a polity founded on a free contract; the second is the story of the European council tradition, which establishes the institutions necessary to sustain freedom, and completes Arendt's ideal of a polity promoting participation and "action." What, in turn, do each of these stories tell us about Arendt's vision of politics?

The American Revolution is important for the happy circumstances surrounding it; it is serendipity and good fortune she stresses throughout this story, to the detriment of all other factors. The image is familiar: blessed by a relative abundance of goods and equality of station, the Americans could make a revolution without the awful necessity of first liberating a large sector of the population from misery and obscurity; the Americans practiced tolerance and enjoyed a plurality of different associations, and these principles were happily incorporated into the Constitution; since they had already tasted the fruits of public freedom in colonial assemblies and town meetings, the Americans refrained from theoretical flights of fancy, and averted the messiness of a revolutionary "dual power"; finally, the Americans, thanks to their unique situation, could frame and implement a constitution without recourse to the crime of violence.

In sum, America's was a "clean" revolution. Indeed, it is the very purity of its beginning that commends it to the storyteller:

> In this respect, the course of the American Revolution tells an unforgettable story and is apt to teach a unique lesson; for this revolution did not break out but was made by men in common deliberation and on the strength of mutual pledges. The principle which came to light during those fateful years when the foundations were laid—not by the strength of one architect but by the combined power of the many—was the interconnected principle of mutual promise and common deliberation.[31]

Where other contemporary philosophers, such as Sartre, have found their image of joint freedom in the impetuous violence of revolutionary combat—in storming the Bastille, say—Arendt finds her image in the sober deliberation and decisive capitalization on good fortune she ascribes to the American Founders.

The second aspect of the story is both more obvious and more subtle: namely, to commemorate the concern with institutional devices and constitutionalism demonstrated by the Founders. The image of the constitution serves a variety of functions in *On Revolution*. On the one hand, it solves the puzzle of the need for absolutes to prevent the appearance of arbitrariness; on the other hand, it overcomes the dilemma of durability. Without recourse to a civic religion, Arendt argues that a constitution can accommodate the inhabitants of a polity within a shared framework of fundamental principles. These principles, venerated from generation to generation, secure the very continuity in time destroyed by the collapse of the Roman trinity of religion, tradition, and authority. To this end, a constitution should be "understood, approved, and beloved" as a "standard, a pillar, and a bond," to quote John Adams. Regarded with the proper piety, a constitution binds each generation back to the beginning, and hence provides the proper ground "in perpetuity" for the recognition of genuine authority; at the same time, it reminds those who come after of the conventional and human origins of their present freedom. Finally, lest the beginning appear capricious, the same principles ought to have limited the very action of the Founders themselves.

When governed by such hallowed principles, the citizens of the public realm are actually "empowered," as recognized agents of a "new power center." This power flows from the citizens themselves, but is housed in the laws. The fundamental laws of the constitution are indeed the tangible expression of isonomy, Arendt's Greek ideal of political freedom.[32]

The moral of this story, however, is far from being unambiguous. For one thing, constitutionalism is scarcely the be-all and end-all of politics. A *constitutio libertatis* that guarantees civil rights and sets limits to government is merely the prelude to freedom, its necessary foundation. Indeed, matters are more precarious than even this statement suggests. For might not contentment with civil liberties, which protect the private pursuit of happiness, slacken the thirst for public freedom? Might not the very perfection of the governmental mechanism breed apathy, and create the conditions for a retreat into those insular concerns that have become the image of "happiness" in America? Have not the generous circumstances attending the American experiment actually helped generate a fatal vascillation between an active commitment to freedom and the passive enjoyment of prosperity? Has not the United States today become the "mass society" Arendt dreaded, a society "intent upon affluence and consumption"? Has not America become the perfect model of a two-party plutocracy where "public happiness and public freedom have become the privilege of the few"?[33]

The truth of the matter is that the framers of the Constitution omitted from their document provision for the organs needed to sustain freedom. While the Founders formulated the principles of freedom, they also limited the public space where this freedom could be exercised, to the representatives of the people. This was the Constitution's flaw, and it may yet prove fatal for the Republic.

It was precisely because of the enormous weight of the Constitution and of the experiences in founding a new body politic, that the failure to incorporate the townships and the town-hall meetings, the original springs of all political activity in the country, amounted to a death sentence for them. Paradoxical as it may sound, it was under the impact of the Revolution that the revolutionary spirit in this country began to wither away, and it was the Constitution itself, this greatest achievement of the American people, which eventually cheated them of their proudest possession.[34]

Under the combined onslaught of private prosperity and a blind patriotic piety, the Americans have virtually forgotten their origins in an act of public freedom. That is why the story of the founding merits retelling, why Thomas Jefferson's ill-fated dream of self-government through a ward system needs to be recalled. But the story of the American founding, by itself, casts a sad light on the matter of creating institutions of public freedom.

So Arendt turns back to that far murkier region of modern history, to plunge deeper into the currents of the European past. There she hopes finally to find paradigms of "political freedom," in institutions of popular participation—for "political freedom . . . means the right 'to be a participator in government,' or it means nothing."[35] Thus unfolds her last story.

The stakes are higher here, for what has been lost is so much greater. After all, the glories of the American Revolution have been recounted many times before; there is scarcely a need to go fishing for "lost treasure" in Philadelphia, since the treasure there is fully visible for those with eyes to see. But the revolutionary councils—the assemblies of the sans-culottes in 1793, the Paris Commune of 1871, the Russian soviets of 1905 and 1917, the *Rätesystem* in Germany in 1918–19, the council system in the Hungarian Revolution of 1956—urgently need to be rescued, not least from the "realists," those dialectical sophists eager to dismiss such institutions as ephemeral experiments foredoomed to failure. Arendt by contrast casts her lot with this "fantastic utopia," and then proceeds to trace the outlines of a new tradition, using bits and pieces of long-forgotten events and devices, scattered across the terrain of European history like so much worthless debris.[36]

Out of this disjunct heritage, she wishes to draw together the image of a political order that would "permit the people to become . . . 'participators in government.'" For this purpose, we require nothing less than "a new type of republican government." Avoiding the mistakes of America's experience, this new form of freedom would "rest on 'elementary republics'" modeled after the assemblies of the sans-culottes; such elementary republics would be federated in such a fashion that a central power would not "deprive the constituent bodies of their original power to constitute."

In her hands, the revolutionary tradition provides a historical testimony that fleshes out Jefferson's rather abstract program for a "ward system"; by linking Jefferson with the image of the revolutionary councils, Arendt reinforces the impression that all free government must be limited and constitutional government. Her ideal, though, is consummated only in the present story:

> If the ultimate end of revolution was freedom and the constitution of a public space where freedom could appear, the *constitutio libertatis*, then the elementary republics of the wards, the only tangible place where everybody could be free, actually were the end of the great republic whose chief purpose in domestic affairs should have been to provide the people with such places of freedom and to protect them.[37]

Armed with this image, Arendt curtly dismisses the self-righteous picture of "free-world democracies" as tranquil islands, blessed by the two-party system, afloat in a sea of dictatorship. For her, "the issue at stake" is precisely "representation versus action and participation"; without a share in public happiness, public freedom, and public power, there is simply no way a person can be called happy or free. Far from preserving the possibility of freedom for posterity, the liberal state has usurped the public realm and ultimately handed public affairs over to bureaucrats, experts, and "professional politicians," who enact before a great mass of powerless spectators a cruel parody of public freedom, if not an intimidating drama of arrogant omnipotence.[38]

But this is scarcely to say that the story of the revolutionary councils is itself free from ambiguity. For the councils, after all, were fated at the outset by their appearance in situations of extreme suffering. The attempts to mollify misery and placate despair pressed the councils, in the logic of their revolutionary moment, toward violence and self-destruction. Indeed, the very image of these free institutions reminds us of the tragic tale of necessity that opens *On Revolution;* and it is only all three stories taken together that convey the pathos of revolution as Arendt understands it. We have come full circle.

Previously I speculated that Arendt's stories might point the way beyond the cycle of futile crime that has scarred modern political history. Now, however, we can see that the path out points back to the beginning itself. There is no exit. The failure is complete. The true spirit of revolution was never embodied in the appropriate organs of public freedom. Indeed, "there is nothing that could compensate for this failure or prevent it from becoming final, except memory and recollection."[39]

Thus, in a final irony, Arendt's fractured utopianism appears as the unwitting heir to Rousseau's unrealized dreams. Like Rousseau, Arendt aspires to show us a perfect image of public freedom, "taking men as they are and laws as they might be." Like Rousseau, she suspects her image will function as a reflection of human fallibility—for what might be almost certainly will *not* be. But the tenor of her inquiry is radically different. For where Rousseau went to work in *The Social Contract* constructing a legitimate political order the way an engineer might set out to design a frictionless machine, Arendt in *On Revolution,* deprived of even a consoling faith in the pure mechanics of government, is reduced to rummaging through "the dustbin of history" (as Trotsky was fond of calling it), in search of those tattered remnants that might be stitched together to restore a patchwork image of human freedom. For Arendt, it is a restoration feasible in memory alone.

We are now in a better position to assess Arendt's political thought. It might as well be said straight off that, to a large extent, her virtues are her faults. Insofar as her philosphy can be condensed into determinate concepts, these concepts can express only a determinate—and hence limited—aspect of the world: what functions as a focusing agent in one field of vision may well become a distorting lens for another. Admittedly, this problem inheres in the appropriation of all great philosophers, for thinkers like poets wrest from language their own unique way of speaking.

At the same time, some of Arendt's distinctions seem of more value than others, just as some make sense in one setting and not in another. To take but one example, consider her distinction between "the political"—for Arendt the realm of "freedom"—and "the social"—the realm of "necessity."

In the course of *On Revolution*, these two concepts successfully perform the rescue mission they were designed for. From the perspective her terminology affords, the importance of the councils and soviets seems indisputable. By contrast, from the standpoint of Marxism, the temptation is overwhelming to concentrate on social, economic, and "cultural" factors, while ignoring the kinds of political possibilities represented by the council tradition. Nor is this surprising.

Socialism at the outset largely defined itself as a movement of economic and technical rationalization. In the beginning, its "politics" were confined to sponsoring new communities that might serve as technical proofs as well as moral paradigms. Until 1848, its political program—at least in France, where some socialist groups in fact became politically active—was largely constructed through alliances with Jacobin liberals (the case of Louis Blanc), or violent declarations of allegiance to the "true" principles of Year II of the Revolution (Auguste Blanqui). This is not the place to develop the point, but I would suggest that these origins of socialism, and its ambiguous relation to the French Revolution, have helped define its subsequent understanding of political theory and practice. I do not think it accidental that the avowed politics of most socialists can, without gross oversimplification, be characterized by either a readiness (however reluctant) to work within the confines of the nation-state, or an eagerness (however tempered) to "smash" this state and orchestrate its "withering away" (the professed solution of anarcho-syndicalists and Marxist-Leninists alike, although they might disagree on the autumnal timetable)— the one option engendering a politics of reform resigned to the elitist principles of the liberal state and party system, the other a politics of force directed by disastrously apolitical principles that issue in arbitrary violence if not the organized terror of totalitarianism.

In beginning to sort out this development, I have found the sharp line Arendt draws between "the social" and "the political" of immense value. Her thinking affords a way beyond the thicket of socialist assumptions: a set of assumptions that, even in the case of Marx's original theory, has hindered as well as helped constructive thinking about the prerequisites and possibilities for human freedom.

On the other hand, divorced from any background in modern social thought, socialist or otherwise, it seems to me that Arendt's concepts rather elegantly miss the point. From the standpoint of her thinking, it might well remain a mystery why the thought of Adam Smith, Karl Marx, Emile Durkheim, Ferdinand Tönnies, Georg Simmel, and Max Weber took the turn it did, toward "the social."

There are, in fact, severe problems with her understanding of "the social" and "the political"—problems, moreover, that inhibit any attempt to critically confront Arendt's stoicism, or to overcome the resignation implicit in the very pathos she so profoundly evokes in *On Revolution*.

In the first place, she far too uncritically deploys a notion of the masses, that, like Jasper's notion, like LeBon's concept of the crowd, Nietzsche's of the herd, Heidegger's of *das Mann*, and Ortega y Gasset's of *masas* (to mention only its most illustrious ancestors), depicts the homogenization of experience far too monolithically, and assigns the blame, usually by innuendo, far too one-sidedly. The absurdities to which this way of thinking leads are often tucked away by Arendt in some passing remark. Consider this couplet: "American prosperity and American mass society increasingly threaten the whole political realm. The hidden wish of poor men is not 'To each according to his needs,' but 'To each according to his desires' "—as if the poor were the architects of American consumerism.[40] Henry Ford would have been amused.

In the second place, the rigidity of her concept of "the political" hides from view a host of phenomena that today press upon thoughtful observers of society with justifiable urgency. I have in mind, for example, her failure to explore adequately the political dimensions of technology. On her definition a part of "the social," technology according to Arendt can be at best the handmaiden of liberation, abolishing poverty and want, at worst the demiurge of affluence, ensuring an empty plenitude which merely lures the soul from public virtue. Hence Arendt's rather fantastic appreciation for Lenin's quip that communism equals "electrification plus soviets."[41]

But the greatest mischief caused by her concept of "the social" derives from the passivity it entails. At one point in *On Revolution*, for example, she remarks that happiness and the release from suffering are goods that "unfortunately, no political action can deliver."[42] Now in one sense, of course, this remark is profoundly true. But in another sense, it is just as profoundly false, for it suggests that joint efforts at alleviating misery are doomed to miscarry and are somehow contaminated by "necessity," while political acts are not. Why? Her very concept of "the social" prevents us from asking, let alone answering, this question.

A series of suppressed questions now erupt. Why should the will to coexist be confined to the realm of "politics"? Is there any sound reason why (to employ the distinction developed in *The Human Condition*) much that is now labor cannot be transformed into work, and the workplace made into a locus of joint effort, of work undertaken according to principles arrived at through discussion? Is mere efficiency the eternal curse of material fabrication? Why should compassion remain a private virtue in an age when the prevalent forms of economic life not only entail extreme personal suffering and exploitation but also help define the parameters of "public policy?" Why should the amelioration of suffering be left to what apologists for capitalism are fond of dubbing "the private sector," as if that sector did not promote much of the suffering, as if politicians did not already welcome businessmen as fellow "civic leaders?" Such questions, while not entirely foreclosed, become difficult to penetrate with Arendt's categories.

It is at this point, though, that the context for Arendt's own thinking ought to be restored. It is by stubbornly adhering to her concepts that she manages so effectively to brush history—and current events—against the grain. When applied to the era's prejudices, so sated with subtle sociology and finely tuned economics, her thought has the effect of an austere tonic, its very severity restoring a sense of balance.

At the same time, this context defines the limits of Arendt's political thought: after all, its context-bound character scarcely recommends extending her theory too far afield.

Which brings me to my last point. Taken in isolation, Arendt's constructive political theory—her "ideal," such as it is—seems more elliptical than substantive. While her background in continental philosophy may account for her attraction to a contract theory that emphasizes human artifice rather than natural law, it does not make that theory any more plausible.

Consider for a moment one of the objections to contract theory raised by Hume in A Treatise of Human Nature. There he argues that, since promises are unintelligible and entail no obligation apart from a previously existing set of other social and moral (and linguistic) conventions, the faculty of promising cannot function as the sole basis for social and political order. In short, political principles can by no means be established ex nihilo, as the contract theorist and Arendt would like. The moral fabric of human coexistence cannot be conjured up through a sheer world-building will to live a life in common—or sustained merely through the veneration of a written constitution. I suspect that carrying through this thought—that the political realm is inextricably bound up in the customs, traditions, and spirit of a people—would inevitably lead toward the kind of reflection on the social realm and its conventional forms that Arendt so fastidiously avoids.[43]

Another example: Rousseau in The Social Contract was at pains to eliminate any concept of "tacit consent" from the vocabulary of politics. He argued, reasonably enough, that human beings could not legitimately be considered bound by the acts of their ancestors unless they actively bound themselves back, in a new act reaffirming the old principles. The price he paid, as Arendt accurately notes, was the abandonment of any guarantee that fundamental principles would be preserved over time. But that risk, Rousseau might have added, is only the authentic burden of public freedom.

Arendt, by contrast, neatly dodges the entire issue of tacit consent, largely through a set of overly agile definitions. She so defines "power," for example, that "real" and "legitimate" power, in contradistinction to mere consent, must rest on "reciprocity" and "mutuality." But given her admiration for America's "constitution worship"—which seems to entail a kind of tacit consent in the form of "veneration," rather than the active and necessarily mutual binding-back proposed by Rousseau—we may well wonder what sense to make out of this fine distinction. In effect, Arendt's effort to distill a redemptive image of the past in concepts leads her to dissolve one of the hard political choices Rousseau thought through with a bitter consistency.

Hannah Arendt's importance lies elsewhere. Thanks to the unique steadfastness of her thinking, she is able to cast a penetrating light on phenomena critical for our time. In particular, she has directed our concerns back to the institutions and devices appropriate to freedom in the modern world.

And Arendt, for all of the difficulties in her method, provides a model, I believe, for using the past to think about the possibilities of the present. Without falsely elevating history into a transcendent font of truth, she is able to extract moral significance from previously mute fragments of the past. By preserving some of those stories that merit retelling, she has made it easier for us to take our bearings, to make sense out of our past, and to understand what matters in our predicament. In all this, she remains true to the highest human hopes, without attempting to rescue a discredited theory of "natural law" and "natural right." Rather, she well understands that political thought today stands exposed, resting on a past that is contestable and jeopardized, and on a fragile and ill-formed will, shared by some, to found together a life of freedom. If her task was to focus our thought, to cultivate our will, and to educate our desire, then in this Arendt has surely succeeded. For in the special power of her images, she had that most precarious of political skills, the gift of "fanning the spark of hope" amidst the embers of the past.[44]

NOTES

1. This essay is dedicated to Stan Spyros Draenos, who helped me clarify its guiding themes. Thanks are also due my colleagues Bruce Miroff and William Galston, who thoughtfully commented on an earlier draft.

2. This statement is not intended to slight *The Human Condition*, thus far her major statement in philosophy, or *The Origins of Totalitarianism*, her most sustained piece of detailing the horrors rather than the promise of the modern age.

3. Hannah Arendt, *On Revolution* (New York: The Viking Press, 1965), pp. 21, 28.

4. See Hannah Arendt, "What is Freedom?" in *Between Past and Future* (New York: The Viking Press, 1968), pp. 153, 171.

5. By 1919 the German Communists could afford to recognize in the self-governing Soviets only their own reified reflection; their tactic became support for the Soviets only where Bolsheviks commanded a majority. See Arendt, *On Revolution*, p. 262; on the search for absolutes, see pp. 156, 160–61. Robespierre's words, quoted on p. 39, summon a truly weary sense of inevitability: "Tout a changé dans l'ordre physique; et tout doit changer dans l'ordre moral et politique."

6. See ibid., p. 87. Compare Edmund Morgan, *The Birth of the Republic* (Chicago: University of Chicago Press, 1956), p. 156. Summarizing the fight over ratification, he remarks that the Federalist victory "was obtained by the narrowest of margins and by methods that cannot be defended."

7. See Arendt, *On Revolution*, p. 153:

To believe that the short-lived European postwar constitutions or even their predecessors in the nineteenth century, whose inspiring principle had been distrust of power in general and fear of the revolutionary power of the people in particular, could constitute the same form of government as the American Constitution, which had sprung from confidence in having discovered a power principle strong enough to found a perpetual union, is to be fooled by words.

Compare Gordon S. Wood, *The Creation of the American Republic, 1776–1787* (Chapel Hill: University of North Carolina, 1969), p. 513: "In short, through the artificial contrivance of the Constitution overlying an expanded society, the Federalists meant to restore and to prolong the traditional kind of elitist influence in politics that social developments, especially since the Revolution, were undermining." A study of James Madison's arguments, in *The Federalist Papers* and elsewhere, will support Wood's case.

8. Arendt, *On Revolution*, p. 260. An integral part of the attire that distinguished the sans-culottes in 1793 was the pike, symbol of popular armed might. See Albert Soboul, *The Sans Culottes*, R. I. Hall, tr. (New York: Anchor Books, 1972), p. 223 and 158–62, where the enthusiasm of the sans-culottes for violence is discussed. It is worth remarking that a primary demand of the Paris Communards of 1871 was arming the people; indeed, it was an aim of the Americans in 1776 as well as the Russians in 1917 (Petrograd had a Workers *and* Soldiers Council). For Russia, see Oskar Anweiler, *The Soviets*, R. Hein, tr. (New York: Pantheon Books, 1974), pp. 103–11, on Petrograd. For America, see Pauline Maier, *From Resistance to Revolution* (New York: Alfred A. Knopf, 1972), pp. 244–45, 286; and Article II of the Bill of Rights: "A well-regulated Militia, being necessary to the security of the Free State, the right of the people to keep and bear arms, shall not be infringed." It is incredible that Arendt, for all of her talk of Rome, Machiavelli, and revolution, does not discuss at length the relation between armed might and freedom— especially since Machiavelli's *virtù*, for example, strongly connotes military virtuosity. Who, indeed, were most of the heroes of ancient Rome?

9. Compare Arendt, *On Revolution*, p. 267 and Anweiler, *The Soviets*, p. 112: "The soviets of 1917 soon became the battleground of various political tendencies. . . ."

10. See Arendt, *On Revolution*, p. 55 and compare p. 243.

11. For her appreciation of Benjamin's theses, see her "Introduction" to Walter Benjamin, *Illuminations*, R. Zohn, tr. (New York: Harcourt Brace Jovanovich, 1968), pp. 12–13. For her attitude toward history in *On Revolution*, see pp. 45ff. where she criticizes Hegel's philosophy of history. Note also her somewhat cryptic rebuke to the Marxists on p. 51: "What the men of the Russian Revolution had learned from the French Revolution . . . was history and not action."

12. Benjamin, *Illuminations*, pp. 255, 262, 263. The quotes, in order, are from these §§ VI, V, XVII, and XVI.

13. Ibid., p. 96. Also, Hannah Arendt, *The Human Condition* (New York: The Viking Press, 1959), p. 164.

206 / HANNAH ARENDT

14. Franz Kafka, *Diaries, 1914–1923*, C. Greenberg, tr. (New York: Schocken Books, 1949), p. 195. The preceding quote is from *Illuminations*, p. 257 (thesis VII).

15. Compare Arendt, *On Revolution*, p. 11. The definition of tradition comes from the "Preface" to *Between Past and Future*, p. 5; the last quote, from "What Is Authority?" in the same volume, p. 94.

16. Arendt, "Introduction" to Benjamin, *Illuminations*, pp. 50–51.

17. Arendt, *On Revolution*, p. 81. The remark about social scientists appears on p. 67. It need scarcely be added that linking Rousseau, however indirectly, with such sentiments is utterly preposterous. For more on Rousseau, see pp. 65, 76–77, 92–93.

18. These quotes from Rousseau occur in *The Social Contract*, Book II, Chapter I ("It is absurd that the will should bind itself") and Book II, Chapter III ("Every citizen should express only his opinion . . . without any communication"). Compare Arendt, *On Revolution*, pp. 162, 171.

19. Arendt, *Between Past and Future*, p. 164. Emphasis is mine.

20. It is this willingness that sharply distinguishes Arendt from Leo Strauss and his disciples.

21. Arendt, *On Revolution*, p. 161; *Between Past and Future*, pp. 14, 28. A comparison with Benjamin's critique of social democracy in his "theses" is interesting.

22. Arendt alludes to the passage and quotes a small fragment of the last paragraph in *Between Past and Future*, p. 30; the complete text—I have quoted only the culmination of Nietzsche's argument—appears in Walter Kaufman, ed. and tr., *The Portable Nietzsche* (New York: The Viking Press, 1954), p. 485.

23. See Arendt, *The Human Condition*, p. 183. For further evidence of this outlook, developed using Heidegger's 1947 essay on Plato, see "What Is Authority?", in *Between Past and Future*, pp. 119–41; also "On Humanity in Dark Times," in Arendt, *Men in Dark Times* (New York: Harcourt Brace Jovanovich, 1968), pp. 10–11, especially.

24. Arendt, *The Human Condition*, p. 17.

25. Martin Heidegger, *An Introduction to Metaphysics*, Ralph Manheim, tr. (New York: Harper and Row, 1961), p. 128.

26. Arendt, *Between Past and Future*, p. 8.

27. Arendt, *The Human Condition*, pp. 38, 178 and *On Revolution*, p. 173.

28. On the "world-building" capacity of men exchanging promises, see Arendt, *On Revolution*, pp. 174–75.

29. Arendt, *The Human Condition*, p. 221. Emphasis is mine. See also p. 214.

30. Arendt, *On Revolution*, p. 23. On p. 205, she admits that the real

meaning of the beginning could never have been conceptualized before the era of revolutions, which enacted the event in broad daylight. The Romans, by contrast (to take one of her most banal models) kept the beginning "shrouded in mystery, . . . an event which memory could not reach." For her emphasis on "covenanting," see p. 174.

31. Ibid., p. 215. Note how this sentence could stand as a direct response to the Heidegger statement quoted earlier.

32. For the constitution as a solution to the puzzle of the absolute, see *On Revolution*, p. 205. For the metaphor of the constitution as a house see p. 163. For the Roman connection, and "binding back," see p. 199. The status of the holy Roman trinity in Arendt's thought would make an interesting essay in itself. The John Adams quote appears on p. 145. For the relation of perpetuity and authority, see pp. 182–83. On the constituting power, see p. 152.

33. On the constitution as a preliminary, see *On Revolution*, p. 220; on civil *vs.* public liberty, see the telling treatment of Robespierre, pp. 129–30. On the apolitical urge to a perfect mechanism of government, and the ambiguities of prosperity for freedom, see p. 133. On modern America as a consumer society, see p. 135. On the two-party system as oligarchic, see p. 273.

34. Ibid., p. 242.

35. Ibid., p. 221.

36. See ibid., pp. 265–67.

37. Ibid., p. 258 and also pp. 247, 271. For those wishing to investigate the sans-culottes paradigm further, the work of Albert Soboul, cited above (in note 8) is essential.

38. On representation, see *On Revolution*, p. 277. On the happiness, freedom, and power of the public realm, see pp. 258–59. On experts, see p. 276.

39. Ibid., p. 284.

40. Arendt, *On Revolution*, p. 136.

41. See ibid., p. 60. Compare p. 110 and Chapter III of "The Pursuit of Happiness," which almost amounts to a fourth story.

42. Ibid., p. 245. Here she is rebuking the social program of the sans-culottes as futile as well as dangerous.

43. For Hume's argument, see Book III, § 5 of the *Treatise*. To gauge the weight of Arendt's fabrication of the "in-between" realm of appearances must carry, see *The Human Condition*, Chapter VI, § 39, on the "Loss of Common Sense." Hume's connection with Adam Smith is hardly accidental; nor is Hegel's (and thus Marx's) with Montesquieu and his category of *esprit*. Let me add that other theorists ignored by Arendt would be critical to further thinking about the possibilities she suggests: for example, G. D. H. Cole, whose *Social Theory* and *Guild Socialism Re-Stated* could profitably be consulted.

44. Compare Benjamin, *Illuminations*, p. 255 (thesis VI): "Only that historian will have the gift of fanning the spark of hope in the past who is firmly convinced that *even the dead* will not be safe from the enemy if he wins."

Stan Spyros Draenos

THINKING WITHOUT A GROUND: HANNAH ARENDT AND THE CONTEMPORARY SITUATION OF UNDERSTANDING[1]

The thinking of Hannah Arendt begins in the conviction that our tradition of thought lies in ruins. This conviction did not arise in the course of philosophical critique; it was born of her troubled experience in comprehending the appearance of totalitarian domination. What she learned from that experience was that totalitarianism is a novel phenomenon whose

> originality . . . is horrible, not because some new "idea" came into the world, but because its very actions constitute a break with all our traditions; they have clearly exploded our categories of political thought and our standards of moral judgment.[2]

Thus, in trying to comprehend totalitarian terror, Arendt found that "even the evil motives of self-interest, greed, ruthlessness, resentment, lust for power and cowardice" are inadequate explanations.[3] While we can say that radical evil has made its appearance with totalitarianism, still "we actually have nothing to fall back on in order to understand a phenomenon that nevertheless confronts us with its overpowering reality."[4]

The definitive experience for the unfolding of Arendt's thought, then, was the impossibility of explaining or understanding totalitarianism within the terms of reference provided by traditional categories of political and moral theory. The "horrible originality" of totalitarianism meant that there are matters concerning men and the possibilities of their organized living-together about which tradition had nothing to say. The criminal behavior of totalitarianism was unspeakable precisely because our tradition gave us no language or concepts with which to speak about it. If the ground of thought is ultimately the reality to which it gives voice, then the unspeakability of totalitarianism indicates that the ground of traditional political thought has disappeared. In the aftermath of totalitarianism, all thinking about our world is, for Arendt, thinking without a ground. Let us see what this means.

"Thought and reality have parted company," she writes in 1961, ". . . reality has become opaque for the light of thought and . . . thought, no longer bound to the incident as the circle remains bound to its focus, is liable either to become altogether meaningless or to rehash old verities which have lost all concrete relevance."[5] The uncompromising assertiveness of this statement is no mark of arrogance on Arendt's part. Instead, her tone of categorical certainty springs from the unblinking witness she gave to the utter nihilism of totalitarian domination. The task of the *Origins of Totalitarianism*, as she described it, was "to discover the hidden mechanics by which all traditional elements of our political and spiritual world were dissolved into a conglomeration where everything seems to have lost its specific value, and has become unrecognizable for human comprehension, unusable for human purpose."[6] And the struggle to comprehend this process of dissolution was itself an act of resistance to it.

> Comprehension does not mean denying the outrageous, deducing the unprecedented from precedents, or explaining phenomena by such analogies and generalities that the impact of reality and the shock of experience are no longer felt. It means, rather, examining and bearing consciously the burden which our century has placed on us—neither denying its existence nor submitting meekly to its weight. Comprehension, in short, means the unpremeditated, attentive facing up to, and resisting of, reality—whatever it may be.[7]

In this Arendt echoes her teacher Martin Heidegger who, more than a decade earlier, had written: "Reflection is the courage to question as deeply as possible as to the truth of our presuppositions and the exact place of our aims."[8] Only now steadfastness becomes the mind's prime quality, not because radical reflection is hazardous, but because mind must stand its ground against a force that denies all sense and meaning.

In an illuminating exchange with Eric Voeglin, Arendt notes that her classic study "does not really deal with the 'origins' of totalitarianism—as its title unfortunately claims—but gives a historical account of the elements which crystallized into totalitarianism. This account is then followed by an analysis of the elemental structure of totalitarian movements and domination itself."[9] Three years after the completion of the *Origins*, however, Arendt's analysis of totalitarianism's "elemental structure" had itself crystallized into a perception of its essence. That essence she located in the mass experience of loneliness. For totalitarianism, loneliness is an experience that has "served as the foundation of a body politic and whose general mood—although it may be familiar in every other aspect—never before has pervaded, and directed the handling of, public affairs."[10] And loneliness, "the experience of being abandoned by everything and everyone," even one's self,[11] has certain distinctive phenomenal characteristics. In the situation of utter loneliness "man loses trust in himself as the partner of his thoughts and that elementary confidence in the world, which is necessary to make experiences at all. Self and world, capacity for thought and experience are lost at the same time."[12] The loss of confidence in the self and the world creates the condition for totalitarian mobilization in which ideology and terror take the place of thought and experience.[13] The mass loneliness that Arendt determined as the experience upon which totalitarian domination took root thus signifies the loss of a common world of experience, of the shared meaning that constitutes our human reality. As such, mass loneliness also signifies the disappearance of the ground of thought. In its full structure, the disappearance of that ground consists in the dissolution of shared experience, the emergence of an unprecedented form of organization and behavior under totalitarianism, and the definitive rupture, as a consequence, of traditional categories of thought and contemporary realities of experience. "Totalitarian domination as an established fact . . . has broken the continuity of Occidental history. The break in our tradition is now an accomplished fact. It is neither the result of anyone's deliberate choice nor subject to further decision. . . . The nondeliberative character of the break gives it an irrevocability which only events, never thoughts, can have."[14]

Arendt's reflective elaborations of the rupture between traditional thought and contemporary experience issue forth in the wake of this seminal confrontation of mind with totalitarianism. Over a span of nearly three decades, the impassioned, articulate figure of Hannah Arendt moves upon the stage of public discourse to perform the "thinking completion" that follows upon action.[15] Arendt identifies this "thinking completion" as the task of any understanding that lives in the aftermath of momentous events. But it is no coincidence that this notion is also a perfect characterization of her own thinking experience. For the essence of her work is that it does, indeed, realize the thinking completion of a world which the winds of totalitarianism swept away—of a tradition whose final and irrevocable devastation she was condemned to witness. And herein lies the peculiarity of her undertaking in the light of its own understanding. For her thinking lives in the self-awareness that the ground of thought has disappeared. Arendt virtually announces the intention to think without a ground—to think in defiance of its disappearance.

The disappearance of a ground for thought means the collapse of the rudimentary framework within which the tradition of thought—with all its antinomies and internal debates—unfolded. And here this means, most fundamentally, the final playing out of the hierarchical relationship between the *vita contemplativa* and the *vita activa*—the obliteration of every last spiritual authority that transcends, and thereby provides binding standards of judgment for, the doings and activities of men. But with the collapse of tradition, something else is lost as well. And it is here, I think, and not with the loss of tradition itself, that her central concern lies. That "something else" is the meaningful presence of the past in the present. Arendt's thought is provoked by the apprehension that we have lost not tradition, which she considered hopelessly dead, but that, having lost tradition, we are in danger of forgetting the past as well. "With the loss of tradition we have lost the thread which safely guided us through the vast realms of the past . . . without a securely anchored tradition— and the loss of that security occurred several hundred years ago—the whole dimension of the past has also been endangered. We are in danger of forgetting. . . ."[16] And the danger of forgetting the past imposed a unique burden on the understanding.

> . . . the task of preserving the past without the help of tradition, and often even against traditional standards and interpretations, is the same for the whole of Western civilization. Intellectually, though not socially, America and Europe are in the same situation: the thread of tradition is broken, and we must discover the past for ourselves—that is, read its authors as though nobody had ever read them before.[17]

In the wake of tradition's end, Arendt's thinking seeks to disclose the meaning of the past outside the framework of any tradition. It is the past, and not the tradition, she desires to redeem from the abyss of time to which the modern sensibility consigns it.

But what is the significance of preserving the past? Isn't it just a hindrance to our movement into the future—a nightmare we only wish were over and done with? Some reflections of Ortega y Gasset express starkly the essence of Arendt's concern. "Man," writes Ortega, ". . . has no nature; what he has is history."[18] And setting this existential fact in the context of the break in tradition, he continues in the same essay:

> Man set outside himself is brought up against himself as reality, as history. And for the first time, he sees himself forced to a concern with the past, not from curiosity, nor in search for examples which may serve as norms, but because it is all he *has*.[19]

To the extent that Ortega's formulations enter the sphere of ontological speculation, they distort Arendt's concern.

In keeping with the worldly orientation of her thinking, Arendt self-consciously refuses to elaborate ultimate philosophical positions and commitments. Indeed, the very radicalism of her thought depended on it. This refusal is nowhere more apparent, not to say problematic, than in her only attempt at "philosophy," *The Life of the Mind*, and accounts for the elusiveness of that work when read with philosophical concerns in mind, however schooled these concerns might be in Heidegger's "destruction of metaphysics." Nonetheless, we shall see that the situation of Ortega's "man set outside of himself" is analogous to the situation of Kafka's *He* who, as Arendt interprets it, also finds himself driven back into the past. Taken metaphorically, the situation of Ortega's "man set outside himself" expresses the eminently practical intention that informs Arendt's remembrance of the past. If we have forgotten or are rapidly in the process of forgetting our past, this means nothing less than that we have forgotten what we are. And if this is our situation, then to remember the past involves no exercise in utopian idealism or philosophical abstraction. On the contrary, only by so doing might we restore the sense of ourselves and thereby gain some practical bearings by which to orient ourselves toward the future. For without a sense of ourselves, we fall easy prey to the efforts of behavioral scientists and systems analysts to remake us in the image of their truly abstract and meaningless theories.

We say, then, that Arendt's ambition is to restore the meaning of the past for the present, and to do this without reliance on traditional thought. Now the past exists only in our present remembrance. And to forget the meaning of the past means no less than to forget what we are. To remember this meaning, however, has been the function of the reflective activity from which theoretical understanding springs.

> If it is true that all thought begins with remembrance, it is also true that no remembrance remains secure unless it is condensed and distilled into a framework of conceptual notions within which it can further exercise itself.[20]

It is this further exercise of remembrance that is exactly the function of tradition insofar as it is held authoritative—that is, insofar as it lives. For tradition, according to Arendt, "orders the past, hands it down (*tradere*), interprets it, omits, selects and emphasizes, according to a system of pre-established beliefs."[21] And the significance of a tradition of thought, while it lives, is just its ability to articulate living experience, to secure it conceptually, and to have the ambition, at least, of guiding and providing a measure for, as well as interpreting, practice. Since living tradition—that authoritative manifestation and meaningful embodiment of the past in the present—is irrevocably dead and in ruins, Arendt's thinking necessarily seeks a remembrance that does not speak from any theoretical tradition. And more radically, since the tradition of thought in its broadest sense is dead, not out of inattention or lack of care, but because its ground has dissolved, so to speak, before our very eyes, Arendt's thinking cannot even seek to stand on the ground of any tradition. For her thinking begins and moves within the conviction that the ground itself has disappeared. And it has disappeared precisely because the one experience we do all share and cannot forget is that, by exploding our traditional political and moral categories, totalitarianism has destroyed the validity of our tradition of thought.

The problem then is as follows: Denied reliance on any received language, concepts, or categories, how can thinking find its way? Arendt claims that thinking finds its way by locating itself and learning to move in the gap between past and future. It is Kafka's parable of *He,* she says, that describes this gap to us. And her interpretation of the parable articulates a metaphor for the thinker that is radically different from the one that expressed its conceptual foundation—namely, Plato's parable of the Cave. In Plato's story, the thinker leaves the deceptive and transient appearances of this world behind, only to return to it with the vision of the world of Being fixed in his mind's eye. As we shall see, no such transcendence of worldly conditions, however temporary, is permitted to man in the gap.

In examining her interpretation of the Kafka parable, in the "Preface" to *Between Past and Future,* we do no more than turn Arendt's thought back upon itself. For, while the gap between past and future may offer the fullest illumination to the "contemporary conditions of thought,"[22] as she puts it, it also expresses the internal problematic of her own thought—her effort to think in the self-awareness that the ground of thought has disappeared. It is not surprising that this preface offers the key to the way of her thought. Fundamentally it is Arendt's reflection on the circumstances and experience of writing the essays onto which it opens. Those essays were written over a period of two decades following the completion of the *Origins of Totalitarianism,* and thus unfold in the wake of her realization of the end of tradition.

According to Arendt, the parable begins just at the point where action and the experiences arising from it call for thinking remembrance to preserve them for the present and allow them to exercise themselves on the future. In the parable, a "he" is engaged in battle with two forces, one coming from the infinite past, and the other from the infinite future. The past, as we might expect, is "pressing" him upon the future, while, oddly, the future is driving him back on the past. This image, Arendt says, is the perfect metaphor for the condition of thought as it has always existed. In other times, however, this gap between past and future was paved over by tradition. It is only with the loss of tradition that the gap has revealed itself in its true character, and engaged the thinker in the wearisome struggle Kafka describes.

The story, however, does not end there. "He," we find, would like to leap beyond this struggle entirely and assume the role of an umpire. Arendt identifies this desire as the dream of metaphysics to transcend the time-boundedness of existence, and to enter a realm of supersensual reality. Significantly, Arendt herself seeks a more modest accommodation to the hostile conditions that prevail in the gap. She modifies the parable somewhat in order to allow for a deflection produced by the battle. This deflection enables the embattled thinker to move back and forth between past and future along a parallelogram of forces whereby, it is hoped, he can gain enough distance to achieve the impartiality of an umpire without leaving time altogether. She declares that the essays that follow are exercises, intended to teach us not what to think, but only how to move in this gap. The problem of truth she keeps in abeyance, though she holds out the hope that the gap is "the only region perhaps where truth eventually will appear."[23]

Let us look at Arendt's interpretation in terms of her own thinking. She says that as long as tradition lived, it paved over the gap between past and future, and allowed us to walk with confidence between them. But with the break in tradition realized irrevocably by totalitarianism, the ground upon which categories of thought were stabilized is replaced by a mere location—by a location of being in time. This situation poses a new challenge for thinking of which Ortega's "man set outside himself" seems unaware.

"Man set outside himself," or literally, man that does not know what he is, is indeed helpless in confronting the future. He is driven back into the past in order to recover the sense of what he is. But this remembrance of himself becomes highly problematic because, as Arendt notes, "Remembrance . . . is helpless outside a pre-established frame of reference."[24] But if, with the disappearance of a ground of thinking, there is no longer a frame of reference for the man in the gap between past and future, there is, at least, one point of reference from which he can begin to think—namely, the shared experience of the end of tradition. This point of reference is itself, of course, radically temporal. Instead of a groundwork of concepts that paves the way from the past toward the future, we have only a groundpoint that, like the navigator's polestar, orients thinking and fixes the location of our being in time. What are the consequences for thought?

Since, as Arendt puts it, "tradition itself has become part of the past"[25] the tradition of thought, along with everything else that has passed, is being forgotten. To remember it can no longer mean to assert its truth which, under contemporary circumstances, would be an empty enterprise. For with the disappearance of a ground in reality to which it gives voice, the tradition of thought is devoid of truth. Nevertheless, to remember the past without the aid of tradition does not mean to forget the tradition of thought. For the tradition of thought constitutes an important structural element of the past. Tradition once enshrined a determinate aspect of the past in the present. While it lives, "tradition puts the past in order, not just chronologically, but first of all systematically in that it separates the positive from the negative, the orthodox from the heretical, that which is obligatory and relevant from the mass of irrelevant or merely interesting opinions and data."[26] In the light of the disappearance of tradition from our world, and of our losing hold of the past as a consequence, the meaning of the past must be thought in a new way. This meaning cannot be thought through some set of categories handed down from the past or accepted from a spiritual or intellectual authority. Rather, it must be thought through remembrance itself. The reflective glance of remembrance always realizes experience, which, in turn, can be rendered coherently only as a story. Thus, to remember a past in which our living-together was once housed by tradition is to tell its story. And to tell its story is to reveal it as phenomena in shared living experience. This is a thinking through of the ground of thought that can preserve its meaning for the present, but only at the cost of abolishing any remnant of the authority of the past over our thinking.

To show just to what extent Arendt's thinking is free of this authority and is not, as is often believed, a reassertion of Plato or Aristotle or someone else, we may simply note her story of the origins of tradition. For, according to Arendt, it was the political experience of the binding force of the past, realized through the sacredness with which the Romans regarded the founding of their city, that introduced tradition into the West, and made it possible for Greek thought to become authoritative in the first place. Thus it was in a

> primarily political context that the past was sanctified through tradition. Tradition preserved the past by handing down from one generation to the next the testimony of the ancestors, who had first witnessed and created the sacred founding and then augmented it by their authority throughout the centuries. . . . The notion of spiritual tradition and of authority in matters of thought and ideas is here derived from the political realm and therefore essentially derivative. . . . the historically all-important fact is that the Romans felt they needed founding fathers and authoritative examples in matters of thought and ideas as well. . . . The great Greek authors became authorities in the hands of the Romans, not of the Greeks.[27]

But Arendt's story has more than one irony. It is not just that the Romans and not the Greeks took the Greek authors as authoritative. The experience of foundation, without which neither authority nor tradition as we have known them would have come into being, remained conceptually unarticulated within the tradition of political thought itself. And it remained conceptually unarticulated, Arendt claims, because "Greek concepts . . .

simply eliminated from historical consciousness all political experiences which could not be fit into their framework."28 It was only with Augustine's assertion that "the seat of the mind is in memory" that we encounter "the conceptual articulation of the specifically Roman experience which the Romans themselves, overwhelmed as they were by Greek philosophy and concepts, never achieved."29

Arendt's subtly nuanced tale of the origins of tradition is itself exemplary of her thinking through the ground of traditional thought. It obviously stands beyond the authoritative claims of tradition itself. But more than that, it points to a peculiarity in the way of her thinking which has led to endless misunderstandings, and even, I suspect, to a degree of self-misunderstanding on her part. This peculiarity lies in the fact that Arendt does not think in concepts. Instead she evokes experience and, like all master storytellers, relies upon the latent evocative power of words to do so. Hence the centrality of her famous etymologies and distinctions to the unfolding of her thought. The problem is the temptation to transform the constellation of interrelated distinctions by which she has penetrated the depths of the past into a systematic set of categories by which to continue or re-establish the tradition of discourse called political theory. It is exactly this temptation we must resist if we are to learn what Arendt has to teach. How so?

We have seen, in her story of the origins of tradition, that Arendt's undertaking involves a radical critique of traditional theory—a critique that is part and parcel of her effort to preserve the meaning of the past outside the framework of any tradition. We could easily expand upon this aspect of her work by turning to her critical interpretation of Plato, whose imposition of philosophy on politics she criticizes in order to defend the dignity of the political realm. In doing so, we would have to underscore the rudimentary distinction she draws between philosophical contemplation and political action—a distinction she carries through to Heidegger's *Being and Time*.30 But this distinction does not in actuality define two categories of thought. It belongs to the story she tells of the encounter of philosophy and politics in ancient Athens—an encounter eventful for the life-experience of Occidental understanding. To transform that distinction into a pair of categories would wholly pervert its nature and significance.

In sum, Arendt's remembrance cannot provide us with a new "framework of conceptual notions" by which the past can continue to exercise itself. That is, it cannot equip us with the means to confront the future. For the loss of tradition from which her thinking unfolds is no simple matter of the dissolution of traditional standards of behavior and traditional categories of thought, in whose place new standards and new categories have emerged. Rather, it signifies the dissolution *per se* of categories that speak their meaning through time, and of standards of behavior that inform lives and create a bond across the generations of men who enter and leave the world. Under these conditions, the point of Arendt's work is that it provides a lasting testimony which, while not establishing or re-establishing any tradition, fittingly memorializes a kind of greatness that, for good or ill, we no longer understand.

But if it is to a realization of the futility of thinking that Arendt's outlook leads us, why should we be concerned with her thought at all? Do we not face here yet another romantic protest against modernity? I think not. On the contrary, Arendt is one of the essential thinkers of our times who, when read properly, illuminates critical aspects of the modern situation with which thinking must come to terms.

Let us return to the situation of thinking in the gap between past and future. For Arendt, the location of being in time "can only be indicated but cannot be inherited or handed down from the past."[31] And this is a perfectly natural consequence of her understanding. With the loss of tradition and the ground from which it alone might be rebuilt, the mind becomes embattled and loses its freedom of movement—its ability to move with confidence through and across reality. And, under the stress of the battle, the thinker is in danger of being overrun by the blind march of time—that is, of succumbing thoughtlessly to whatever the course of things may be. The intention of Arendt's location of being in time is to regain this freedom of movement for the mind by restoring the capacity of thought to literally remember a past we are forgetting. And while her thought cannot, by its very situation, provide concepts and categories with which to confront the problems of our world, what it does do is call thinking back to that world. Indicative of the resounding force of this call in her work is the fact that the turn of her later years from politics to thinking took as its point of departure the case of Adolf Eichmann and the thoughtless banality of his evil, as if, even in thinking about thinking, she refused to leave behind worldly concerns for the abstractions of the mind's self-reflection.[32] How we can emulate Arendt's example without merely following in her footsteps remains, I think, an open question. On this matter, we must begin, at least, by taking to heart Arendt's warning that "each new generation, indeed, every new human being, as he inserts himself between an infinite past and an infinite future, must discover and ploddingly pave [the gap] anew."[33]

According to Arendt, the gap between past and future has now become a fact of political relevance, which relevance is "to be confronted anew, without religious trust in a sacred beginning and without the protection of traditional and therefore self-evident standards of behavior, by the elementary problems of human living-together."[34] Since we live it daily, we need no authority and no methodology to confirm the validity of this truth. And if we were to place it in the wider context of Arendt's thought, and then follow out the immanent logic of her position, we would have to conclude that thinking must await a new beginning in the political realm. For without a new foundation of freedom and authority, which she understood to be the always defeated intention of the revolutions that have punctuated the last two centuries, thinking cannot gain a ground from which to speak the meaning of our experience once again. But in reaching this conclusion, we would be embracing her thought as a conceptual structure, while ignoring the significance of her thinking as an exemplary orientation of mind to world. For Arendt, it was always the world itself that provided the matter of thought. And if she turned to the authors and texts of the past to think those matters through—to literally permeate them with thought—it was not from a need for authority, or out of longing for a dead past, but because she believed, I suspect, what George Seferis expressed poetically:

> *As pines*
> *keep the shape of the wind*
> *even when the wind has fled and is no longer there*
> *so words*
> *guard the shape of man*
> *even when man has fled and is no longer there.*[35]

NOTES

1. Robert M. Tostevin posed the question this essay attempts to answer. That answer was originally presented in the form of a commentary at the Conference on the Work of Hannah Arendt, held at York University, November 24–26, 1972. In all essentials it is unchanged here.

2. Hannah Arendt, "Understanding and Politics," *Partisan Review*, Vol. xx, no. 4 (July–August, 1953), p. 379.

3. Hannah Arendt, *The Origins of Totalitarianism*, 2nd ed. (Cleveland: Meridian Books, 1958), p. 457.

4. Ibid.

5. Hannah Arendt, "Preface," *Between Past and Future* (New York: The Viking Press, 1960), p. 6.

6. Arendt, *The Origins of Totalitarianism*, p. viii.

7. Ibid.

8. Martin Heidegger, "The Age of the World View," *Measure*, Vol. II (1950–51), p. 269.

9. Hannah Arendt, "Rejoinder to Eric Voeglin's Review of *The Origins of Totalitarianism*," *Review of Politics*, Vol. xv, no. 1 (January 1953), p. 78.

10. Included in the 2nd ed. of *The Origins of Totalitarianism*, p. 461. Originally published in *Review of Politics* (July 1953) as "Ideology and Terror: A Novel Form of Government."

11. Ibid., p. 476.

12. Ibid., p. 477.

224 / HANNAH ARENDT

13. Compare ibid., pp. 473–74.

14. Arendt, *Between Past and Future*, pp. 26–27.

15. Ibid., p. 6.

16. Ibid., p. 94.

17. Ibid., p. 204.

18. Ortega y Gasset, "History as a System," in *History as a System and Other Essays Toward a Philosophy of History* (New York: W. W. Norton, 1941), p. 217.

19. Ibid., p. 230. Emphasis is his.

20. Hannah Arendt, *On Revolution* (New York: The Viking Press, 1963), p. 222.

21. Hannah Arendt, letter in *The New York Review of Books* (January 1, 1970).

22. Arendt, *Between Past and Future*, p. 13.

23. Ibid., p. 14.

24. Ibid., p. 6.

25. Arendt, letter. (See note 21.)

26. Hannah Arendt, "Walter Benjamin," in *Men in Dark Times* (New York: Harcourt Brace Jovanovich, 1968), pp. 198–99.

27. Arendt, *Between Past and Future*, p. 124.

28. Ibid., p. 136.

29. Ibid., p. 126.

30. Arendt, *Men in Dark Times*, pp. viii–ix.

31. Arendt, *Between Past and Future*, p. 13.

32. Hannah Arendt, *Eichmann in Jerusalem* (New York: The Viking Press, 1965), and also "Thinking and Moral Considerations: A Lecture," *Social Research*, Vol. xxxviii no. 3 (Autumn 1971).

33. Arendt, *Between Past and Future*, p. 13.

34. Ibid., p. 141.

35. George Seferis, "On Stage" in *Three Secret Poems*, Walter Kaiser, tr. (Cambridge: Harvard University Press, 1969), p. 31.

J. Glenn Gray

THE ABYSS OF
FREEDOM—AND
HANNAH ARENDT[1]

At the very end of her life Hannah Arendt was at work on giving written form to philosophical reflections on the nature and operation of willing as the source of our freedom. These reflections will be perceived to be the distillation of her life-long study of political theory and practice. They were to be the second series of her Gifford Lectures. She had already delivered at Aberdeen ten lectures on *Thinking* and was planning to follow the lectures on *Willing* with concluding essays on *Judging*, all three under the title, "The Life of the Mind." Unfortunately for us, death came to her when she had barely completed a penultimate draft of her thoughts on the will. Though she was sixty-nine years old, her sudden death can only be regarded as untimely. For those who knew her mind with some intimacy it was evident that she regarded judging to be her particular strength and in a real sense a hoped-for resolution of the impasse to which the reflections on willing seemed to lead her. As Kant's *Critique of Judgment* enabled him to break through some of the antimonies of the earlier critiques, so she hoped to resolve the perplexities of thinking and willing by pondering the nature of our capacity for judging.

Her lectures on the will had been especially intractable and laborious to formulate. More than once she told me on the telephone, "The will is not my thing," and it was not difficult to detect in her voice the torment that the work was causing her. So unusual was the complaint in her case that I did not dare to reply: "Oh yes, it is, Hannah. Throughout your life you have been primarily concerned with the issue of individual and political freedom. Now you are searching for its philosophical basis in human willing, well aware that the problem has baffled the best minds of our heritage."

Her difficulties were compounded, I believe, by the fact that her great mentor, Immanuel Kant, whose thoughts on judging were to serve as a guide to the concluding part of "The Life of the Mind," failed utterly to satisfy her on the nature of willing. His *Critique of Practical Reason* she considered an avoidance of the real issue because Kant believed the will to be another form of reason. She was convinced on the contrary that to think and to will are fundamentally different activities of the mind, deriving from distinct mental powers (as she titled them, "faculties" or "organs"). Moreover, Kant resolved the problem of man's freedom by locating its source in the noumenal world, whose very existence we could never establish but in which we could rationally believe. Like her, Kant experienced the question of human freedom as the paramount one of his entire intellectual life. But Hannah Arendt could not accept his conclusion that its reality must be a matter of rational faith. Her thinking was too deeply rooted in history and politics to permit such acceptance, and she was also too persuaded of the primacy of the world of appearances.

In the earlier lectures she had concluded that thinking removes us from the world of appearance, making manifest invisible realities by which we are aided to interpret the everyday world of spectacle and event, that is, to reveal its sense and meaning. Nevertheless, this duality of the visible and the invisible is emphatically not the Kantian dualism between phenomena and noumena. In all her writing Hannah Arendt remained resolutely attached to seeking solutions to the riddles of life and thought within a humanistic rather than a religious framework. This in spite of the fact that her researches on the history of the idea of willing taught her quickly that it has a theological origin. The will was a "discovery" of the Apostle Paul and more especially of

Augustine, with whose thought she became acquainted early as a graduate student and doctoral candidate in Germany and whose ideas on the will remain pervasive in her final work. For a less heroic thinker than Hannah Arendt the fact that her favorite thinker, Kant, as well as the "discoverers" of the will, had grounded it firmly in otherworldly reality might have been an insuperable deterrent. This fact she found troubling enough, but so firm was her conviction that "freedom is the *raison d'être* of politics" that she struggled to the end to give freedom a philosophical description and foundation without recourse to any transcendent principles.

Nonetheless, she was disturbed by the large number of philosophers who either denied the will's very existence or refused to grant it any distinctness from thinking or desiring. In tracing the history of the will in Western thought she concluded that the Greek philosophers had little conception of the will as an independent power of the mind, though Aristotle had some intimation of it in his notion of forethought (*proairesis*) or the power of choice between alternative courses of conduct. Even more disturbing to her was the discovery that most philosophers of the Christian era refuse to believe that the will is anything but an artificial construct, a figment of the imagination. Though nineteenth-century German idealists like Schelling briefly elevated the will to the status of primary being, their twentieth-century successors repudiate the will in the manner of the late Heidegger or deny its reality altogether like Gilbert Ryle.

Confronted by this persisting tendency of philosophers and persuaded that the existence of free will is what makes us really human, Hannah Arendt attacked with all her polemic skill the dominant tradition. The substance of her own position can be simply stated. The hallmark of willing is our power to initiate something altogether new, something that we realize every instant we can also leave undone. Our will is the originator of actions that are not explicable by preceding causes. Such actions spring from the incalculable power of willing and are as spontaneous and unpredictable as life itself, which the will closely resembles. In contrast to reason, the will is our organ for the future; it possesses the power to make present to the mind the not-yet dimension of reality. As such it is the very opposite of remembrance or recollection of the has-been, which is so beloved by thinkers. She notes the interesting fact that the word "will" is a modal auxiliary of the future tense in our language, an indication of our capacity to make the future a genuine tense of time as it so rarely is for philosophic thought. According to her, the will is immeasurably freer than either thought or desire in its capacity to act or refuse to act—or, in her formulation, to will and to nill—at every instant.

Her charge against philosophers as a class is that they are unable to acknowledge the future as such an authentic tense. She quotes Bergson approvingly in his claim that thinkers are simply unable to conceive of "radical novelty and unpredictability." The fatal weakness of historical accounts of the will is that they have been undertaken by "professional thinkers," a term she derived from Kant but with a pejorative flavor missing from his use of it. Because these thinkers are committed to the life of theory, they seek to interpret the world rather than to change it, according to the old complaint of Karl Marx. At heart philosophers are displeased with freedom, she believed, because the notion of an action that is contingent constitutes a threat to their love of order and intelligibility. The idea of necessity is much more comfortable for theoreticians, and the familiar circumstance that after anything has actually happened, it seems to have been inevitable furthers the philosophic preference for necessity. And this is not all. The very notion of a free will raises the specter of evil, long regarded as the most intractable problem for thought. Confronted with the possibility that evil possesses an equal status in the nature of things as its opposite, most thinkers from antiquity to the present day have sought to interpret it as merely a deficient mode of the good. When one adds to this that our normal mood while under the influence of will is one of tenseness, disquiet, and care in contrast to the peace and serenity that is the goal of contemplative thought, there is little wonder that thinkers are unable to give a just account of the activity of will. As she summarizes in a trenchant sentence: "The will's mix of fear and hope always *wills* to do something and thus implicitly holds in contempt sheer thinking whose whole activity depends on 'doing nothing.' "

These are serious charges and deserve to be taken seriously by those of us who like to lay claim in some degree to the title of philosopher. Before coming to grips with these ideas, however, I want to review her conclusions in the final lecture on the will, which follows her sketch of the history of the will in Western thought. As we would expect from her, she follows relentlessly the logic of her analysis in the opening one, which I have summarized inadequately enough in the foregoing. Following Augustine she believes that the will individuates us radically, is indeed the very source of the principle of individuation, by removing us from the common world of our fellow men. The will establishes our singular identity and forms our distinctive character. Let me quote her summary statement of the matter:

> For this individual, fashioned by the will and aware of the fact that it could also be different from what it is... always tends to assert its "I myself" against an indefinite "they," all the others which I as an individual am not. Nothing indeed can be more frightening than this notion of a solipsistic freedom, that is, the "feeling" that my isolated stand as distinguished from all others is due to free-will, that nothing and nobody can be held responsible for it than I myself.[2]

The "abyss of freedom," which forms half the title of her final chapter, is the outcome of a philosophic analysis that treats the exercise of the will outside of community and reaches the impasse of an isolated ego caught in the toils of willing and nilling. In an effort to escape this impasse she turns to the idea of political freedom, which understands willing in terms of "being able to do what we ought to will." In contrast to thinkers, men of action understand willing as the I-can and achieve through action a sense of the "we." For Hannah Arendt action is always communal in essence, as such in stark opposition to the solitariness of thought. The "we" is older than the "I," just as the I-can precedes in time the I-will. Hence she seeks the root of our inner conviction of being free by recourse to political history. She believes the most elemental kind of freedom is the liberty to go or to move, unrestrained by bodily disease or an external master. Liberation from restraint is prior in time and in logic to the idea of freedom as the power to begin anew.

Her inquiry into the political meaning of freedom leads her back to the mysterious "in the beginning" when men of action endeavored to found political freedom after the fact of liberation from oppression. They thought of this new beginning as a *novus ordo seclorum* (a new order of the ages), which forms the other half of the title of her concluding chapter. She investigates two great foundation legends of Western civilization, the Judaic and the Roman, both of which were also important to our American Founding Fathers after their liberation from Britain. The Jews and the Romans, she discovers, believed they knew something of their own beginnings as a human plurality or we-consciousness; both distinguished sharply the negative sense of liberation from the positive sense of constituting freedom as a stable, tangible reality. To her disappointment, however, she finds that these men of action when confronted with the upsetting fact that they might do whatever they pleased looked for a precedent, the Hebrews to a god outside the temporal order who created heaven and earth, the Romans to the destruction of Troy and the legend of Aeneas as founding father of Rome. Their new order of the ages turns out to be a restoration or re-enactment of an earlier order. These founders, or in fact restorers, tend to be divinized in their turn by later generations. She notes that even the secular men of the Enlightenment who founded the American republic found it necessary to appeal to "nature and nature's God" as justification for their new order of the ages.

So it develops that men of action are hardly more pleased with freedom as a spontaneous new beginning than are the philosophers. They can face the opaqueness of the future only by recourse to precedents for their will to bring something new into existence. Hannah Arendt concludes her lectures on the will by returning to Augustine's idea that the freedom each of us possesses is rooted in our natality. We are "doomed" to be free by the very fact of being born, the primary beginning for everyone. This ground of freedom is opaque and unsatisfactory, she admits, as indeed it is. But she promises to "open" or "resolve" the impasse into which she has been led by investigating our faculty of judgment, which, alas, she did not live to write.

At stake for her throughout these lectures, it seems fair to observe, is the endeavor to justify the principle of individuation, whose very core is the freedom each of us experiences daily when we rise from sleep and decide what to do or refuse to do with the approaching hours. With the existentialists she shared a passionate faith in the openness of the future and the contingency of events in that future. Only if we possess the courage to accept such contingency can we take responsibility for shaping our individual characters and for exerting our will upon tomorrow and tomorrow and tomorrow. Though the philosophical ground of such freedom eluded her until the close of her life, Hannah Arendt did not permit herself to doubt that the reality of freedom is disclosed in our individual capacity to act into a future whose only certainty we seek to provide for in writing "a last will and testament." In a sense not simply metaphorical, these lectures on the will are her own final testament to a life-long endeavor to relate a passionate philosophical conviction of freedom to political community in the panorama of history.

In seeking to come to grips with her interpretation, I shall be less concerned with justifying or rejecting this or that idea than with thinking alongside her, so to speak, in reliance on the ancient Greek proverb "two going together, one sees before the other." It is important to remember that her "Life of the Mind" lectures are not propounding a set of propositions, teaching a doctrine, or writing another critique in the manner of Kant. Instead her focus is on mind as a life, an Aristotelian dynamism in which thinking, willing, desiring, judging, and the like are

observed phenomenologically as activities in and upon the world.
In these lectures Hannah Arendt was delineating an outlook on
total experience, at once deeply personal and profoundly objective,
an *out*look in the nearly literal sense. Even for those most in
sympathy with her ideas, it is an outlook easy to misunderstand.
One reason is its comparative independence of even those
predecessors to whom she felt most deeply indebted; another is the
subtlety of her critical reflections, which developed from one book
to the next without undergoing the reversals that have become
fashionable nowadays. Though her thought is deeply rooted in the
Western heritage, in the classical Greek and Roman as much as
Continental philosophy of the last two centuries, it is in fact very
contemporary, nearly *avant-garde*, in its sensitivity to reigning
moods and persuasions. If in certain opinions she seemed old-
fashioned, harking back to the Enlightenment and to Plato,
Aristotle, and Augustine, in reality she intended to be unfashionable by resolutely opposing much conventional wisdom of our
age.

Her most thought-provoking insight for me is the theological
origin of the will in the experience of Paul and Augustine and its
infusion into the history of thought as a distinctively Christian
element. With the Apostle Paul the will was discovered at the core
of the inner conflict between soul and flesh, reason and desire,
causing him to cry out: "The good that I want to do, I fail to do,
and the evil that I do not want is what I do." Such conflict between
soul and flesh and spirit Augustine perceived more profoundly by
locating its source within the will itself, in a broken and divided
will that incessantly calls up a counter-will to negate what we
command ourselves to do. In this experience of the I-will-and-I-
cannot by contrast to the Greek emphasis on the I-will-and-I-can,
Hannah Arendt locates the birth of modern individuality or what
existentialists prefer to call human subjectivity. She recognized
that Paul and Augustine could escape their inner turmoil only by
transforming willing into loving by recourse to God's grace. That
is, they escaped the solipsism of the turbulent will by passionate
faith in and love for a transcendent Being who returned them to

the community of the faithful. Though she could not resolve in this fashion the division of mind that the will introduces, Hannah Arendt was certain that Christian experience had made an advance over classical philosophy by its discovery of the very principle of individuation. In short she believed that our will and not our intellect is the real locus of freedom. The turbulence of willing makes us aware of the sheer contingency of our actions, which is the recognition that we could as well not act or could do something utterly different every instant. This awareness of contingency alone assures us that we are not mere links in the chain of natural causation.

How does one respond appropriately to this insistence on the central role of contingency? I find it necessary to acknowledge that I have hitherto failed to take with sufficient seriousness the function of will in interpreting man and his world. Since college days I have accepted Aristotle's conception of freedom as our capacity for choice between alternative modes of conduct and have resisted current threats to such voluntarism in the forms of behaviorism and other fashions of positivism. But I have not allowed myself to think of freedom in the radical sense of the will's power to initiate something new, spontaneously, in separation from intellect and desire and so incomparably freer than they. When I have encountered such thoughts in Sartre and the early Heidegger, though clothed in different terminology, I accorded them short shrift. The lasting value of Hannah Arendt's lectures lies in their compelling us to give reasons for assent or dissent from her account.

What troubles me most in her insistence on the reality of the contingent is its threat of meaninglessness. If we are barred from founding freedom of the will on faith in a transcendent being or in a Kantian noumenal world, what remains? Does the feeling of freedom not indeed become a doom in the Sartrean sense, a burden and a curse? Though she has convinced me that willing is that activity of the mind which individuates us radically, even isolates us from all others and pervades us with a sense of utter futility, I cannot believe that this is the whole of freedom or

individuality. Who of us has not had the experience of Housman:
"I a stranger and afraid/ In a world I never made," or more
appropriately in this context: in a world I only made?

Yet surely genuine individuality is more and other than this.
The consciousness of individual freedom comes to us, so I believe,
when thinking and willing do remove us temporarily from all
community and reveal us to ourselves in all our finitude, that is, in
our impotence and contingency as well as our uniqueness and our
possibility. But possibility when understood profoundly seems to be
at the root of all real freedom, for it carries the promise of the
achievement of true individuality. Such individuality in contrast to
the individualism of mere willing appears when we move in
thought and act from intimate to ultimate matters or from
particular to general concerns. As communal beings we belong to
others and to the surrounding world; as unique persons we belong
only to ourselves. In concert, thinking and willing propel us from
the one pole of the particular and unique to the other pole of the
general and the communal, and ever back again. That none of us
can dwell for long in any equilibrium is simply a mark of the
unstable union of thinking and willing. We achieve individuality
only when we are able to hold both poles in momentary balance, to
realize in meditation or action the particular and communal
components of our being. It is then that our will is sufficiently
harmonious to enjoin us to act. I believe that Hannah Arendt
might not have demurred, for in an earlier essay she wrote: "Only
where the I-will and the I-can coincide does freedom come to
pass."[3]

But I would go a step further to note that only where thinking
and willing interact does genuine individuality, in contrast to mere
individualism, emerge. The principle of individuation that our
will discloses is quickly countered by the principle of community
as our belonging to others and to the world. Reflection forces this
recognition upon us in much the same way that action does the
discovery of the "we." Though thinking may remove us from the
world of appearance, as Hannah Arendt claims, it does not thereby

isolate us in the manner of willing. On the contrary, we find in the invisible world, as did Socrates, a whole company of counselors, living and dead. They suffice to assure us that this invisible world of thought is also real and individuation is no more fundamental than community. We live and move and have our being in communication as much as in our solitary, skin-enclosed flesh and mind. Though the principle of individuation may have been revealed most starkly to Paul and Augustine, they were equally persuaded that "we are members one of another." In contrast to the earlier Greek political *koinonia* or the later Greek conception of friendship, they transferred the locus of community to a mystical realm of believers. For them too such community was both temporally and logically prior to individuation.

Certainly such moments of the harmonization of thought and will are rare in our experience. As Goethe once wrote: "Only he deserves freedom like life itself who must daily conquer it anew." Constantly we fall back into purely private existence or lose ourselves in gregariousness. There are many perversions of intimacy and ultimacy that cause us to miss in dailiness any keen awareness of either pole, much less experience their occasional union. In separation from willing, thinking has a natural desire to dwell in recollection of a past that becomes present to it, just as willing in isolation propels us to draw the future into our present. The former reconciles itself easily to the way things are, the latter is impatient with every existing state of affairs. Our usual state of mind or mood is an ever-changing balance of the two, nearly as random as our desires, which act upon both thought and will in diverse ways.

The difficulty of discovering the ground or ultimate source of our individual freedom, which Hannah Arendt's lectures reveal to be as intractable a problem for political practice as it has always been for philosophical theory, is a peculiarly vexing one. It resists our conceptual analysis because part of freedom's essence lies in the future. Like we ourselves, it appears to be always in becoming, never in total being. If we could once achieve a timeless perspective in which our beginning and endings were linked, the dilemma would presumably not exist. Existing as we do only "for the time being," a haunting figure of speech, we are thrown back on feeling and opinion in this search for a ground. Our vague, if powerful, conviction of being initiators of some project on which we are engaged at any time is far from a coherent account that distinguishes between relatively rare acts of ours and mere behaving in accordance with the laws of natural causality which mostly govern us. It is one thing to cry that we are "born free, free as the wind" in the words of the popular song, quite another to discover how we are free to act into and upon the enduring present and future. Yet inquiry never ceases.

I prefer to approach the problem of freedom's ground in terms of the limits to our freedom. It appears evident from experience that we are freer at one time than at another and that some persons are freer than others in both thought and action. If I ask myself when I experience an increase of freedom in thought, I answer at once: it happens when I understand something that previously baffled me. Anyone who has struggled in frustration to understand a segment of experience and finally succeeds in perceiving its relatedness to the rest of his knowledge will call himself freer than he was before. Commonplace as this observation is, I wonder if many of us grasp its full implications. Stated simply, each of us expands the limits of his freedom to the extent he truly appropriates the heritage of previous generations. Plato spoke of re-collecting in the profound sense of making one's own the enduring discoveries of other minds. In the same vein Hegel wrote of *Erinnern* (remembrance) in its etymological meaning of "making inner" what has been and holding it in present being. Both distinguished this activity from that of gaining factual knowledge; neither would assert that the person who has much information is freer than one who does not. Rather it is the discovery of principles that promotes the sense of power inherent in the mind's freedom. Such principles are to be found in the rare works of any heritage that have transcended the particular time, place, and circumstances under which they were formed or composed. Though not independent of their tradition, they succeed in gaining a partial revelation of things as they are, a revelation that provides succeeding ages a secure base for building further. To the extent any of us really appropriates these principles, we achieve a degree of freedom.

In short, I believe that we discover one source of our freedom in the activity of appropriating some of these creations of art and science, religious imagination, and philosophic reason. The Greek thinkers separated the activity of *poiesis*, of making or fabricating such works, from *praxis*, those actions of practical life which issue in political and economic institutions in the widest sense. These activities belong to a different order, *poiesis* alone surpassing the limitations imposed by a particular stage of culture. It does so by enabling us to see with the eye of the mind something of the beauty of the real in all its awesome splendor and terrible power. Yet seeing by the aid of these "poetic" works will not alone assure us that our freedom is grounded in the nature of things. If we are to achieve any notable degree of liberation from external causality we must respond to such appropriation by "doing the beautiful," in Hannah Arendt's phrase. If the former is primarily the product of thinking, response to it may be primarily the work of will. Yet it is an error, as I have said, to believe that either is exclusively the activity of thinking or willing in separation. It is likewise wrong to believe that willed response follows after appropriation in a temporal sense merely: logical priority is quite a different matter from the temporal. In wonder some have experienced the beauty of creation only by doing the works of beauty, while others require first the experience of wonder in the already created before they can respond. In either case the borders of our freedom are expanded when we recognize in thought the beauty of the real and respond by doing the beautiful in whatever sphere of life. Such "making" in the philosophical sense enables us to transcend to some degree the human anthill or beehive. We gain in freedom when we acknowledge in thought freedom's inner reality and in doing the beautiful its power to relate us to the world of others and to nature. Only by such seeing and responding can we escape the abyss of freedom and glimpse its source. In those rare moments when thought and will coincide do we learn that our individual lives have a ground of their own.

Let me try to make more concrete what is implicit in this idea of "seeing" and "responding" to the beautiful. When an artist or thinker devotes years of his life to the creation of a work that he hopes will be a fitting response to his wonder and delight in existence and to his unease and torment as well, what does this reveal of the ground of freedom? Such a person will answer at once that he feels both compelled by his task and aware that he could abandon the work at any time. This awareness of constraint and contingency are as intimately intertwined as are thinking and willing. A thousand times he may despair at the recalcitrance of the material he seeks to shape in accordance with a more or less clear vision of the completed work. Will it ever be done in halfway satisfactory fashion? A thousand times hope of success in the future will impel him onward, either to begin afresh or transform what already exists. He lives through the days in a complex mood of fear and hope, conscious of the brevity of life and the immense difficulty of every art, *ars longa, vita brevis*. In moments of hope he knows a delight that surpasses everything, for in creating the new, as Plato early discovered, there is a momentary escape from the tyranny of time by the achievement of "deathlessness." Yet this is not the real goal, at least consciously, for the genuine artist or thinker. As the "maker" he becomes ever less central, the work itself ever more so.

In doing the beautiful, if anywhere, the intimate and ultimate dimensions of our brief lives are bound together. Momentarily we attain individuality through awareness that as singular beings we belong to a communal world. As creators we are projected into the not-yet of willing and the has-been of thinking; both become simultaneously present to us. We are constrained to dwell for the time being in both realms. We live "between past and future," as the title of one of Hannah Arendt's books suggests. In our best moments as makers or doers of the beautiful, we escape the one-sidedness of past and future and are not stretched along time's continuum. Nor are we torn by the tension between the poles of the intimate and the ultimate, particularity and communality, because we are engaged in work that is for ourselves and for others at one and the same moment. Then and only then do we realize that our freedom is not without a ground.

However, the brevity of such experiences teaches us all too poignantly that the future is a genuine tense of time, as Hannah Arendt insisted. Against the philosophic tradition she is right in maintaining that thought by itself cannot do justice to the unpredictability and contingency of this future. At least I have been persuaded by her that contingency as sheer spontaneity and utter novelty belongs to our freedom as night belongs to day. Previous philosophy has been only too fond of drawing its substance from memory as the mother of all the Muses, including its own muse. Whatever our strictures against her reflections on the will, they challenge some of us to reexamine our Aristotelian or Kantian conclusions about the relation of freedom to willing.

Moreover, there is something peculiarly contemporary about Hannah Arendt's insistence on the importance of contingency in our lives. Against these happy occurrences I have just mentioned must be weighed the vast number of unintelligible events and blind surds in individual and collective history. Even the happy few, perhaps especially they, know hours and days when the senselessness and futility of life as a whole relativize those moments when thinking and willing are fused in them. The fear that "life is a tale told by an idiot" mocks all our attempts to make sense of the whole of experience, even any considerable segment of it. To reduce this existential dilemma to a problem of evil, as philosophers lamely do, and "solve" it by calling evil a deficient mode of the good is to be woefully out of touch with the living, breathing present. Hannah Arendt's long preoccupation with the life of action was governed by a passion to come to terms with evil in this existential sense. She knew of its intimate association with freedom and with willing, knew that the best and the worst in us spring from the same source.

Did she also suspect that the freedom of the will to initiate the radically new may likewise initiate something utterly destructive? Far from making us mere functionaries, a broken and divided will may unite itself on occasion in denial of existence and in hatred of the beautiful. As the root and ground of the principle of individuation, I believe that the will in isolation from thought can spawn those who are enemies of creation. Occasionally they are not deficient beings, idiosyncratics, but full-fledged individualities whose single-mindedness is directed upon destruction.

In them the natural will to happiness is overpowered by the habitual will to spread misery. Their freedom arises in a monstrous yearning for chaos. Though few of these destroyers achieve historical importance, they continue to appear in every age and in many groups of every nation. I do not wish to imply that an ideal type of such individuals can be made coherent nor do I intend to absolutize the evil any more than I do the good. Instead I believe that the world, not just our human world, contains more than a few surds by which bad chance and blind contingency rule supreme. It lies in the nature of human freedom that some beings can dedicate themselves to these surds. If freedom can make us truly human, it can likewise make us devils—and devils who are not fallen angels. Though most human evil is banal and without ontological roots, being error or sensual greed, lust or weakness of the will, and so on, radical evil is surely as deeply grounded in the nature of human beings as is freedom itself. When we praise freedom as a supreme good, we should not forget this dark possibility that lives within it.

The theological discoverers of the will could cope with this negative side of freedom because they held an absolute faith in God's supremacy in human willing. For an age that no longer accepts man's divine origin and governance, freedom of the will becomes an altogether different matter. In her chapter on Duns Scotus, whom Hannah Arendt praises as the one thinker who was willing to pay the price of freedom by accepting contingency and elevating the will above our reason, I fear she fails to acknowledge sufficiently that God's will was absolute for Scotus. It is one thing to declare an act good because God wills it, another to say with the unbelieving Nietzsche that my willing makes an act good. When Nietzsche later discovered the doctrine of eternal recurrence, he abandoned his notion of the will to power as the substance of reality and fell back into the early Greek teaching of the cyclical nature of time. But here Hannah Arendt was unable to follow him, for she was persuaded of time's linear nature and consequently of the genuinely new in history as in the life of each of us.

She wanted to take over, if I interpret her correctly, certain Judaic and Christian insights into the nature of time, freedom, and the will without their foundation of belief in the reality of a transcendent Being. This led her into an impasse, as she was sufficiently honest to admit. At the end of her lectures she could only point back to Augustine's assertion that freedom is something we are born with and by virtue of this fact we are "doomed" to be free. That such an assertion is opaque and unsatisfactory she was the first to admit, as I have already pointed out. Life itself is not very different, so she frequently remarked to me in moments of discouragement. I believe that her work on judgment would have reunited thinking and willing, which the first two volumes so sharply sundered. The impasse was by no means acknowledged by her as a defeat, only as a challenge.

Yet the difficulty of finding a philosophical ground for our feeling of freedom, a bottom to its abyss, remains for each of us. In the absence of a secure faith in God as originator and sustainer of the will, we are left without a ground of freedom except what thinking in conjunction with willing can supply. Though I am convinced that we can glimpse in the enduring works of *poiesis* a source or origin of our freedom, these epiphanies are fleeting and insufficient to sustain us over the arid stretches in every lifetime. When we seek to give conceptual formulation to these epiphanies we invariably falter. Therefore, freedom remains an abyss over which we construct bridges of various sorts according to our individual talents and the stage of development we have attained at any moment.

W hile pondering Hannah Arendt's pages on freedom of the will, I have been frequently struck by the wide divergence of her conclusions from the heritage of German idealism in which she was reared. Evidently her emigration to America involved much more than a change of residence. For example, in her penultimate chapter on Nietzsche and Heidegger, titled "German Idealism and 'The Rainbow Bridge of Concepts'" she quotes Nietzsche to the effect that German philosophy is the most fundamental form of homesickness. It is dominated throughout by a longing for the ancient Greek world and an era in which man's mind was truly at home in the world. In order to attain this home German thinkers, Nietzsche charged, had built a "rainbow bridge of concepts," a bridge that in her interpretation even Nietzsche himself and later Heidegger also crossed despite their early revolts against it. In a rare moment of personal disclosure she writes in this connection: "I did not want to cross 'the rainbow bridge of concepts' perhaps because I am not homesick enough, at any event because I do not believe in a world, be it a past world or a future world, in which man's mind, equipped for withdrawing from the world of appearances, should or could ever be comfortably at home."

An arresting sentence this, one that sums up her thoughts on the will almost better than any other. It voices on the one hand her enduring rebellion against the mind's tendency to seek peace and serenity in a realm apart from the daily world of spectacle and event in which we are ever immured as singular and communal beings. On the other hand, it implies her independence of the tradition in its assertion that willing, not thinking, should have preeminence in understanding what it means to be a human being. In effect she answers Kant's famous question: What is man? by calling him a being engaged in bringing into existence by an act of will what was never before present. If that will keeps him forever anxious, full of care, making him a question to himself, it likewise distinguishes him from all other creatures in holding so much of his essential being in the future tense of time. To ask oneself in conclusion whether she is right in this assessment of the human condition is to ask how adequately human beings are defined by the will to freedom.

My own response is a somewhat nuanced one. I believe with her that the possession of freedom *is* the distinctive character of human existence. We attain the full human estate to the extent that we are constantly dissatisfied with the measure of freedom we have attained at any given moment. Yet freedom is not for me as exclusively associated with beginnings alone as Hannah Arendt seems to believe. Freedom of the mind rather than the will is not only the capacity to begin something new but also to carry through whatever we have initiated. It is a character of thinking and acting which pervades both throughout their course, sometimes growing and at other times diminishing. Rightly or wrongly, I fall into abstraction when I try to think of freedom apart from such activities. Neither the beginning of an activity nor its end-product seems as likely to be free as the development itself. Once we have reached the solution of a problem or completed a project, restlessness sets in, testifying to the wisdom of her insight into the close relation between life itself and our freedom. Yet beginnings are hardly identical with freedom, either, though they may be a vivid manifestation of its promise. To me freedom's reality lies in our persisting endeavor to accomplish well the tasks that we set for ourselves. Freedom is a constituent of those human activities which aim at a goal other than freedom itself, a goal Hannah Arendt characterized in an earlier essay as the achievement of meaning in our lives through the search for belonging.

In pursuit of that end there is place in my view for homesickness, which seems to be a legitimate emotion on occasion, in any case nearly inescapable for anyone who seeks to make sense of his existence. Perhaps because I am not as alienated from German thought as she, I do not find it either impossible or undesirable to feel at home in the world for however brief a time.

In any event I do not share the Augustinian or contemporary existentialist conviction that our minds are essentially homeless. Instead I prefer to believe in their hidden origin in nature's vast economy. In its unending search for reconciliation of the human spirit with nature and history, German idealism has become on the whole unacceptable to our contemporaries. Still there are those of us who hold that twentieth-century subjectivity must seek a fresh path to reuniting the individual with his fellows and to environing nature. In the search for a new union of the intimate and the ultimate, we can ill afford to neglect either the ancient Greek heritage or the recent German one. The abyss of freedom requires bridges, not only conceptual ones to be sure, if we are ever to understand ourselves aright and begin to claim our historical and natural heritage.

NOTES

1. J. Glenn Gray died before he could see Hannah Arendt's manuscript "On Willing" in print.

2. Citations are from the unpublished manuscript "On Willing," later published as *The Life of the Mind*, Vol. II (New York: Harcourt Brace Jovanovich, 1978).

3. Hannah Arendt, *Between Past and Future* (New York: The Viking Press, 1960), p. 160.

Michael Denneny

THE PRIVILEGE
OF OURSELVES:
HANNAH ARENDT
ON JUDGMENT

After Hannah Arendt's death in December 1975, friends found in her typewriter the title page, with two epigrams, of her projected work on *Judging*, which was to join *Thinking* and *Willing* as the third and final part of *The Life of the Mind.*[1] She had been working on this book—which may turn out to be her magnum opus—since 1961 when she went to Jerusalem to observe the Eichmann trial. To those who had followed her thinking on these matters for so long, there was a strange irony involved. She had first addressed these issues publicly in a course at the University of Chicago in the spring of 1966 entitled "Reconsiderations of Basic Moral Propositions, Socrates to Nietzsche." The course dealt with thinking and willing, the two faculties she found consistently behind the various propositions basic to Western morality. The lectures on thinking (and conscience and consciousness) were brilliantly original and stimulating; those on the will difficult and puzzling. And it became increasingly clear that the heart of the matter lay in judgment. But surprisingly, the discussion of this faculty was constantly postponed and, in the end, it was treated only summarily in the very last lecture.

Something similar seemed to happen over the next decade. The time required to deal with thinking, and especially with willing, expanded vastly beyond Arendt's expectations and occasionally she seemed slightly demoralized by the whole project. The invitation to give the Gifford Lectures, however, presented her with a welcome opportunity to force herself to work out—or at least to write down—her reconsiderations and be done with it. She had delivered the first series on *Thinking* and had written those on *Willing* in draft form, although their delivery was interrupted by a heart attack. When she died she was about to write the first draft of the lectures on *Judging*, due to be given at Aberdeen a few months later, in spring 1976. She seemed confident she could write them out in a couple of months and, after her struggle with the will, judgment would probably have been easy sailing. Unfortunately for us, we have only the two epigrams on the title page and the intent.[2]

Under the circumstances, the two quotations she selected merit close attention. The first, from Cato, was quite familiar; she had used it in a variety of contexts over the years: "The victorious cause pleases the gods but the defeated one pleases Cato." Its meaning for her is fairly clear.[3] Unlike Hegel who would make history (success) the ultimate judgment on action—*"Die Welt-geschichte ist das Weltgericht"*—Cato (and, Arendt insisted, Kant) would give the last word to the judging spectators, for it is they who make an event at home in history or not. Neither success nor naked power determines the significance or grandeur of an event. Only the spectators, who constitute the space of history (memory) into which all actions and works of art fall and thus appear at all, can pass ultimate judgment on an event or action by the quality of their attention. This could be considered the political function of judging; action, the central category in Arendt's political thought, is matched by judgment as the faculty that responds to and evaluates actions.

The second epigram is more unusual; it is from Goethe and it goes as follows:

Könnt' ich Magie von meinem Pfad entfernen,
Die Zaubersprüche ganz und gar verlernen,
Stünd' ich, Natur! vor dir ein Mann allein,
Da wär's der Mühe wert, ein Mensch zu sein.

(Faust, II, 11404-7)

Of course, one cannot interpret this fragment with any certainty regarding Arendt's meaning, yet it does tease us into thought on many levels. These words might best be considered a marker, a sign that judgment is a faculty that goes beyond the political sphere ("ein Mann *allein*"), perhaps even beyond the moral. But any meditation that begins here leaves behind an interpretation of Hannah Arendt's work and starts the process of thinking along with her, treading the paths that she had entered upon but had not the time to follow along, perhaps the most fitting response to her work, certainly the one that would have pleased her most.

I propose to consider first the more limited significance of judgment within the realm of politics and political theory, pointed to by the quotation from Cato, and then turn to wider and more difficult questions suggested by the quotation from Goethe.

"The defeated cause pleases Cato."

With the wisdom of hindsight it is now fairly clear that the whole corpus of Hannah Arendt's political thought can be articulated around two foci: the concept of action and the significance of judgment in the world of opinion.[4] These two interdependent themes reveal the startling—albeit not systematic —internal unity to be found throughout her diverse writings.

Arendt's major endeavor was an attempt at the reconstruction of political thought, which, she argued, had come to an end on the level of theory due to the collapse of the Western tradition in general and had, on the practical level, been drained of significance by the extraordinary political events of the twentieth century, which traditional political theory was simply inadequate to deal with. To this reconstruction her central contribution is her redefinition of the concept of action, for action—its nature, ways, and institutions—is, she argues, the central subject matter of political thought.

With that peculiarly brilliant historical sense she so often displayed, Arendt pinpointed, illuminated, and then rejected the ancient metaphysical interpretation of action, which had attempted to understand the actions of men with the same philosophical categories used to analyze the movements of bodies. She thereby released action from a false identification with motion in general and allowed the phenomenon to emerge in its own shape. By analyzing and tracing to its origin the concept of rule, the center of traditional political thought and loosely analogous to the notion of law governing the movement of bodies, she rediscovered its original elements—initiating and carrying on— which had virtually disappeared under the strained analogy to physical motion. It was then easy for her to display the inadequacy of the concept of rule, as traditionally used, to the phenomena of political life. This entire traditional misconstruction of the nature of action she traced to classical metaphysics with its two-world theory (reality/appearance or Being/Becoming), which naturally distorts, if it does not completely dissolve, the phenomenon of action. From Plato on, all political philosophers—and all political philosophers, she sharply observed, were philosophers first, which turns out to be their major problem—had turned away from the world of motion and the tumultuousness of the public life. When forced to confront the political world, the historical world, the changing world, they were uniformly dismayed by its "melancholy haphazardness" (Kant) and drawn away by the ontological weight and conceptual clarity of the sky of ideas—the eternal, the unchanging, the true.

The net result of Arendt's liberation of political thought from classical metaphysics is that the nature of action as well as its elemental conditions—natality, mortality, and plurality—stand forth in a theoretical clarity they have never possessed before. It might at first seem odd that *political* philosophers, even political *philosophers,* had overlooked such very obvious determinations of the human condition—the fact that men are born, that they die, and that they are many—but then we remember Thales falling into the well and the laughter of the Thracian maid (of course, Thales could make his points too). In any event, from these three facts—natality, mortality, and plurality—one could ultimately spin most of Arendt's political thought and one would be inexorably led to the paramount importance of judgment and opinion.

This indeed went against virtually the entire tradition of political theory, not to speak of philosophy. For classical thought the central faculty in these matters is reason, that part of man which allows him to approach closest to the eternal, motionless— and thus true—realm of Being. For modern thought the central faculty had been the will, which enables man to participate in movement or process, which was now seen as the very substance of reality. Classical philosophy, which found truth only in the immutable, had an obvious difficulty in accounting for action and the world of politics, which, after all, is characterized by movement and change, in Arendtian terms natality and mortality. At first modern philosophy seemed much more adequate, being armed with the dynamic concept of the will. But the will, unfortunately, ran roughshod over the third condition of politics— plurality. The will cannot brook diversity or contradiction; a will that contradicts itself collapses into nonexistence. Already Augustine had seen that to will and to nill simultaneously results in paralysis, that is, the absence of will. When the concept of the will was applied to the political realm, the problem inevitably seemed to be to unify the diversity of wills into one general will—Hobbes's Leviathan or Rousseau's *volonté générale*. And this unity of the will with itself throughout all its members obviously destroys the fact of plurality. The problem of action is solved by creating a new subject that acts—a Leviathan or monster, a general will, a state, a class, a race. Under the concept of the will, the plurality of men shows itself as a multiplicity of self-wills; the diversity of opinion (an opinion is only diversity of opinion or it is nothing) appears as a chaos of self-interest; and judgment is degraded into the calculating handmaiden of selfishness. In short, plurality appears as the war of all against all and the task of politics (and of the political philosopher) is to end this original civil war by abolishing plurality.

It was against this state of affairs in political theory that Arendt attempted to reassert the primacy of judgment and the plurality of opinion. For in the "True Twentieth Century"[5] reality had come to mimic theory in an uncanny way, as Arendt showed so brilliantly in her discussion of Hobbes in *The Origins of Totalitarianism*. Although it may at first have seemed that she came slowly to her new estimate of judgment in her later, post-Eichmann, writings, it seems clear in retrospect that it was there, at least by negative implication, in her early analysis of totalitarianism; the path of thought from her first major book to her last unwritten work now appears as the natural unfolding of the discoveries she made in her investigation of totalitarianism.

Totalitarianism is a frighteningly real version of modern political theory based on the metaphysics of the will. Totalitarianism seeks to abolish the plurality of men, which gives rise to the diversity of opinion, by first atomizing a society by means of terror into utterly discrete units and then melding them into a new, gigantic actor on the stage of history—the race, the proletariat, the party. The individual ceases to stand in his own unique place (thus the need for uprootedness, at least spiritually if not physically, and the constant emphasis on *movement*, not a party but a movement) and he becomes a cog, a cell—essentially a "unit of historical energy"[6] conveying the will of the Leviathan. Since the individual has lost his specific place and become totally "coordinated" to all others, he has lost his unique perspective on the whole, which gives rise to necessarily diverse opinion. With the loss of these specific and unique and multiple perspectives, the world that arises among them, the world we share in common, disappears, for the worldliness of the world derives from the plurality of perspectives just as the three-dimensionality of a physical object arises from our ability to see it from different angles. Since the common world constitutes what we usually call reality (as opposed to our inner life of dreams or any transcendent realm of Being), our sense for reality—common sense or judgment—withers and is replaced by the mechanical logic of one idea, that is, by ideology.

It was in the schoolroom of totalitarianism that Arendt learned that plurality is one of the basic determinations of the human condition; to put it simply, the attempt to abolish plurality renders the human condition monstrous, as was demonstrated once and for all in the concentration camps. If followed to its ultimate extreme, the politics of the will leads to the abolition of the human race through self-destruction—as Dostoevski with his uncanny insight foresaw in *The Possessed,* when Kirilov, unfolding the mad dialectics of the will, proves that it all ends logically in suicide, which is the only true self-creation, the moment when man becomes God. Kirilov's mad logic stands as an eerie foreshadowing of Hitler's eventual Final Solution, which entailed the destruction of all the peoples of the earth with the exception of ten thousand chosen SS men and their wives, who would produce a new race of gods. This insanity and the nightmare visions it has left with us constitute the central fact of the twentieth century, as the French Revolution was the central fact of the nineteenth century. Morally, imaginatively, and intellectually it is our burden and our insight, the revelation of our time.[7] It is immensely to Arendt's credit to have recognized this fact and to have had the sheer courage to do the necessary thing, to fix her mind and her spirit on this phenomenon, to respond according to her ability, which, of course, for her meant to try to understand.

So it was in theoretical recoil from the reality of totalitarianism that Arendt unsystematically disassembled both the modern and ancient metaphysical theories of politics and came to the central role of the faculty of judgment—which can be defined as the capacity to accept the human condition of plurality. While reason requires that I be together with myself in the conscious dialogue called thinking and the will requires that I be identical to myself, only judgment requires that I be together with my fellow men. Arendt insisted that Kant in his *Critique of Judgment* had grounded plurality as no other philosopher had, making the presence of others an *a priori* prerequisite for the very existence and operation of the faculty. "Here Kant viewed man not as a natural being, a member of a species, nor as a transcendent end-in-himself, but as an earthbound creature, living in communities, by no means autonomous, entirely dependent on each other for their mental qualities (for without others one could not think or judge)."[8] In turn, Arendt found judging "one if not the most important activity in which this sharing-the-world-with-others comes to pass,"[9] and tentatively speculated that judgment or taste might well be the paramount faculty for man as a political being.

As Arendt never tired of pointing out, if it is the peculiar lot of men that they neither are simply there like objects, nor easily slip into the scheme of things as do the other animate creatures, but must make their own place, then it is the task of politics to construct and care for this place and to make sure that it is a fitting abode for men. For this task judgment is easily the paramount faculty. Judgment (or taste) Arendt declared, "decides not only how the world is to look but who belongs together in it"[10]—the preeminent question of the political life. Furthermore it does so while honoring the fact of human plurality, itself the expression of natality and mortality.[11] Judgment incorporates plurality into its very operation, both accepting the diversity of men, which caused a common world to spring up between us in the first place, and yet providing the means for the resolution of the conflict inherent in diversity, a means which paradoxically intensifies our experience of diversity *and* commonness simultaneously.[12] By divesting political theory of its reliance on ancient and modern metaphysics, which have collapsed in any event, Arendt has shown that judgment is the central operating principle of the human condition and of any theory of politics that is to be adequate to that condition.

Indeed, it is in these passages on judgment and taste, added almost as an afterthought to "The Crisis in Culture," her contribution to the rather dated discussion of mass culture so popular with intellectuals in the fifties, that one finds her most original contribution to political thought. The sixteen pages that form Part II of the essay are an utterly brilliant and startlingly original meditation on one sentence Thucydides attributed to Pericles. Here we find the distilled essence of what she had learned and what she could contribute to political theory: the necessity, the primacy, the nobility of judgment for the political life. In terms of the tradition, these remarks make a new beginning, but Arendt herself evidently never considered extending them into a systematic account of judgment in the realm of politics. When at last she was prepared to turn her attention to judgment, the context was much vaster than the political realm, encompassing "the life of the mind" and concerned with the entire moral—and perhaps metaphysical—condition of man.

What is for us a new beginning for political thought was for her, perhaps, almost a resting place, theoretically the furthest reach of her political thinking, originally aroused by an anguished recoil from the "True Twentieth Century." It would be possible, and perhaps desirable, for a scholar to work through Arendt's writings and systematically reassemble them from this perspective, showing in detail how it all fits together and thereby giving us a theory of judgment in the realm of politics.[13] Arendt, however, having reached this insight, was content to sketch in the essentials and to point the direction. Her reconstruction of judgment in political life remained a sixteen-page addendum to a minor essay, oddly parallel to the unwritten work on judgment in moral life that she left behind.

". . . *ein Mann allein*"

One suspects that matters might have rested here if Arendt had not gone to Jerusalem to cover the Eichmann trial for *The New Yorker*.[14] Here she received a jolt whose impact was to set the course of her thinking for the next fifteen years, for she realized that this trial "touched upon one of the central moral questions of all time, namely upon the nature and function of human judgment."15 Now the faculty of judgment has received relatively little attention in the Western philosophical tradition. Neither in politics nor in morality has it been considered of paramount importance, usually being considered a minor, subordinate faculty. Aside from Aristotle, Shaftesbury, some men of letters in the Enlightenment, an occasional jurist, and, of course, Kant, it has scarcely been noticed. Certainly it has received nowhere near the intense thought lavished on the faculty of reason or the will. Nevertheless, Arendt became convinced that, as judgment was central to a new theory of politics built around man's capacity for action within the realm of freedom, so the vast moral dilemmas which totalitarianism had brought to the fore revealed with new clarity the central role of judgment in the moral life. Previously she had been concerned with totalitarianism as a political phenomenon, attempting to understand how this huge system of evil had come into being and how it worked. Confronted now by Eichmann, one individual, the deeper and far more disturbing moral implications forced themselves on her attention. Under the impact of totalitarianism, "All the moral norms of behavior in the Western tradition collapsed overnight and it seemed as if the original nature of morals (*mores*—custom, manners) and ethics (*ethos*—custom, habit) had suddenly revealed themselves for what they were—that is, customs or behavior patterns which could be changed as easily as table manners. This arouses our suspicions that morality never was more than that—as if morality was a dream from which we had been suddenly awakened."16

While sitting in Jerusalem watching the strange figure of Eichmann, the entire matter came home to Arendt in its stark simplicity. She found herself asking, "What's wrong with this man? Didn't he have *any* ability to tell right from wrong?"—a question that goes to the heart not only of Western political thought but of our entire moral tradition as well. Certainly Eichmann was not insane. He could function and apply the rules of conduct given him well enough; he was able to exercise what

Kant would call determinative judgment, the ability to subsume the particular under a general concept or rule. What he was incapable of was Kant's reflective judgment. And here Arendt's seizure of part of Kant's esthetic philosophy for morality has enormous implications.

Eichmann's problem, or rather our problem with Eichmann, comes from the fact that he judged according to the rule only too well. In fact, that's all he ever did; he never looked at the particular case in front of him and tried to judge it without a rule. And the rules society gave him to work with were criminal. Traditionally, of course, crime is the individual's failure to live by the rules; in this situation, the rules had failed the individual, the respectable voice of society and the righteous command of the law both urged him toward criminal actions—a state of affairs that baffles our traditional notions of public and private conscience, legality, and the origin of moral feelings. For instance, in court, "Eichmann said he recognized that what he had participated in was perhaps one of the greatest crimes in history, but, he insisted, if he had not done so, his conscience would have bothered him at the time. His conscience and morality were working exactly in reverse. This reversal is precisely the moral collapse that took place in Europe."[17] At the other extreme, Arendt had seen from experience that "those few who were still able to tell right from wrong went really only by their own judgments, and they did so freely; there were no rules to be abided by, under which the particular cases with which they were confronted could be subsumed. They had to decide each instance as it arose, because no rules existed for the unprecedented."[18] And so for Arendt the philosophical question arose: How can the individual judge matters of right and wrong for himself, without reliance on the general code established by society at large? To put it technically, can one judge the particular without reference to a general concept or a universal rule?

In the context of philosophy this is a radical suggestion. Socrates initiated the Western philosophical tradition by pointing out that "yes, we judge this person to be beautiful and that object to be beautiful, but to do so we must have an idea of what beauty is, otherwise we could never know that *this* is beautiful; so then, what is Beauty?" This question (or rather this form of question) shifted the attention of philosophers once and for all from the here and now of particulars to the transcendent realm of ideas (in Nietzsche's terms, from *diesseits* to *jenseits*). It became the accepted assumption of Western thought that the world around us (Becoming) could be understood only through the illumination of a transcendent, intelligible world (Being); that the particular could be understood only by reference to the universal. Arendt, to the contrary, insisted that this two-world theory had collapsed in the nineteenth century and with it the entire Western tradition; a position she argued brilliantly in her studies of Kierkegaard, Nietzsche, and Marx.[19] In this perspective, totalitarianism appears as an example—albeit an extreme instance—of what happens when men are left without any universal concepts or rules (any transcendent ordering) and try to fill the vacuum by means of the will, the only faculty of man that is self-creating, as Duns Scotus pointed out when he said that nothing could cause the will except the will or it would not be will.

It is important to any real understanding of Arendt not to see these matters as only a technical problem of philosophy or as relevant only to the admittedly extreme situation of totalitarianism, when indeed "the chips are down." The basic and urgent assumption behind this entire philosophical discussion is that the field of human interaction—politics and morality—is today without any universal rules or standards. Totalitarianism is situated at the dead center of the "True Twentieth Cenutry" precisely because it illuminates with harsh clarity the essential crisis of our epoch, a crisis easily lost sight of in the less dramatic confusions of our everyday life.

Upon reflection, few would disagree that the loss of any transcendent ordering is the hallmark of our situation today. Those "realities" that previously seemed to stabilize, support, and guarantee human values have strangely lost their power. Formerly this was the function of tradition, concretely the cities of men hedged about by their laws, which were there before the individual was born and which survived his disappearance; more basically of the household of nature, which surrounded, limited, and nourished the cities; and ultimately of God or natural law, which constituted the fundament of an ordered cosmos. Both the cities and nature offered permanence to mortal men and were felt to underwrite the human endeavor, while the Divine Fundament offered the ultimate guarantee of meaningfulness. The city, with its relative permanence and greater generality, transcends the life of the individual; nature with its ever-presence transcends cities, which were founded in time and will eventually disappear; the Divine Fundament of the cosmos transcends the local household of nature on the earth. With each transcendence a new order of reality is placed alongside a previous one, characterized each time by greater lastingness and wider generality; thus each can be used as a source of measure, of value, much as a yardstick is placed alongside an object we wish to measure. The entire Western tradition, it would seem, accepts this structure: that the measure must transcend what is measured, that Becoming can be understood only in the light of Being. Arendt was among the few who recognized that this simple structure, which had previously organized virtually all of Western culture, had broken down, and her sharp insight connected this fact intimately with the phenomenon of totalitarianism.

Today, she argued, we are witnessing the reversal of these relations between the orders of reality. Somehow the mobility and impermanence of the individual life has infected the product of human hands to the point where not only are our use objects increasingly made to be interchangeable and disposable, the cities that house them have been set into motion: within our lifetime and before our eyes we can see them grow and decline, differentiate and transmute themselves almost like living organisms. The rise and fall of Rome was a phenomenon of centuries, but when we argue about the life and death of American cities, we are considering a few decades at most; and the pace of physical change is increasing. Nor does nature any longer offer a reliable framework. Mary McCarthy, in her essay "A Touch of Nature,"[20] has pointed out the uncanny reversal by which our cities—"meant to enclose, and not to expand"[21]—have begun encroaching upon nature. The city no longer stands as a bulwark and shelter against the forces of nature; rather we now try to protect what is left of nature from the forces that men have unleashed. We fence it in, zone it as national parks, hire policemen to protect it, and enact laws against pollution. Our unnaturally living cities paradoxically threaten the decay of nature—a reversal Nietzsche recognized when he said, "the wasteland grows"—and tomorrow we may find ourselves visiting the ruins of nature as today we visit the ruins of Rome. On a deeper level we have astonishingly reversed the most basic relations of life and death. With the modern weapons of war, the pollution released into the environment, and massive ecological intervention, we have for the first time brought the threat of death to the *household* of nature itself, as opposed to its individual inhabitants. In the realm of nature death was not an irrevocable ending, but a phase promising rebirth in the sempiternal cycle of life everlasting. The *possibility* of destroying all life, of terminating nature, has radical consequences; whether it is ever actualized, the existence of this possibility,[22] whose reality today no one can sensibly deny, has altered the human condition far beyond any Copernican reversal and will be as vast in its impact as the shift from hunting and gathering to agriculture and urbanization in terms of its ultimate consequences. It is absurd only on the surface to say that nature is now no more than an outworn cultural tradition—like grand opera—bereft of its own power and dependent on the fickle benevolence of humanity for its continued existence.

It is surprising that the theologians have not been more alert to this change in our situation. One would have expected that Christian thinkers, who, after all, believe in a Creator God, would have been the first to raise the hue and cry over endangered species, for when the last dodo bird disappeared from the face of the earth, the Creation—the handiwork of God—was altered *irrevocably* by the actions of men. This ultimate irrevocability is an utterly new dimension of human action. The possibility that the actions of men could now lead to the destruction of all life on the earth means that man has now come into a power previously thought to be restricted to God, a power of destruction equivalent in extent (for all practical purposes) to the power of creation. Previous generations could imagine God destroying the world through water or fire; it is for us to imagine this desolation caused *inadvertently* by the ignorance or foolishness of men. Whether God is dead as Nietzsche proclaimed or has simply withdrawn from man as Heidegger would have it, is unclear; what *is* clear is that the Divine Fundament, upon which all traditional moral authority rested, simply lost its relevance when it lost its exclusive power. Today neither the city, nor tradition, nor nature, nor the Divine Fundament of the cosmos offers a firm ground and measure for human action.

In this situation it is understandable that the will has emerged as the only faculty of man that is self-creating (the *will* wills to will or it doesn't exist) and rests on no ground outside itself (for if there is a cause of the will other than the will it isn't will). But politically the will leads to totalitarianism and morally to an existential "ethics" in which value rests on no "ground" nor is derived from any higher "source" but is freely posited or asserted over the abyss—in other words, the product of the will. In this case one may say to a Hitler, "I will kill you (to assert my values)," but not, "You are wrong." "This I refuse to believe," said Hans Jonas in a profound essay on these matters and Arendt clearly shared his position. In the end, an existential "ethics" based on the will boils down to "might makes right," which simply means there is no such thing as right. It is impossible that anyone who forces his imagination to contemplate "the gassed and burnt children of Auschwitz, the defaced, dehumanized phantoms of the camps,"[23] cannot but believe that this is wrong. Not that if it were in our power we would not allow such things to happen—an irrelevant consideration for they were not in our power and they did happen and it was quite possible that Hitler could have won the war and gotten away with it—but that these things were basically, fundamentally wrong, that ethics are not simply a matter of table manners that can be changed at will, that morality is not just a dream from which we have been awakened in our times but that our times are a nightmare from which we need to awake.

Thus the real dimensions of the "True Twentieth Century" begin to emerge as Arendt perceived them, concentrated with blinding clarity in the phenomenon of totalitarianism that stands not as an aberration but as the true focal point of the human condition today. Stripped of the stabilizing support of his cities and tradition, of nature, of the Divine Fundament, man "stands alone" in the midst of a wasteland, a moral vacuum, that grew as his power grew. No longer sure of the distinction between right and wrong but with his power increased beyond measure, man confronts today the ultimate *moral* crisis of his career on earth.

". . . *ein Mensch zu sein.*"

In this situation judgment offers the only alternative to the will as a means of solving "the problem of man's self-orientation; that is, the task of making oneself at home in existence without fixed points of support," which according to Auerbach was the pressing necessity first felt at the very beginning of the modern age by Montaigne.[24] Our basic values are no longer underwritten by any "transcendent" reality and we find ourselves in much the same position as those writers of the seventeenth and eighteenth centuries who first developed and explored the notion of judgment and taste, which Kant then translated into conceptual terms and systematized in the *Critique of Judgment*. These men were confronted with a similarly sudden collapse of "values," although in their case, while they were ultimately interested in ethics, the discussion tended to center around that other field of value, esthetics.

The root of the problem can be traced back to the precise moment the modern age began, when the telescope first revealed the scandalous optical illusion of millennia and men felt they could no longer trust their senses. In the most momentous philosophical act of the modern age, Galileo distinguished the primary qualities (objective, in-themselves, real) from the secondary qualities (subjective, for-us, illusory). The former— length, weight, velocity, and all qualities suited to objective, mathematical measurement—inhere in the objects themselves. The latter—color, smell, taste, etc.—being the accidental results of our peculiarly human modes of perception, exist only for us. This epistemological/ontological dichotomy, expressed most program- matically in Descartes's division of reality into *res extensa* and *res cogitans*, became so deep and extensive as to virtually constitute the grain of modern thought. Such division of Being into objective and subjective was to have momentous consequences, the first and most obvious of which was the suddenly problematic nature of value, whether in esthetics or ethics. As far as I know, little notice has been taken of the fact that these two suddenly became separate and major fields of philosophical enquiry, whereas traditionally they had tended to be subordinate disciplines, tightly integrated into general philosophical thought. Nor as far as I know has anyone commented—perhaps because of its obviousness—on the startlingly low quality of thought in both these fields for the last four centuries. While modern philosophy can point to profound masterpieces in the fields of ontology, social theory, epistemology (especially), and other branches of philosophy, the quality of even the best discourse in ethics and esthetics has been abysmal, a tedious and surprisingly shallow oscillation between theories of objectivity and subjectivity, the rational and the sentimental, the ruled and the arbitrary, etc. Since these two fields comprise the area where human values are at stake, this is a notable development.

From the beginning those thinkers who developed the theory of taste or judgment were in opposition to the subjective/objective dichotomy which has ruled modern thought and which, in the final analysis, makes the existence of value not only problematic but impossible. To put it crudely but quite adequately, this dichotomy means within the field of esthetics that beauty is either in the eye of the beholder (in which case, such a thing as *beauty* doesn't exist and we are left with only subjective preference), or it subsists in the object (either as an element or a pattern of elements) and yet has completely and mysteriously eluded our most intense scrutiny, although it is in full view and instantly recognizable. Those writers who rejected this sterile dichotomy developed the notion of taste—one of the few faculties of man whose discovery can be dated with historical precision: the word was coined by the Spanish Jesuit Baltasar Gracián in the early seventeenth century— as a faculty that perceived realities that were neither subjective nor objective. Here is not the place to trace the development of that tradition, initiated by Gracián and most fruitfully developed by Shaftesbury, whose thought has startling and profound affinities with that of Arendt. Let it suffice to say that this century-and-a-half-long discussion was absorbed and translated into conceptual terms by Kant in his *Critique of Judgment,* which remains the clearest exposition of these notions (although Shaftesbury is perhaps the richer and more profound thinker on this subject, precisely because of his remoteness from professional philosophy).

The question before us is how the individual can judge questions of value (in the present discussion, beauty) if it is neither an objective fact nor a subjective assertion, that is, if he is not to rely on any objective rule recognized by society (remembering how badly such rules had failed the Eichmanns of this century) and if the assertion, "This is beautiful," is to have more meaning than merely subjective preference (so that we may say of the crimes of this century, "This is wrong."). To put it philosophically, can one judge the particular without reference to a general concept or universal rule, and can that judgment have any validity beyond the judging subject, that is for others?

This, Kant asserted, is indeed the case and the faculty for such judgments he termed reflective judgment, to distinguish it from determinative judgment, in which we have the concept and merely place the particular under it. Reflective judgment comes to the fore most readily in the field of esthetics. When something appears to us we can say, "This is beautiful," or, "This is ugly," even though we do not have any absolute rule that tells us what makes a beautiful object and even though we don't have a worked-out definition of beauty. If Kant had been an Englishman he might have noticed that the same sort of reflective judgment seems to work in the common-law tradition, where a jury pronounces in each given case what is just, though clearly nobody has an idea of what *justice* is; and furthermore, a sense for justice develops through case precedents much as a taste for beauty develops through the appreciation of exemplary models of artistic excellence.

We cannot, obviously, say of something, "This is a trapezoid," if we don't have any idea of what a trapezoid is. But already at the beginning of philosophy Socrates had been puzzled by our ability to say, "This is beautiful," when, upon examination, it became quite apparent that we don't know what *beauty* is. Unfortunately Socrates, and following him the entire Western philosophical tradition, overlooked a very simple fact: the fact that it *is* a fact that we *can* and *do* make judgments and that, all things considered, there is a surprising amount of agreement about such judgments. The average Greek may not have known what beauty was but he knew a beautiful youth when he saw one and he recognized beautiful poetry when he heard it. Upon such general agreement the canon of Western culture—the classics—has been based and over twenty-five centuries there has been vastly more agreement than disagreement about it. It seems a curious quirk of our philosophers that, being unable to offer a suitable explanation of how something could be the case, they tend to disregard the overwhelmingly significant fact that it *is* the case—oddly parallel to the tendency in philosophical ethics that allows one, having proved that evil is conceptually impossible or theft a contradiction in terms, to disregard the fact that people continue to go around murdering and robbing each other.

When Kant investigated this curious faculty of esthetic (reflective) judgment, he found it worked in the following way. Some object appears to us. We do not, when judging esthetically, refer it to an objective concept but rather to our self and our feelings: we say, "This pleases me," or "This displeases me." This feeling of pleasure/displeasure normally accompanies all appearance; it is parallel to the "I think" that accompanies all our conscious mental operations. It would be difficult to imagine an appearance not calling forth at least this minimal feeling response; difficult but not impossible, as we see in the example of a man who has no taste whatsoever, a man who eats alone every night and gets so he doesn't even notice what he is eating, a very lonely man. Normally, however, we can say of anything that appears to us that it pleases us or it doesn't. Of itself, this subjective statement makes no demand on the opinion of anyone else.

However, when we say of something, "This is beautiful," we not only mean that it pleases us but that it will please others too, or that it ought to please others. What right do we have to make such a claim? According to Kant, what changes this *dokei moi*, the subjective "it seems to me," to a judgment of taste is our ability to look at the same thing from the perspective of other people. We do not judge as they might judge; our judgments are not identical with their judgments (which would be empathy), but we judge from their point of view. By the utterly mysterious power of the imagination, that strange ability to make present what is absent and to make ourselves absent from our immediate presence and present to some absent perspective, we are able to put ourselves in the other's position and see, not as he sees, but how it looks to us from his point of view. In this way we free ourselves from the subjective constraints inherent in the fact that as unique individuals we are always situated in some utterly specific spot, and while we do not flip ourselves out of the subjective plane into some altogether universal, objective realm, we do lose enough of our inherent partiality to be able to judge impartially (though not "objectively") for all judging persons.

If this object pleases me independently of my particular subjective situation, it ought to please the other independently of his particular subjective situation: thus, the validity of an esthetic judgment Kant called general, as opposed to universal (i.e., objective) validity. Without losing the *human* perspective altogether, we transcend the subjective and assert that impartially seen it *is* beautiful. This type of statement cannot be demonstrated; we cannot coerce the minds of other men into agreement by the force of logic or the power of reason, and in this sense there is no arguing about taste. We can only "woo their consent" as Kant put it; that is, encourage others to make the same imaginative leap, to view the phenomenon from the various perspectives of their fellow men. And in this sense, of course, there is no end to arguing about taste and the essence of that talk is precisely, as Boileau, the originator of modern criticism, understood so well, Kant's "wooing," the attempt to persuade others to see as we see and share our values. In this context, we might be tempted to say that the appreciation and judgment of beauty not only presupposes the plurality of men but that the activity it gives rise to, critical discourse, concretely articulates and celebrates that plurality.

Behind this discussion stands a notion that beauty could exist neither in the eye of the beholder nor as an objective quality embedded in the object. Rather beauty is seen as a quality of the *relation* that exists between the beholder and what appears to him, a peculiarly pleasing and life-enhancing quality these writers sought to promote by improving the taste of men, that is, by sharing the disinterested pleasure they felt. Of course, the urge behind this is the desire to share our world with our fellow men—and the emphasis is on *our* world, not the objective world, not the rational world, but the world as experienced from the human, though not the subjective, perspective. And it is only in the human world that we belong and neither in the rational world where, as Aristotle perceived, we only tarry for a while, nor in the objective world whose cold immensities chilled Pascal. Only the human world can offer men an abiding home.

The relevance of these ideas of beauty and of the nature of

value to morality and politics is obvious. Although Kant withheld questions of right and wrong from the sphere of reflective (esthetic) judgment—moral judgments being rationally compelling for him—Arendt herself was convinced that in doing so he had made a major mistake.[25] The phenomenon of totalitarianism has taught us that justice, for instance, can no longer be conceived as subjectively grounded in the assertion of the will, a culturally specific pattern of behavior that can be changed "as easily as table manners" whenever some dictator gains total control of the implements of violence and communications, nor as the tracing out of some mythical natural law that is peculiarly impotent in the face of criminal "transgressions." Justice can be conceived—and defended—as a certain quality or modality of the relations between men, a quality we want to defend and enhance for we wish to live with each other on the basis of equality and respect. We may wish to live this way or we may not; nothing beyond ourselves forces us to or helps us to. But if we wish to avoid the will,[26] with its ultimately murderous dialectic, as the only source of value, then the faculty of taste (judgment), which attunes us to relations between men and between men and appearance, does indeed offer us a means of "making ourselves at home in existence without fixed points of support."

In a world denuded of any transcendent realm, which seems to be our situation today, the curious faculty of judgment would appear to be the only source of value that respects the nature of the human condition. The will seems unable ever to escape its absolute particularity and singularity and would tend to abolish the fact of plurality and diversity; one may even suspect, along with Nietzsche, that it reacts with abhorrence to the fact of natality and mortality, the ultimate limits imposed by the fact that the human condition is "given" to us and not self-created. Judgment alone can find standards—from the old German words *stehen* and *ort*, a standing place—around which we can rally and for which we strive that they may prevail. It is our great misfortune that Hannah Arendt did not live to explore these matters and it is our great fortune that she pointed the way.

Postscript: The Privilege of Ourselves

Although one may agree with Bernard Crick's recent assessment of Arendt: "Rereading her, I am convinced that even yet her stature has been underestimated. There is a view of political and social man just as comprehensive as those of Hobbes, Hegel, Mill, and Marx; and, to my mind, one far more flattering to humanity"[27]—it is probably unnecessary and certainly too early to try to judge the relative value of her contribution to political and philosophical thought. To my mind, her investigation of judgment will be her preeminent contribution to political and moral philosophy, establishing as it does a wholly new point of departure for thinking about these matters, one that breaks from virtually the entire Western tradition since Plato; while her greatest achievement of the spirit will remain *The Origins of Totalitarianism*, in Crick's judicious words, ". . . her greatest, but most pell-mell and least philosophical work."[28] But it might also be worthwhile to consider not only the specific theoretical content but also the source and peculiar quality of her work, that unique blend of erudition, passion, intellect, and writing that makes the ways she applied her mind appear so illuminating and relevant, when the more conventional brands of scholarship and intellectual activity so often seem to have lost touch with the times and therewith their claim to be a subject of serious intellectual and cultural interest to those not professionally engaged in them.

It is somehow fitting that the most important legacy Arendt left to us deals with the matters of judgment, taste, and common sense. Those lucky enough to have known her were often struck by the vigor with which she exercised these faculties, though it usually took some time to realize that this enormously powerful theoretical mind was directed by a shrewd, down-to-earth common sense—an extraordinarily rare combination. Shaftesbury was convinced that the faculty of taste, developed and exercised, resulted in the gift of "the privilege of ourselves," a striking formulation for a man so intimately aware of the nuances of Latin.

For privilege comes from the Latin words *privus* (single, one's own) and *lex* (law), as if there could be a "law for one," a law that addresses itself to the single person and the unique set of circumstances, rather than to the abstract generality of mankind and circumstance. In a similar vein Hans Jonas once made a most accurate characterization of Arendt when he declared, at the end of hours of conversation, out of a friendship that went back nearly half a century, and not without some exasperation, "Ja, she is such a *sovereign* creature!"

This quality of "sovereignty," which shone forth so clearly in her person and in her works, makes clear that she fully enjoyed "the privilege of herself" to an uncommon degree, as if she had discovered that peculiar "law" that applied only to the single case and steadfastly held to it. And this thought brings to mind Arendt's oft-repeated elucidation of the Greek concept of happiness: *eudaimonia*, she explained, had nothing to do with a subjective feeling or state of the self, it was properly understood as the well-being (*eu*) of one's *daimon*, that power controlling the destiny of the individual which she identified as the "who" we are, as opposed to any "what" we might be. This "*daimon* who accompanies each man throughout life, who is his distinct identity" cannot be seen by the individual himself; as if it peeked out from over his shoulder, it "appears and is visible only to others."[29] Such *eudaimonia* has perhaps many possible sources, but Sophocles, in a favorite passage of Arendt's, suggested one that seems apt in her case. The last chorus of the *Antigone*, rendered freely as Arendt once did in conversation, though not as far as I know in any published work, would go:

> *Our happiness* [eudaimonia] *depends*
> *On wisdom all the way.*
> *The gods must have their due.*
> *Great words by the proudly confident*
> *Answering back the hammer-blows of Fortune*
> *Bring wisdom, finally, in the end.*

Arendt's understanding was startlingly different from the normal reading of this passage and from our usual ideas about wisdom.[30]

Wisdom, she suggested, was not somehow there, internally, and then expressed in great words; rather the words came first, as a pure *action,* a courageous response and measuring up to the disasters of fate with the most profoundly human resource man has, language. As the doer of great deeds makes nobility manifest in the world, so that probably all our values and standards ultimately derive from the individual and remembered acts of heroes and saints, so the sayer of great words makes wisdom manifest. This, of course, stands on its head our everyday notion of wisdom, the vague idea of a sage who considers his words carefully before speaking. Sophocles, Arendt insisted, was suggesting that the speaking itself must have greatness—must be raised to its highest innate excellence, its particular *virtù*—then the words so spoken would give us food for thought, and meditation upon them could bring wisdom. For this greatness of speech, the preeminent requirement would be courage, which Churchill once called the "premier virtue for it alone can guarantee all the others,"[31] the courage to answer back the blows of Fortune with words that match them. This response with words—for which one must mobilize *both* the intellect and the spirit—is a peculiarly human form of assuming responsibility. Etymologically speaking, which no doubt would please Arendt, the word *responsibility* has three distinct but tightly connected elements of meaning: to declare the presence of that which is present; to declare oneself present; and to declare a bond between oneself and that which is present to one. In common language we may say to face the facts and to stand up and be counted, which together mean to respond to the facts, to declare ourselves in regard to them. That this was Arendt's own understanding of what she was doing is clear from an essay she wrote after finishing *The Origins,* which ends with the words, "If we want to be at home on this earth, even at the price of being at home in this century, we must try to take part in the interminable dialogue with its essence."[32] What this requires is stated in one of the rare "methodological" comments—always significant and usually overlooked by academic readers—Arendt made in the preface to the first edition of *The Origins of Totalitarianism*:

> The conviction that everything that happens on earth must be comprehensible to man can lead to interpreting history by commonplaces. Comprehension does not mean denying the outrageous, deducing the unprecedented from precedents, or explaining phenomena by such analogies and generalizations that the impact of reality and the shock of experience are no longer felt. It means, rather, examining and bearing consciously the burden which our century has placed on us—neither denying its existence, nor submitting meekly to its weight. Comprehension, in short, means the unpremeditated, attentive facing up to, and resisting of reality—whatever it may be.[33]

The Origins of Totalitarianism will probably stand as her greatest work because it is—however pell-mell—an act of astonishing intellectual courage and moral responsibility, an act not of a professional working in her field but of a person answering back the great hammer-blows of Fortune. For this act of intellectual courage she was amply rewarded, for it opened all the many avenues her thought was later to take. For us, in quieter though no less ominous times, it should serve as a reminder of what intellectual activity is all about.

NOTES

1. This piece of information was given to me by her assistant, Jerome Kohn.

2. This calls to mind a comment Kafka makes in his diary: "Moses failed to reach Canaan not because his life was too short, but because it was a human life."

3. Here I am following my own notes from a lecture Arendt gave at Chicago, in February 1971, on Kant's *Critique of Judgment*. She introduced the quotation from Cato in this form and proceeded to explicate it in these terms.

4. This section owes much to Ernst Vollrath's paper, "Hannah Arendt on Judgment and Opinion," which was delivered at the Conference on the Work of Hannah Arendt at York University, Toronto, in 1972; it began as my comment and response to that paper, delivered at the same conference. I would now amend my assertion about the internal unity of Arendt's thought (around action and judgment), having read Ron H. Feldman's brilliantly original and convincing essay, "The Jew as Pariah: The Case of Hannah Arendt," the introduction to his collection of Arendt's essays on Jewish themes, *The Jew as Pariah: Jewish Identity and Politics in the Modern Age* (New York: Grove Press, 1978), which shows that this philosophical position is even more fundamentally grounded in Arendt's early reflections on her own concrete position as a Jew in the modern age.

5. This is the phrase used by the Russian poet Anna Akhmatova to distinguish the essential reality of our age from accidental facts; it manifested itself to her in the Stalinist terror.

6. This phrase is from Harold Rosenberg's essay on Eichmann, "Guilt to the Vanishing Point," in his *Act and the Actor: Making the Self* (New York: The World Publishing Company, 1970). See also his essay on the Communist Party as historical agent, "The Anthropologist's Stone," in *Discovering the Present* (Chicago: The University of Chicago Press, 1973). In fact, virtually *all* of Rosenberg's work—the art criticism as well as the general essays on society, literature, and politics—is of enormous relevance to anyone interested in Arendt's thought, for the thread that runs through everything he writes like "an obsession [is] the identity of an actor, individual or collective, sham or genuine, forming itself through acts" (Preface to *Act and the Actor*, p. xxi). He and Arendt are the most important contemporary thinkers on the nature of action and, although they were great friends personally, I'm not aware that anyone has pointed out their unique convergence, from different perspectives, on this one theme.

7. Such language easily makes one self-conscious but in this instance it seems called for. It might be pointed out that "the burden of our times" was the "morally apt if uninformative title" (Bernard Crick) of the first English edition of *The Origins of Totalitarianism*.

8. This is taken from my own notes of Arendt's course on Kant's *Critique of Judgment*, given at the University of Chicago in February 1971.

9. Arendt, *Between Past and Future* (New York: The Viking Press, 1968), p. 221.

10. Arendt, "The Crisis in Culture," in *Between Past and Future*, p. 223.

11. Arendt distinguished human plurality from the sheerly numerical multiplicity of the other animal species, which she conceived, perhaps unfairly, as mere replicas whose identity lay with their species-being (*Gattungswesen*) rather than in their individuality—carbon copies as opposed to individuals. Similarly birth and death had a different reality for humans—the beginning of something new and a final ending—than they could have for other animals, in this view.

12. Politically, of course, the institutionalization of judgment, and consequently plurality, is the republic, which Arendt articulates in great detail in *On Revolution*. In esthetic matters, it would be the theory of taste, its ideal practical form, the Republic of Letters. How Arendt would have dealt with these matters in the moral realm in her unwritten book on judging is much more difficult to conceive.

13. Something like this has been attempted by Ernst Vollrath in *Die Rekonstruktion der Politischen Urteilskraft* (Stuttgart: Ernst Klett Verlag, 1977), dedicated to Arendt.

14. One very strong reason for believing this is the odd existence of the essay, "Understanding and Politics," which she published in the *Partisan Review*, Vol. xx, no. 4 (July–August 1953), pp. 277–92. In many ways this essay anticipates the major themes of the first volume of *The Life of the Mind: Thinking,* which was not to appear until 1978, twenty-five years later. She remained utterly dissatisfied with the essay and even appeared to be somewhat embarrassed about it, saying once in conversation that she had "bitten off more than I could chew and was quite out of my depth" and she resisted attempts to convince her to republish it in book form in one of the collections of essays. Not until after the Eichmann trial did she return to these themes.

15. Arendt, *Eichmann in Jerusalem* (New York: The Viking Press, 1964), p. 294.

16. From my own notes of Arendt's lecture course at the University of Chicago, "Reconsiderations of Basic Moral Propositions," in Spring 1966.

17. Ibid.

18. Arendt, *Eichmann in Jerusalem*, p. 295.

19. Arendt, *Between Past and Future*, "Tradition and the Modern Age," p. 17.

20. Mary McCarthy, "A Touch of Nature," *The Writing on the Wall* (New York: Harcourt Brace Jovanovich, 1971), p. 173.

21. Hans Jonas, *Philosophical Essays* (Englewood Cliffs, N.J.: Prentice-Hall, Inc., 1974), p. 5.

22. For the philosophical distinction between possibility and actuality on the one hand and reality (and necessity) on the other, see Kierkegaard's *Philosophical Fragments,* the section "Coming into Existence" (Princeton:

Princeton University Press, 1962), p. 90. Possibilities can be either real or unreal and real possibilities—the fact that a wealthy farmer may disinherit his son—can be the decisive *reality* of a situation, whether that possibility is ever *actualized* or not.

23. This quotation and the following one are from Hans Jonas's essay, "Immortality and the Modern Temper," *The Phenomenon of Life* (New York: Harper and Row, 1966), p. 270. The essay, which Jonas describes as a "groping journey," is dedicated to Arendt and shows one of the most profoundly metaphysical minds now at work grappling with the same issues of action and value that preoccupied Arendt. As with Rosenberg, they were great personal friends and Jonas's work is enormously illuminating to a reader of Arendt, not least because it makes startlingly clear—this essay is almost a case study of it—the powerful *moral* attraction of the two-world theory of traditional metaphysics. In his later work, especially in *Philosophical Essays,* Jonas may have gone beyond Arendt, whose recognition in the preface to *The Human Condition* that what she is about to describe is a state of affairs that has already passed away, was oddly without consequence in much of her later work —although she had been heard to say that her basic mistake in writing *The Human Condition* was to consider the determinants of the *vita activa* from the perspective of the *vita contemplativa,* when the latter, based on the transcendent realm of the traditional two-world theory, had already collapsed. Jonas recognizes that "all previous ethics—whether in the form of issuing direct enjoinders to do and not to do certain things, or in the form of defining principles for such enjoinders, or in the form of establishing the ground of obligation for obeying such principles—had these interconnected tacit premises in common: that the human condition, determined by the nature of man and the nature of things, was given once for all; that the human good on that basis was readily determinable; and that the range of human action and therefore responsibility was narrowly circumscribed . . . these premises no longer hold." He goes on to contend that "with certain developments of our powers"—for instance, the fact that today "Nature [is] a human responsibility . . . surely a *novum* to be pondered in ethical theory"—*"the nature of human action* has changed" and that "the changed nature of human action changes the very nature of politics." (See pp. 1, 9, and 12 of "Technology and Responsibility: Reflections on the New Tasks of Ethics," *Philosophical Essays,* (Englewood Cliffs, N.J.: Prentice-Hall, Inc., 1974).

24. Erich Auerbach, *Mimesis,* tr. by W. R. Trask (Princeton: Princeton University Press, 1974), p. 311.

25. From my own notes of Arendt's course on Kant's *Critique of Judgment,* given at Chicago in February 1971.

26. I realize that here—and in many other places in this essay—I have grossly simplified matters and have glided over many difficulties. It is not

sensible to simply reject the modern metaphysics of the will in favor of judgment and let it go at that. Arendt rejected classical metaphysics with its two-world theory but, as her essay on "Thinking and Moral Considerations" made clear, she understood that there was a valid experiential ground for this viewpoint—the relation of the invisible to the visible and the experience of thinking. The collapse of the old account of these matters not only lets the original phenomenon show up more clearly but also urges us to try to give a new account. Now the metaphysics of the will has guided the thinking of our philosophers for the last three centuries. There must be some experiential ground for this; philosophers may be silly, but they're not that silly. If we demolish will to make room for judgment, we should also look at the concrete ground that led to the theories of the will as well as at the relation between the will and judgment. These matters are extremely difficult and perhaps the second volume of Arendt's *Life of the Mind* (on the will) will shed some light on the subject.

27. Bernard Crick, "On Rereading *The Origins of Totalitarianism*," in this volume, p. 44.

28. Ibid., p. 43.

29. Arendt, *The Human Condition* (Chicago: University of Chicago Press, 1958), p. 193.

30. The conventional translation of this passage reads:

> *Our happiness depends*
> *on wisdom all the way.*
> *The gods must have their due.*
> *Great words by men of pride*
> *bring greater blows upon them.*
> *So wisdom comes to the old.*

So it is rendered by Elizabeth Wyckoff in *The Complete Greek Tragedies*, David Grene and Richmond Lattimore, eds. (Chicago: University of Chicago Press, 1959), Vol. II, p. 204. This conventional translation reduces the closing words of the *Antigone* to a rather trite Greek moralism, of little interest to anyone. Grammatically the original Greek could bear Arendt's reading, a reading which could be further supported by an examination of Sophocles's other work.

31. This is a quotation that Arendt often used in conversation.

32. Arendt, "Understanding and Politics," p. 292.

33. Arendt, "Preface to the First Edition," *The Origins of Totalitarianism* (New York: Harcourt, Brace & World, Inc., 1966), p. xxx.

Melvyn A. Hill

THE FICTIONS OF MANKIND AND THE STORIES OF MEN

> . . . in the paradoxical situation of the first human be-
> ing, as it were—she was compelled to grasp everything
> for herself as if encountering it for the first time.
>
> Hannah Arendt
> Rahel Varnhagen

Hannah Arendt distinguished her own view of political thinking from the two major contemporary versions of political science in which the study of politics is either modeled after natural science, which reduces the political actions of men to a set of laws that render political behavior predictable, or regarded as a branch of economics that investigates the competing material interests that motivate political rule or social revolution. When she addressed the American Political Science Association in 1960, she invoked a method of understanding politics that must have sounded alien to her professional audience. She said:

> The common and the ordinary must remain our primary concern, the daily food of our thought—if only because it is from them that the uncommon and the extraordinary emerge, and not from matters that are difficult and sophisticated.[1]

"Difficult and sophisticated" are, of course, the methods of a behavioral political science or of a political economy insofar as they proceed from their respective definitions of science and of its proper methods, thereby erecting an elaborate and abstract intellectual apparatus that is placed in between the scientist and "the common and the ordinary" phenomena in the world that constitute the object of his investigation. If his thinking therefore comes between him and the real events of the political world— "the common and the ordinary"—it also prevents him from recognizing and understanding "the uncommon and the extraordinary" events when, in fact, they occur. For these too are reduced to the statistical mean of behavior, or they are cast adrift on the tides of dialectic.

Hannah Arendt's concern with politics as a thinker was provoked by the uncommon and extraordinary rise of totalitarianism in her native Germany and this calamitous event became the test of her understanding. To her mind the only way to approach a form of government—the criminal, totalitarian state—the likes of which had never before appeared in the world, and which defied the political science of her time, was to rethink the way we look at politics in the hope of finding a political science whose premises and methods would clarify rather than obscure what was for her the crucial political phenomenon of her times. In doing so she found that the view of politics underlying behavioral political science and political economy was at least a negative contributing factor in the rise of European totalitarianism—in the sense that they helped to prevent the ordinary citizens from understanding what was happening in their world, thereby depriving them of the kind of perspective on politics that facilitates the political action of citizens, instead of inhibiting it with reductive assumptions about their capacity for action.

Arendt aimed at a way of thinking about politics that remained faithful to this capacity for action among citizens— whether it is at play in a particular event, or at risk—not out of a romantic allegiance to political participation for its own sake, but for a set of reasons that are fundamentally linked. Unless one realizes that the meaning of politics arises from the fact that the political world gives men the chance to manifest their capacity for action by coming together and thereby creating political power, one cannot understand that the meaning of totalitarianism was to destroy this political world, make it impossible for men to act as citizens and impossible, therefore, for them to create any political power—all this while pretending to save the political realm and the citizens by instituting a transcendent world order.

Arendt, thus, took as her point of departure and her method as a political thinker not the sophistications of behavioral science nor of Marxist dialectics, but simply the perspective of the citizen who views the political world as the realm of freedom needed in order to act with others in matters of common concern. She attributed to ordinary citizens a common concern with the well-being of the world in which, for better or worse, they live together. And she addressed her audience, or her readers, in this capacity—as citizens. For it was the thinking of citizens—how they perceive and understand what happens in the world—that she considered critical to political action; critical, indeed, to the question of whether the freedom to act would survive in our century. She believed that the professional concern of political scientists should be the experience of citizens. And she had the old-fashioned idea that one cannot hope to control or direct political events with the aid of a theory that promised some method of prediction. She believed, on the contrary, that the uncertain and the contingent in human affairs inhered in the condition of freedom, and that any attempt to negate their reality provided the basis not for a science but for a fiction that could well provide a plan of action, but would draw people further away from political reality as it was put into effect. She believed, instead, that when we are able to remember and communicate our political experience—so that its meaning is revealed and, in turn, reveals some aspect of the world —we have, indeed, mastered it. And she traced this procedure of mastery through imagining and recounting events to our capacity to tell stories. For her, the stories that citizens tell are the source and remain the touchstone of political thinking.

Arendt devoted many years of work to sharing her understanding of what she took to be the two greatest threats to freedom

in our time: totalitarianism and the "rule by nobody" of bureaucratic government. But she did not believe that it was up to her as
a political thinker to save the political world from them. She always thought that it was up to the citizens. And she wrote for the
citizens—not as a theorist whose perspective transcends the common and ordinary experience of the world, but as one who shared
their concern with the well-being of the world and who, like so
many others, had been overwhelmed by the uncommon and extraordinary events that Brecht had called "the dark times."

Fictions

Hannah Arendt argued that bourgeois politics and its outcome, imperialism, prepared the way for the rise of totalitarianism. Her point of departure was the bourgeois fiction of "tradition." Since the bourgeoisie was fundamentally materialist, their
political practice came down to a clash of social and economic
interests that government had to bring to a compromise to make it
possible to resume business. But the bourgeoisie would not acknowledge material self-interest as the goal of their politics. On the
contrary, they characteristically disguised their interest behind
some appeal to the authority of traditional values, which they invoked to justify and disguise what they wanted and what they
did:

> . . . the bourgeoisie claimed to be the guardian of Western
> traditions and confounded all moral issues by parading public
> virtues, which it not only did not possess in private and busi-
> ness life, but actually held in contempt.[2]

This means that the bourgeoisie could not reflect on what happened honestly. Instead their efforts to adhere to the conventional
fiction of their circle became all the more strenuous as its incon-
gruence with what was really happening became more apparent.

Arendt claimed that Hobbes was the first to realize that in

bourgeois society truth can survive only as long as it does not contradict somebody's profit or pleasure. It is destroyed, "if it is a thing contrary to any man's right of dominion, or to the interest of men that have dominion."[3] In sum, "the public order is based on people's holding as self-evident precisely those best-known truths which secretly scarcely anyone still believes in."[4]

The hypocrisy of the bourgeois regimes was finally exposed by their pursuit of empires and the resulting wars that openly contradicted their "traditions." At this point, when the bourgeois fiction collapsed, one might have expected the people to act as citizens and to recover their capacity to perceive and judge for themselves what was going on. But their conformity to the bourgeois fiction had impaired their capacity for judgment. They only experienced a loss of their so-called traditions in the form of disillusionment, nihilism, and cynicism without a revival of their capacity to think in terms of the real condition of freedom in the political world. As a result the emptying out of the bourgeois fiction made room for the acceptance of the new fictions of the totalitarian parties and regimes, which, with the aid of propaganda, served to legitimize ambitions that were even more criminal.

As the bourgeois fiction collapsed, those who had been accustomed to living unthinkingly and had been dependent on what they were told to believe could keep going only by nurturing the hope for a new fiction to rescue them from the disappearance of conventional belief and conformist habits. The totalitarian parties offered new fictions. Their ideologies provided the consoling new belief that while events had taken a sudden turn for the worse they could be overcome by those who knew the underlying laws of nature or history and who would act violently and ruthlessly to liquidate the natural or historical enemies of progress toward a transcendent world order.

There were three seductive elements to the new fiction proposed by totalitarian ideologies: a "logical" explanation for events that provided an intellectual guarantee against their threatening aspect, an identifiable "enemy" to relieve the people of responsibility for the affairs of their common world, and the illusion of regaining political power by the use of criminal violence against the class or race that offended against mankind.

In the end, far from restoring the public world to the citizens, these ideologies simply delivered the people into the hands of their new, totalitarian rulers. Far from gaining the power to act together in order to change the world, the people found themselves completely isolated from each other and reduced to depoliticized masses. They became incapable of political action, for the totalitarian regime now claimed the exclusive right to take initiatives since it had a monopoly on the legitimacy conferred by the new ideology.

The peoples of Europe, newly subject to totalitarian rule, thus came to occupy a place in relation to their governments that closely resembled the subjection of colonial peoples to their imperial masters at the height of the European empires. Whether in the name of a superior race, class, or civilization, imperial and totalitarian rulers employed whatever means they could devise to pursue the goals they had set their minds on. Hannah Arendt has shown that with the course of time the aims pursued by these rulers increasingly failed to meet the criteria set out by their own ideologies, and often contradicted them. Therefore she concluded that what they really wanted was simply domination for its own sake regardless of what their ideologies originally proclaimed, and in the case of Nazi Germany and the Soviet Union they wanted total domination. One can say, therefore, that the rigid and obsessive "logic" of totalitarian fiction served only to disguise and facilitate its opposite, arbitrary criminalities.

The horrible irony of this story lies in the fact that in order to find a new fiction and a regime to provide an escape from the contingencies of acting in a free world, men became totally subject to the mere will of a group of criminals who cast themselves as heroes in the rescue of "mankind" from its enemies. This bitter deception was practiced once more during the war in Vietnam, and its contradiction was revealed by an American general whose defense of the "freedom" of the so-called free people of South Vietnam was ultimately defined as "to destroy in order to save." At issue, of course, was simply the will of successive American administrations to get their way in Vietnam.

It becomes the mission of those who rule in the name of an ideological fiction to destroy anybody who appears to obstruct their will to dominate, and to do so with the claim that they are out to save mankind. Franz Kafka, in *The Penal Colony,* writes about an imperial administration that has devised an ingenious machine that induces a moment of "enlightment" in a prisoner just before it kills him. He is "saved" as he learns, literally on pain of death, that the will of those who rule has prior claim to his own existence: he is meant to believe that he is destroyed so that he can be saved for civilization. In the case of the extermination camps and the slave-labor camps, the rulers do not resort to even such a bare excuse for criminal domination: saved or damned, the victims have already been forgotten and turned into a mere statistic even before they reach the camps, because they are superfluous.

Following in the steps of modern imperialism, totalitarianism denies the significance of people as citizens of their world and considers large numbers of them superfluous unless they serve the will of their rulers. It denies equally the significance of the world as a public realm where citizens are free to act. Its ideological fictions provide a thin pretext for the assertion of a will to total domination for its own sake. Here the gap between fiction and reality, first opened up under bourgeois rule, suddenly becomes wide enough to permit the extermination of millions of people without any sense of what is being done to them. Terrifying and threatening as this unprecedented form of government is, it remains an extreme political phenomenon in our century, although by no means ruled out as a more common possibility: "As a potentiality and an ever-present danger [it] is only too likely to stay with us from now on."[5]

What has become common and widespread in Hannah Arendt's view, is what she came to call "the rule by nobody." By this she meant the increasing substitution in the mass societies of the free world of bureaucratic management—where nobody can be held responsible for what is done—for government by public participation. Her account of the rise of bureaucracy as a form of government also goes back to her analysis of bourgeois politics, and she sees it as arising from the same premises.

The fiction that sustains mass society consists of the belief that the purpose of the world is to maximize the "good life" of production and consumption, and government is organized to this end by dedicating itself to the "rational," bureaucratic management with the techniques of prediction and control that the social sciences offer. Conformity in mass society therefore consists of thinking of oneself exclusively as a jobholder and consumer, playing a functional role in the economy, and looking forward to the rewards for one's contributions to it.

Once more the reality of the world, and of the freedom it gives citizens to act and to reveal their identity to each other through action, is obscured. Defined as jobholders, men become isolated into their discrete functions in the economy and lose all sense of sharing in a common world, let alone the sense of their capacity to take common initiatives in order to affect the course of affairs. They become increasingly dependent on administrative organizations to govern the world, and give up participation in voluntary associations, so that isolation, passivity and apathy displace their capacity for action.

Arendt believed that the relentless pursuit of accumulation set afoot by capitalism and continued by socialism undermines the public life. While it holds out the promise of abundance, and sets production and consumption as the goals of life, in effect it reduces the world to a giant household subject to a bureaucratic management whose purpose is to control and eliminate the uncertain elements that arise when men act freely in the world as citizens. This requires the virtual elimination of action. One could say that Arendt applied to the condition of the contemporary masses in society in general, what Marx had to say about the condition of the proletariat in the nineteenth century:

The animal becomes human and the human becomes animal. . . . For eating, drinking, and procreating . . . abstractly considered, apart from the environment of other human activities, and turned into final and sole ends . . . are animal functions.[6]

Arendt's critique of the social sciences arises in this context. She sees their development as an effort to amplify the techniques for "rational" administration in mass society, where men have learned to "behave" (or conform) instead of acting. The social scientist's quest for abstract laws that render human behavior predictable coincides with the administrator's goal of controlling men. If the social sciences can reduce human affairs to questions of causality and probability then calculation can replace the need for judgment as the goal *and* the method of those in positions of authority, effectively relieving them of the responsibility that goes with judgment and providing a further element of fiction in their belief that not men but "the laws of mankind" now govern.

Arendt notes that in the development of natural science it was necessary to purge thinking "of all anthropological elements,"[7] and to the extent that this model is followed in the social sciences we also find a universal *theory* that eradicates the individuality of men in the context of its abstract laws. Thus an administration based upon the theories of social science will not take account of the individuality or the plurality of men. Indeed, the greater the control over mass society achieved by the application of the social sciences, the less real the world becomes as the public space where we appear to each other, and through which, if at all, we have the chance to reveal who we are and what we can do.

The use of the social sciences for the rational administration of categories of men and things (in fulfillment of Engel's phrase) is, in effect, an extension of government as the enforcer of bourgeois compromise, so that the replacement of the citizen by the bourgeois is followed by the control of the masses by executive committees of technocrats. Arendt was concerned about the denial of the validity of political experience implied by this attempt at turning the world into a smoothly managed household. And she argued that it is doomed, time and again, to run foul of the reality of human plurality, which it denies with its abstract fictions of a mankind whose behavior can be predicted. At which point the technocrats find themselves unable to grasp what has happened, and can only invent still more elaborate calculations in the hope of improving their controls, as if their administration has failed only because the state of their science is not refined enough for the task.

Hannah Arendt's analysis of the neglect and loss of freedom under the conditions of mass society is not only a development of her analysis of bourgeois politics, but also derives from her more general belief that one cannot talk about politics and economics as a single sphere of activity. Indeed this is the case only when the citizen, concerned with the world, becomes the bourgeois, who sees the world purely in terms of the conflict of economic interests. Then political actors give up their task of judging in terms of a common world and become representatives of class bias and influence-peddlers of even more particular interests.

It is precisely because she recognized the importance of class struggle and the role of economic and imperial interests in shaping political events that she argued that when political institutions become the means to settle economic questions, political freedom is not enhanced, but on the contrary, submits to the underlying rule of necessity that is inescapable in the economic sphere. For her, politics is the realm where the issue is not labor but action, not capital but initiative, not production but power, and not consumption but freedom.

We see now that the point of departure for Hannah Arendt's political thinking is the recognition that what has happened politically—with the emergence of totalitarianism on the one hand, and the rise of mass society with its rule by nobody on the other—is that the capacity for taking initiative in the world has been impaired and the world that men constitute when they act together as citizens has been obscured. The reality of the public world that actually connects us to each other, even as it gives us the room to reveal our individual identities, has been replaced by the imposition of conformity and bureaucracy in the name of a fiction—that unlimited production and consumption is the goal of our worldly existence.

With her concept of freedom, Arendt also criticized the prevailing political theory that sees the world as essentially divided up into the rulers and the ruled, so that the significant question is only the criterion by which you become a member of either class. In her view of freedom, those in authority derive their legitimacy from the power of the citizens who give them support and consent to the laws. Since the participation of the citizenry remains essential, there is no division established between those who command and those who obey. And this freedom that provides access to the realm of action must be constituted by law in order to be secured. Her favorite example of the founding of freedom was the American Revolution.

Freedom gives men the chance to take initiative—to begin something new in the world. Hannah Arendt traced the connection between freedom and initiative to St. Augustine: *"Initium ergo ut esset, creatus est homo, ante quem nullus fuit."* ("That there might be a beginning, man was created, before whom nobody was.") She offered the following interpretation:

> Here, man has not only the capacity of beginning, but is this beginning himself. If the creation of man coincides with the creation of a beginning in the universe (and what else does this mean but the creation of freedom?), then the birth of individual men, being new beginnings, re-affirms the original character of man in such a way that origin can never become entirely a thing of the past; while, on the other hand, the very fact of the memorable continuity of these beginnings in the sequence of generations guarantees a history which can never end because it is the history of beings whose essence is beginning.[8]

"The original character of man" is the source of his unique capacity for beginning, which informs the continuity of history not as a continuous process, but as a "sequence of generations" for whom each end contains the promise of beginning. Politically, the capacity for beginning is manifest in action, by which men take the initiative to constitute their world, and to change and renew it continually.

Hannah Arendt did not believe that the theorist could pre-empt the actor. Nor did she believe that theory—or theories—could take priority over action, and its condition of freedom. She argued that insofar as we think, we think on our own, while, insofar as we act, we act along with others. We can move from the solitude of thinking to the plurality of acting only by introducing our ideas to others in the form of an opinion for them to accept or reject. While the fate of an idea, in thinking, depends on the compelling quality of its truth, the fate of an opinion, in action, depends firstly on the persuasive power with which it is communicated to others, and then on their response to it—whether they believe it answers to their experience and judgment.

The theorist, who thinks by himself, is concerned with the truth, but the citizen, who acts in company, is concerned with persuading others on whom he relies for support and power. A citizen cannot hope to see the result of his action follow the same orderly march toward a conclusion that a theorist expects from his argument. And just as the citizen cannot control the outcome of his action, so the persuasive power of an opinion cannot carry the compelling authority of truth. There is a contradiction in a theorist—or a scientist for that matter—presuming to apply the authority of truth to the rivalry of opinions in action.

This view of theory and action belongs with Arendt's view of the ruler and the ruled. She believed that both of these distinctions implicitly deny the free participation of citizens in politics, for the rulers command while the ruled obey, so that nobody really acts freely in relation to other men. The theorist, however, presides over what men do on the strength of his abstract laws—in modern times he goes so far as to operationalize his theory so that it can be administered, and in this way he literally preempts reality.

Hannah Arendt traces both distinctions back to Plato, in

whose work they appear combined in the concept of the philosopher-king, where the theorist becomes the ruler. And she argues that since Plato, this has indeed been the received view of the role of the political theorist. Consequently, on this issue as well, she steps outside the tradition. Theorizing of a scientific or technical kind belongs only where there is no room for action or debate, in the strictly economic sphere, where men engage in the activities of labor and work, when they produce and consume. Here, of necessity, the category of means and ends governs their activity and their thinking about their activity, which takes the forms of calculation, planning, and administration with the aim of prediction and control. Here efficiency is at a premium and economy can best be served by decisions that are reasoned out by one or a few men, rather than debated by everybody. For what is at issue is not the variety of experience and judgment of what is best for a common world, but simply the correct means to an end.

Stories

Hannah Arendt certainly believed that if one accepted the validity of the *vita activa* as a sphere of activity that finds its condition and end in freedom, then the thinker cannot presume to instruct the citizens on how to act, since this would mean setting thinking above acting. Consequently, the kind of thinking about politics one engages in must remain faithful to acting and to the experience of the political realm, accepted on their own terms; and the form in which the theorist expresses his thinking must respect the free conduct of political life. Storytelling, by which we remember and think through experience, provides the point of departure for her concept of political thinking, precisely because it respects the conditions of action and does not presume to supersede it.

I believe that Hannah Arendt's concept of storytelling—the fundamental form of thinking about experience—is central to the relationship between thinking and acting in her work, though the point is not always clear in her writing and its significance has not been recognized. It has occurred to me that even Arendt herself was not fully aware of the implications of the concept, or at least not in the work published during her lifetime. It informs her political thinking so basically, and is so characteristic of her posture as a thinker, that she may well not have recognized its role in her work. For she may simply not have had the chance to catch herself in the course of her thinking in order to tell us how it is she does what she is doing. I believe that Hannah Arendt did indeed think out of "the incidents of living experience,"[9] and that storytelling is at the root of this kind of thinking. Consequently, we must turn our attention to storytelling in order to grasp the originality of Arendt's view of the political thinker.

Storytelling relates to thinking in terms of remembrance and reconciliation to what has happened. These two aspects are not discrete, but together inform the thinking activity. Hannah Arendt traced the concept of remembering in storytelling to the Greeks. I believe her concept of storytelling as the reconciliation to reality is adapted from Hegel.

Thinking about an experience requires that we remember it and recount it to ourselves. This invariably takes the form of telling a story. Telling the story, then, is the "thinking completion" of the event,[10] it is the form of dialogue in which I think with myself about what has happened. And this Hannah Arendt believed everybody does. It was by no means the preserve of theorists, or what, after Kant, she called "the professional thinkers." She claimed that everybody feels the need to think about their experience in this way, because it is the only way we can become reconciled to reality: "Every person needs to be reconciled to a world into which he was born a stranger and in which, to the extent of his distinct uniqueness, he always remains a stranger."[11] The need for thinking thus arises out of the tension between ourselves as unique individuals and the world of men, which we live in but which confronts us as strange.

For Hannah Arendt, reconciliation does not consist in discovering the cunning of reason in history. In her view it has to do with overcoming one's strangeness in order to make oneself at home in the world. The meaning sought is: how does my experience come about in relation to others and events in the world? What is at issue is the relation of my singular self to the numbers of others in the world, both in terms of the constant surprise that characterizes my experience in the world, and my vulnerability to the contingencies of the world in which so many others are free to undertake initiatives.

In my single self I am not complete; on the contrary, I live as one among the numbers of men with whom I share the world. Therefore I am not the master of my experience and certainly not of events in the world. Frequently, my experiences arise and usually events take place as a result of the initiatives and reactions of others that I cannot predict, so that they take me by surprise. So I feel vulnerable to the world, and a stranger to it. How am I to satisfy my need for reconciliation to what happens in the world?

Remembering an experience or event and thinking through the way various contingencies came into play and gave it shape presents me with its story. In the form of a story its meaning is presented to me, and I have overcome the surprise by understanding how it came about. By making sense of the experience or event in the form of a story I am reconciled to what happened. I no longer feel at the mercy of the contingencies that affect me, but rather I feel that I am their master at the level of understanding: "The story reveals the meaning of what otherwise would remain an unbearable sequence of sheer happenings."[12] I move from being surprised by experience and events to understanding them; just as I move from feeling a stranger in the world to being at home in it. The story is the form that my remembering and thinking with myself takes.

Storytelling offers us the means of reconciliation with reality. But, in effect, it also makes a common understanding of reality, and so, a world, possible for us in our plurality. In this respect storytelling must be understood not just as the primary form of thinking about experience, but also as the primary form of communicating with each other about experience. It makes possible the sharing of experience and reality. Further, when others hear our stories and believe them, they confirm our sense of what has really happened.

Here the experience of plurality comes full circle: first it confronts us unawares with an experience or event, and finally it offers us confirmation of our understanding, thereby making us feel not only master of what has happened, but also at home among others in the world, at the level not just of our own, but of a common understanding.

> If the essence of all, and in particular of political action is to make a new beginning, then understanding becomes the other side of action, namely that form of cognition . . . by which acting men . . . eventually can come to terms with what irrevocably happened and be reconciled with what unavoidably exists.[13]

Storytelling gives us the chance to keep up with what happens in the world. Consequently, in thinking about politics we look for those stories that reveal what is going on, and interpret them so that their ability to illumine reality is enhanced. Thinking about politics is in large part a matter of engaging in the ongoing debate about what has really happened, and thereby contributing to the common sense of reality.

Stories tell us how each one finds or loses his just place in relation to others in the world. And the communication of the story is confirmed when justice has been recognized. Is there any story we tell in which justice is not at issue? It is almost as if we constitute a jury out of our listeners, so that it falls to them to judge the particular view of the case that we present in our story. What they validate is not one's particular relationship to a transcendent realm of meaning, but simply his place in the world:

> Storytelling reveals meaning without committing the error of defining it. . . . it brings about consent and reconciliation with things as they really are, and . . . we may even trust it

to contain eventually by implication that last word which we expect from the "day of judgment."[14]

When those who must live in the world together agree to the meaning of experience, it amounts to a verdict of final judgment simply because that is the only validation of meaning that we can expect from the world.

Now let us consider how storytelling relates to acting. Storytelling addresses the question of how we understand what has happened from the point of view of the present. The story presents a past experience to us by recalling it to mind, thereby raising it to the level of understanding where we can imagine it for ourselves. That is the moment "between past and future" when we can "think what we do." Here the thinking citizen takes reality into account —as he grasps it by imagining through memories in the form of stories—and applies his understanding of it to the task of judging the opinions men offer him. In that moment the citizen takes his bearings in the world. He looks for—and the thinker may offer him—a disclosure of the reality on which to base his judgment. In this respect stories bring the light of the past to bear on present reality. But they also remind us of the promise contained in the present.

The moment that gives us the chance to remember and recount the past not only reconciles us to it, but also brings us the chance to recall our faculty of action. For the end of the story returns us to the present with its promise of beginning something new, which stems from that "original character" of men:

> . . . every end in history necessarily contains a new beginning: this beginning is the promise, the only "message" which the end can ever produce. Beginning, before it becomes a historical event, is the supreme capacity of man: politically it is identical with man's freedom.[15]

Thus stories bring to mind what is otherwise remote, either at a distance, in the past, or so immediate, in our present character, that we cannot see it.

As such, storytelling is related to the imagination, which Hannah Arendt thought of in terms of its specific capacity to put things into perspective for us, or to bring them into focus. The point of focus is always the world: ". . . understanding and judging everything in terms of its position in the world at any given time."[16] But the concern is to understand experience; not just our own, but also the experience of others with whom we share the world:

> Imagination alone enables us . . . to put that which is too close at a certain distance so that we can see and understand it without bias and prejudice, to bridge abysses of remoteness until we can see and understand everything that is too far away from us as though it were our own affair. . . . Without this kind of imagination, which actually is understanding, we would never be able to take our bearings in the world. It is the only inner compass we have.[17]

In enabling us to appreciate the reality of what happens by means of storytelling, the imagination allows us to take the world to heart, and do justice to the fact that we share it with others. Hannah Arendt cited an illuminating evocation of the imagination in the prayer King Solomon utters as he stands in awe of his newly felt responsibility for his people and their world. He calls it "the understanding heart."[18] Storytelling keeps this "understanding heart" alive, so that when one acts one does so in the full recognition of the world that makes freedom possible, and with respect for the citizens with whom one shares it.

The search for the reality of the world and one's fellow citizens—rather than the quest for truth or the laws of behavior—emerges as the central political theme in Hannah Arendt's thinking. This reflects her concern with the tenuousness of our grasp of reality, and, of course, with the radical destruction and the loss of the reality of a common world that she attributed to totalitarianism and the "rule by nobody." But it did not come to her merely as an idea: it grew out of her attempt to think through her own experience of the world, an experience forced upon her rather than ini-

tiated by herself—an experience of flight from the world, such as
it had become, rather than of participation in its affairs. It was out
of her understanding of what it meant to be a refugee that Hannah
Arendt came to understand what it meant to live in the world. This
irony is fundamental to her political thinking and suggests how it
was that somebody who was not herself *engagée*, should have devoted so much of her work as a thinker to a concern with the
conditions of political action.

Hannah Arendt rarely wrote about her own experience, but
when she was awarded the Lessing Prize by the city of Hamburg
she responded ironically to the occasion of being publicly honored
in the country she once had to flee, in part by reflecting on the
difference between a government based upon "the emergency
measure of a restoration," and one based upon the new beginning
of a revolution, and partly by making thinly veiled allusions to
what her experience as a Jew in Germany had meant to her.

She was forced to flee and to accept the fact that her flight—
the need to be "on the run"—represented the only reality the world
permitted her:

> Flight from the world in dark times of impotence can always
> be justified as long as reality is not ignored, but is constantly
> acknowledged as the thing that must be escaped . . . Those
> in flight must remember that they are constantly on the run,
> and that the world's reality is expressed by their escape.[19]

This "reality," however, is an expulsion from the world and presents the danger of losing oneself in the "irreality" of isolation. In
the face of it, as she reports,[20] she maintained her freedom by
thinking, since acting to change the world had become impossible.
Her thinking was concerned with the meaning of her flight and of
the destruction of the world by the Nazis that made it necessary. It
gave her the chance to put the terrifying events in perspective, and
came not readily, but in flashes:

> Instead of the truth . . . there are *moments of truth*, and
> these moments are actually the only means of articulating

this chaos of viciousness and evil. The moments arise unexpectedly like oases out of the desert. They are anecdotes, and they tell in utter brevity what it was all about.[21]

These anecdotes were the stories by which the imagination gave shape to the events and experiences of the time. When she was safe, however, it became possible to tell them to others, and through this communication to confirm the reality of her experience and at the same time recover those with whom she could share a world.

To reestablish her *philanthropia*—the "readiness to share the world with other men"[22]—she communicated at first with those with whom she could feel some bond of trust—"some rather obscure brotherhood"[23]—who were the readers she imagined as she wrote the story of totalitarianism. And this gave rise to her entry into "public life," not for the sake of "success," but in order to initiate the task of reconciliation and face the challenge of a new beginning:

> Even those among us who by speaking and writing have ventured into public life have not done so out of any original pleasure in the public scene, and have hardly expected or aspired to receive the stamp of public approval. . . . These efforts were, rather, guided by their hope of preserving some minimum of humanity in a world grown inhuman while at the same time as far as possible resisting the weird irreality of this worldlessness—each after his own fashion and some few by seeking to the limits of their ability to understand even inhumanity and the intellectual and political monstrosities of a time out of joint.[24]

What drew Hannah Arendt to political thinking was her own need for reconciliation with events, which proved to be the condition for renewing her own sense of the reality of the world:

> We are contemporaries only so far as our understanding reaches. If we want to be at home on this earth, even at the

price of being at home in this century, we must try to take part in the interminable dialogue with its essence.[25]

But understanding was not enough; communicating it with others was a necessary step in regaining her sense of humanity, after having had it denied because she was a Jew: "We humanize what is going on in the world and in ourselves only by speaking of it, and in the course of speaking about it we learn to be human."[26] Storytelling could effect a reconciliation even with the experience of the inhuman and the monstrous, and it could overcome the "weird irreality of this worldlessness" with its promise of a new beginning, which is precisely the conclusion that Hannah Arendt drew when she came to the end of her story in *The Origins of Totalitarianism*.

This account of Hannah Arendt's own political experience and her reconciliation to it points out a further dimension of storytelling. In those "dark times" when the world itself is obscured by fiction and no longer perceptible through the categories by which men think, or when it has been liquidated by totalitarianism or supplanted by the "rule of nobody," storytelling carries an additional burden of significance: it actually makes thinking in terms of the world possible, even when the world itself and the political imagination of those around us are in a state of ruin. This is the kind of thinking that gave Hannah Arendt the freedom to recognize reality even in the "irreality" forced on her in flight. And it is the kind of thinking that she would remind us of when freedom has not simply been forgotten, but when it has virtually been ruled out of the political agenda of our century.

Hannah Arendt's experience of politics in its most catastrophic form is the point of departure for her political thinking. Insofar as her thinking has an immediate bearing on acting, it lies in keeping the political imagination alive to the possibility and requirements of freedom. She does not attempt to theorize away the vulnerability and contingency that inheres in our plural existence in the world, but tries to think them through to the point of reconciliation in each instance, so that we can continue to act and accept the actions of others. Far from being the specialized concern of a philosopher or scientist, her thinking is simply a more self-conscious version of the ordinary thinking of citizens:

> I have always believed that no matter how abstract our theories may sound or how consistent our arguments appear, there are incidents and stories behind them which, at least for ourselves, contain as in a nutshell the full meaning of whatever we have to say. Thought itself—to the extent that it is more than a technical, logical operation which electronic machines may be better equipped to perform than the human brain—arises out of the actuality of incident, and incidents of living experience must remain its guideposts by which it takes its bearing if it is not to lose itself. . . . The only gains one might legitimately expect from this most mysterious of human activities are neither definitions nor theories, but rather the slow, plodding discovery and, perhaps, the mapping survey of the region which some incident had completely illuminated for a fleeting moment.[27]

Telling the stories that "contain as in a nutshell the full meaning of whatever we have to say" is in fact the primary form of thinking and communicating for the citizen and the political thinker.

Exactly how does the work of the political thinker differ from the ordinary storytelling and interpreting of stories among citizens? I believe there are two ways in which this distinction arises: in the task of selecting stories, and in the skill with which they are discovered and told.

In what she called "my old-fashioned storytelling,"[28] Hannah Arendt was in effect telling those stories that she believed were critical for the recognition of reality in our time: they revealed the meaning of crucial political events. The political thinker, like the historian Herodotus whom she cites, "examines witnesses and obtains truth through inquiry,"[29] which is to say that he gathers the stories. Then he selects those that he believes shed light on experience, and interprets the way in which they do.

He is not simply an anthologist, but records stories as he follows the "guideposts" of experience.

Inevitably it is his own sense of the critical events and experiences that informs his selection of the significant stories. These then become "paradigmatic models," or ideal types, that inform his political imagination and can be shared with contemporaries and preserved for posterity: "they survive splendidly in thought to illuminate the thinking and doing of men in darker times."[30] In a world where the authority of traditional doctrines no longer bridges the gap between one generation and another, this preservation and interpretation of stories provides the only means by which the past can continue to throw its light on reality for the generations to come. In making his selection, therefore, the political thinker attempts to provide a record of experience that will stir the political imagination of future generations into life, and give them the means to see through the fictions of their age and beyond its worldlessness.

The story gives one the best chance to recapture or imagine what the experience was like, or how the event took place. The point is not that the story is true—or that storytelling leads us to "the truth"—but that it is faithful to the reality of what happened, and so conveys its meaning. What is at issue is simply whether one can recognize the experience in the story; and that recognition is indeed the hope that Hannah Arendt held out in her political thinking: the moment when what was too far away to see clearly, or too close to be seen at all, comes into focus in its worldly significance, so that we see where we stand in relation to what has happened and we can think what we do.

If the story is faithful to the experience, it is not, and cannot even aim to be, a re-creation of the experience. It makes no claim to scientific replication. Stories are always inventions or, as Hannah Arendt preferred to say, discoveries. Storytelling is an art rather than a science. In telling a story the minute elements that formed part of the experience or the event have to be sorted out and given an intelligible order. Details have to be sacrificed, information selected, emphasis placed, a sequence created, speeches modified,

situations viewed from different angles—all in the attempt to discover and reveal what happened in a way that is faithful to reality
and at the same time illuminates it, so that the experience or event
becomes recognizable for what it is in the form of the story.

How can we distinguish a story from a fiction? Only by
whether we recognize the experiences and events in its telling
rather than a series of unified abstractions. Here the criteria of the
possible and the probable come into play, which, according to
Aristotle, make up the realm that poetry illuminates. For the story
offers us a plot that must appear possible and probable, otherwise
we cannot recognize the words and deeds of men in its account of
them.

The plot emerges from the conflict of a set of characters and
shows how an event is shaped from the interplay of the actors.
Thus it allows us to judge whether it does justice to our sense of
human plurality—of how men are likely to act and react in relation
to each other. If we recognize the unfolding of contingencies in the
story as possible and likely, we also learn that it has taken place.
It was Vico who first argued that we can understand and know
what men do themselves from their stories, because we know them
as the authors of their deeds.[31]

The political thinker has to be a good storyteller: one who is
particularly alert to the way things happen in the world, and can
reveal their course by means of a plot. For he wants to illuminate
the world as a scene of action—not as the staging ground for
social processes and interlocking systems. Telling stories is critical
to his work, because stories account for what happens in terms of
initiatives, rather than by an abstract chain of cause and effect that
obscures the interplay of men. Even where events appear to run
away with men, the skilled storyteller is there to find the origin of
events in what people did and said to each other.

The political thinker as storyteller is out to maintain the reality
of the human dimension of the world against any attempt to veil it
in fiction:

. . . be loyal to life, don't create fiction but accept what life is giving you, show yourself worthy of whatever it may be by recollecting and pondering over it, thus repeating it in imagination: this is the way to remain alive.[32]

In this interpretation of an Isak Dinesen short story, Hannah Arendt formulated the dilemma with which existence confronts us —as much in the sphere of private as of political life: do we reconcile ourselves to "what life is giving" by our ability to think through experience in the form of stories, or do we attempt to "create fiction" out of life by narrowing the access to experience to a set of ideological preconceptions? The fictions of mankind have a deadening effect on existence; the stories of men alert the imagination to the possibilities of living and acting.

NOTES

1. Hannah Arendt, "Action and the Pursuit of Happiness," paper delivered at the Meeting of the American Political Science Association, September 1960, p. 2.

2. Hannah Arendt, *The Origins of Totalitarianism*, Part III (New York: Harcourt Brace Jovanovich, 1968), p. 32.

3. Hannah Arendt, *Between Past and Future* (New York: The Viking Press, 1968), p. 230. Her reference is to *Leviathan*, Chapter 11.

4. Hannah Arendt, *Men in Dark Times* (New York: Harcourt Brace Jovanovich, 1968), p. 11.

5. Arendt, *The Origins of Totalitarianism*, p. 176.

6. Karl Marx, "First Manuscript: Alienated Labor," in Erich Fromm, *Marx's Concept of Man* (New York: Ungar 1968), p. 99.

7. Hannah Arendt, "The Archimedean Point," *Ingenor VI* (Spring 1969), p. 8. She is quoting Max Planck.

8. Hannah Arendt, "Understanding and Politics," *Partisan Review*, Vol. XX, no. 4 (July–August 1953), p. 392.

9. Arendt, "Action and the Pursuit of Happiness," p. 2.

10. Arendt, *Between Past and Future*, p. 6.

11. Arendt, "Understanding and Politics," p. 377.

12. Arendt, *Men in Dark Times*, p. 104.

13. Arendt, "Understanding and Politics," p. 391.

14. Arendt, *Men in Dark Times*, p. 104.

15. Arendt, *The Origins of Totalitarianism*, p. 176.

16. Arendt, *Men in Dark Times*, p. 7.

17. Arendt, "Understanding and Politics," p. 392.

18. Ibid.

19. Arendt, *Men in Dark Times*, p. 17.

20. Ibid., p. 9.

21. Hannah Arendt, "On Responsibility for Evil," in Richard A. Falk, Gabriel Kolko, and Robert Jay Lifton, eds., *Crimes of War* (New York: Vintage Books, 1971), p. 500.

22. Arendt, *Men in Dark Times*, p. 25.

23. Ibid., p. 17.

24. Ibid.

25. Arendt, "Understanding and Politics," p. 392.

26. Arendt, *Men in Dark Times*, p. 17.

27. Arendt, "Action and the Pursuit of Happiness," p. 2.

28. Ibid., p. 10.

29. Arendt, *Between Past and Future*, p. 285, note 1.

30. Hannah Arendt, "Home to Roost: A Bicentennial Address," *The New York Review of Books*, Vol. XXII, no. 11 (June 26, 1975).

31. It is unfortunately beyond the scope of this essay to trace the influence of various thinkers perceptible in Hannah Arendt's work. In her essay, "Karl Jaspers: Citizen of the World?" in *Men in Dark Times*, she discussed his concept of communication among thinkers in "a realm of spirit where all are contemporaries" (p. 85). It goes without saying that the novice who enters this realm tries to learn what he can from the others. So, of course, did Hannah Arendt.

32. Arendt, *Men in Dark Times*, p. 97. The quote is taken from the story, "The Blank Page," from the collection, *Last Tales*.

Hannah Arendt

ON HANNAH ARENDT

In November 1972, a conference on "The Work of Hannah Arendt" was organized by the Toronto Society for the Study of Social and Political Thought and sponsored by York University and the Canada Council.

Hannah Arendt was invited to attend the conference as the guest of honor, but replied that she would prefer to be invited to participate. Naturally, she was. In the course of numerous exchanges over the three days of the conference she spontaneously revealed aspects of her thinking and the style of her thinking in response to direct questions, or statements, or challenges, as well as in response to the papers read. Fortunately we arranged to record the discussion with a view to later publication.

What I have presented here is a series of her exchanges with, and excerpts from, some of her longer responses to various participants, some of whom are major thinkers and writers, while others may not be known to the reader. The selections were chosen either because they touch on controversial aspects of Arendt's thinking, or because they cast further light on difficult areas of her work. They have been presented not in the order of the conference, but according to the major themes and concerns that they reflect.

These exchanges went back and forth in the course of debate, and to find an accessible written form for them I have had to exercise a degree of discretion in taking them out of their context in the ongoing discussion. My principal aim was to make Arendt's thinking apparent, while trying to do justice to the concerns and criticism of her interlocutors. Since this is a book about her work, I have edited the transcripts so that the reader may have the chance to enjoy a glimpse of what Hannah Arendt was like interpreting her own work before all comers. It may appear to the reader that she gets the last word too often, but as this may be an artifact of the editing let me say that I do not mean to suggest that she always managed to satisfy her critics and enlighten her challengers! Further, in keeping with my intention of preserving the flavor of the conference, I have not attempted to "English" the occasionally foreign syntax or diction of the participants.

Melvyn A. Hill

List of Contributors

C. B. Macpherson , professor emeritus of political economy, University of Toronto

Christian Bay, professor of political economy, University of Toronto

Michael Gerstein, consultant on Social Services, Halifax, Nova Scotia

George Baird, architect and associate professor in the School of Architecture, University of Toronto

Hans Jonas, professor emeritus of philosophy, The New School for Social Research, New York City

F. M. Barnard, professor of political science, University of Western Ontario, London, Ontario

Mary McCarthy, writer, Paris

Richard Bernstein, professor of philosophy, Haverford College, Haverford, Pennsylvania

Albrecht Wellmer, professor of sociology, University of Constanz, Constanz, W. Germany

Hans Morganthau, university professor of political science, The New School for Social Research, New York City

Ed Weissman, associate professor of political science, York University, Toronto

Thinking and Acting

Hannah Arendt: Reason itself, the thinking ability which we have, has a need to actualize itself. The philosophers and the metaphysicians have monopolized this capability. This has led to very great things. It also has led to rather unpleasant things—we have forgotten that *every* human being has a need to think, not to think abstractly, not to answer the ultimate questions of God, immortality, and freedom, nothing but to think while he is living. And he does it constantly.

Everybody who tells a story of what happened to him half an hour ago on the street has got to put this story into shape. And this putting the story into shape is a form of thought.

So in this respect it may even be nice that we lost the monopoly of what Kant once very ironically called the professional thinkers. We can start worrying about what thinking means for the activity of acting. Now I will admit one thing. I will admit that I am, of course, primarily interested in understanding. This is absolutely true. And I will admit that there are other people who are primarily interested in doing something. I am not. I can very well live without doing anything. But I cannot live without trying at least to understand whatever happens.

And this is somehow the same sense in which you know it from Hegel, namely where I think the central role is reconciliation—reconciliation of man as a thinking and reasonable being. This is what actually happens in the world.

·   ·   ·

I don't know any other reconciliation but thought. This need is, of course, much stronger in me than it usually is in political theorists, with their need to unite action and thought. Because they want to act, you know. And I think I understood something of action precisely because I looked at it from the outside, more or less.

I have acted in my life, a few times, because I couldn't help it. But that is not what my primary impulse is. And all the lacunae which you would derive just from this emphasis I would admit, almost without arguing, because I think it is so very likely that there the lacunae are.

.   .   .

C. B. Macpherson: Is Miss Arendt really saying that to be a political theorist and to be engaged are incompatible? Surely not!

Arendt: No, but one is correct in saying that thinking and acting are not the same, and to the extent that I wish to think I have to withdraw from the world.

Macpherson: But to a political theorist and a teacher and a writer of political theory, teaching, or theorizing is acting.

Arendt: Teaching is something else, and writing too. But thinking in its purity is different—in this Aristotle was right. . . . You know, all the modern philosophers have somewhere in their work a rather apologetic sentence which says, "Thinking is also acting." Oh no, it is not! And to say that is rather dishonest. I mean, let's face the music: it is not the same! On the contrary, I have to keep back to a large extent from participating, from commitment.

There is an old story that is ascribed to Pythagoras, where the people go to the Olympian games. And Pythagoras says: "The one goes there for fame, and the other goes there for trade, and the best ones sit there in Olympia, on the amphitheater, just for looking." That is, those who *look* at it will finally get the gist out of it. And this distinction has to be kept—in the name of honesty, if no other.

.   .   .

I do believe that thinking has some influence on action. But on acting man. Because it is the same ego that thinks and the same ego that acts. But not theory. Theory could only [influence action] in the reform of consciousness. Did you ever think about how many people whose consciousness you will have to reform?

And if you don't think about it in these concrete terms then you think about mankind—that is, about some noun which actually doesn't exist, which is a concept. And this noun—be it Marx's species-being, or mankind, or the world spirit, or what have you—is constantly construed in the image of a single man.

If we really believe—and I think we share this belief—that plurality rules the earth, then I think one has got to modify this notion of the unity of theory and practice to such an extent that it will be unrecognizable for those who tried their hand at it before. I really believe that you can only act in concert and I really believe that you can only think by yourself. These are two entirely different—if you want to call it—"existential" positions. And to believe that there is any direct influence of theory on action isofar as theory is just a thought thing, that is, something thought out —I think that this is really not so and really will never be so.

.   .   .

The main flaw and mistake of *The Human Condition* is the following: I still look at what is called in the traditions the *vita activa* from the viewpoint of the *vita contemplativa*, without ever saying anything real about the *vita contemplativa*.

Now I think that to look at it from the *vita contemplativa* is already the first fallacy. Because the fundamental experience of the thinking ego is in those lines of the older Cato which I quote at the end of the book: "When I do nothing I am most active and when I'm all by myself, I am the least alone." (It is very interesting that Cato said this!) This is an experience of sheer activity unimpeded by any physical or bodily obstacles. But the moment you begin to act, you deal with the world, and you are constantly falling over your own feet, so to speak, and then you carry your body—and, as Plato said: "The body always wants to be taken care of and to hell with it!"

All this is spoken out of the experience of thinking. Now I am trying to write about this. And I would take off from this business of Cato. But I am not ready to tell you about it. And I am by no means sure that I will succeed, because it's very easy to talk about the metaphysical fallacies, but these metaphysical fallacies— which are indeed metaphysical fallacies—has each one of them its authentic root in some experience. That is, while we are throwing them out of the window as dogmas, we have got to know where they came from. That is, what are the experiences of this ego that thinks, that wills, that judges; in other words, that is busy with sheer mental activities. Now that is quite a mouthful, you know, if you really go at it. And I cannot tell you much about it.

.   .   .

I have a vague idea that there is some pragmatic business in this question, "What is thinking good for?"—as I formulate what you all here say: "Why the hell are you doing all this?" and "What is thinking good for independent of writing and teaching?" It's very difficult to put that down, and certainly more difficult for me than for many.

You see, with the political business I had a certain advantage. I, by nature, am not an actor. If I tell you that I never was either a socialist or a communist—which was absolutely a matter of course for my whole generation, so that I hardly know anybody who never committed themselves—you can see that I never felt the need to commit myself. Until finally, *schliesslich schlug mir [einer mit einem] Hammer auf den Kopf und ich fiel mir auf:* finally somebody beat me over the head and, you can say, this awakened me to the realities. But still, I had this advantage to look at something from outside. And even in myself from outside.

But not here [with this business of thinking]. Here I am immediately in it. And therefore I'm quite doubtful whether I will get it or whether I won't. But anyhow I feel that this *Human Condition* needs a second volume and I'm trying to write it.

.   .   .

Christian Bay: I have a very different concept of the calling of a political theorist from that of Hannah Arendt. I should say
that I read Hannah Arendt with pleasure, but out of esthetic
pleasure. She is a philosopher's philosopher. I think it is beautiful
to follow her prose, and her sense of unity in history, and to be
reminded of all the great things the Greeks have said that are still
somehow pertinent today. I think, however, from my point of view,
there is a certain lack of seriousness about modern problems in
much of her work.

I think perhaps her most serious work is her book, *Eichmann
in Jerusalem:* her pointing out with such force how Eichmann is in
each of us. I think it has great implications for political education,
which, after all, is the ancient theme of connectedness with politics. Yet I find this lacking in so much else of Hannah Arendt's
work. Perhaps our ability to decentralize and to humanize will
depend on the extent to which we find ways of coping with, com-
bating, and surpassing Eichmann in ourselves, and become citizens
—in a sense so radically different from the customary use of
this term.

I get very impatient with abstract discussions at length on
how power differs from violence. I would like to know not only
what is justice in a world whose injustice we all abhor, but how
can the political theorist make us become more committed and
more effective in fighting for justice—and for that matter, for
human survival, which is the number-one problem.

I was disturbed when Hannah Arendt said that her desire is
never to indoctrinate. I think that *this* is the highest calling of the
political theorist: to attempt to indoctrinate, in a pluralist universe, of course. If we are serious about problems like survival, like
justice, then it seems to me our first task is to overcome the sea of
liberalism and tolerance, which, in effect, amounts to one opinion
having as much justification as another. Unless we passionately
care for certain opinions I think we will all be lost, in that events
will continue to be allowed to take their own course: power tend-
ing to be ever more asymmetrically distributed, while the liberal

institutions permit the economic masters to continue to enrich themselves at the expense not only of the poverty of the rest of us, but of our access to knowledge, to information, to understanding.

I want political theorists of my kind to be men and women of politics first, committed to try to educate ourselves and each other about how to resolve the urgent existential problems that we are up against. And one last point on that. It was possible to say with Stuart Mill a century ago that in the long run truth will prevail in a free marketplace of ideas. But (a) we don't have much time, and (b) there is no free marketplace of ideas.

Hannah Arendt, what can we as political theorists do to see to it that the existential issues—which sometimes have true and false answers—are brought home to more of our fellow citizens, so that they become citizens in the ancient sense?

Arendt: I am afraid the disagreement is quite huge and I will just touch on it.

First of all, you like my book *Eichmann in Jerusalem* and you say that I said there is an Eichmann in each one of us. Oh no! There is none in you and none in me! This doesn't mean that there are not quite a number of Eichmanns. But they look really quite different. I always hated this notion of "Eichmann in each one of us." This is simply not true. This would be as untrue as the opposite, that Eichmann is in nobody. In the way I look at things, this is much more abstract than the most abstract things I indulge in so frequently—if we mean by abstract: really not thinking through experience.

What is the subject of our thought? Experience! Nothing else! And if we lose the ground of experience then we get into all kinds of theories. When the political theorist begins to build his systems he is also usually dealing with abstraction.

I don't believe that we have, or can have, much influence in your sense. I think that commitment can easily carry you to a point where you do no longer think. There are certain extreme situations where you have to act. But these situations are extreme.

And then it will show who is really reliable—for commitment—and who is really willing to stick his neck out.

But these other things—that you saw in the development in the last years—are more or less things of the public mood. And the public mood may be something which I like, and the public mood may be something which I dislike, but I would not see it *my* particular task to inspire this mood when I like it, or to go on the barricades when I dislike it.

The unwillingness of people who actually are thinking and are theorists to own up to this, and to believe that this [thinking] is worthwhile, and who believe instead that only commitment and engagement is worthwhile, is perhaps one of the reasons why this whole discipline is not always in such very good shape. People apparently don't believe in what they are doing.

I cannot tell you black on white—and would hate to do it—what the consequences of this kind of thought which I try, not to indoctrinate, but to rouse or to awaken in my students, are, in actual politics. I can very well imagine that one becomes a republican and the third becomes a liberal or God knows what. But one thing I would hope: that certain extreme things which are the actual consequence of non-thinking, that is, of somebody who really has decided that he does not want to do [i.e., to think] what I do perhaps excessively, that he doesn't want to do it at all—that these consequences will not be capable [of arising]. That is, when the chips are down, the question is how they will act. And then this notion that I examine my assumptions, that I think—I hate to use the word because of the Frankfurt School—anyhow, that I think "critically," and that I don't let myself get away with repeating the clichés of the public mood [comes into play]. And I would say that any society that has lost respect for this, is not in very good shape.

.   .   .

Michael Gerstein: I wonder, as someone who is or feels himself to be a political actor, how would you instruct me? Or wouldn't you instruct me at all?

Arendt: No. I wouldn't instruct you, and I would think that this would be presumptuous of me. I think that you should be instructed when you sit together with your peers around a table and exchange opinions. And then, somehow, out of this should come an instruction: not for you personally, but how the group should act.

And I think that every other road of the theoretician who tells his students what to think and how to act is . . . my God! These are adults! We are not in the nursery! Real political action comes out as a group act. And you join that group or you don't. And whatever you do on your own you are really not an actor—you are an anarchist.

·   ·   ·

George Baird: One of the revelations to me in *The Human Condition* was the argument which, as I understand it, sprang partly from Machiavelli: that glory and not goodness is the appropriate criterion for political acts. And, indeed, in *The Human Condition* Miss Arendt argues that goodness may even prove to be radically subversive of the political realm.

Now it seems to me that implicit in all that is a kind of dramatic challenge to the motivations of political activists as I've understood them typically in the world. On the other hand, Miss Arendt has, in her essay on Rosa Luxemburg, expressed her admiration for what I believe she calls Luxemburg's sense of injustice as the springboard for *her* entry into the political sphere.

It might clarify the discussion *vis-à-vis* all these pleas for guides to political action if Miss Arendt would try to clarify the relationship between her austere sense of glory—rather than goodness—as the appropriate criterion (which is an extremely tough and unfashionable position in the modern world), and her admiration for Luxemburg. Somewhere there must be a relationship which sustains those distinctions but which clarifies the situation.

Arendt: This business with goodness was not brought up by me but by Machiavelli. It has something to do with the distinction between the public and the private. But I can put it differently. I would say that in the notion of wanting to be good, I actually am concerned with my own self. The moment I act politically I'm not concerned with me, but with the world. And that is the *main* distinction.

Rosa Luxemburg was very *much* concerned with the world and not at *all* concerned with herself. If she had been concerned with herself, she would have stayed on in Zurich after her dissertation and would have pursued certain intellectual interests. But she couldn't stand the injustice *within the world.*

Whether the criterion is glory—the shining out in the space of appearances—or whether the criterion is justice, that is not the decisive thing. The decisive thing is whether your own motivation is clear— for the world—or, for yourself, by which I mean for your soul. That is the way Machiavelli put it when he said, "I love my country, Florence, more than I love my eternal salvation." That doesn't mean that he didn't believe in an after-life. But it meant that the world as such is of greater interest to me than myself, my physical as well as my soul self.

You know that in modern republics religion has become a private affair. And actually Machiavelli was arguing that it *be* private: "Don't let these people into politics! They don't care enough for the world! People who believe that the world is mortal and they themselves are immortal, are very dangerous characters because we want the stability and good order of *this* world."

.   .   .

Hans Jonas: That there is at the bottom of all our being and of our action the desire to share the world with other men is incontestable, but we want to share a certain world with certain men. And if it is the task of politics to make the world a fitting home for man, that raises the question: "What is a fitting home for man?"

It can only be decided if we form some idea of what man is or ought to be. And that again cannot be determined, except arbitrarily, if we cannot make appeal to some truth about man which can validate judgment of this kind, and the derivative judgment of political taste that crops up in the concrete situations—and especially if it is a question of deciding how the future world should look—which we have to do all the time dealing with technological enterprises that are having an impact on the total dispensation of things.

Now it is not the case that Kant simply made appeal to judgment. He also made appeal to the concept of the good. There is such an idea as the supreme good however we define it. And perhaps it escapes definition. It cannot be an entirely empty concept and it is related to our conception of what man is. In other words, that which has by unanimous consensus here been declared dead and done with—namely, metaphysics—has to be called in at some place to give us a final directive.

Our powers of decision reach far beyond the handling of immediate situations and of the short-term future. Our powers of doing or acting now extend over such matters as really involve a judgment or an insight into or a faith in—I leave that open—some ultimates. For in ordinary politics as it has been understood until the twentieth century we could do with penultimates. It is not true that the condition of the commonwealth had to be decided by the really ultimate values or standards. When it is a matter, as it is under the conditions of modern technology, that willy-nilly we are embarking on courses which affect the total condition of things on earth and the total future condition of man, then I don't think we can simply wash our hands and say Western metaphysics has got us into an impasse and we declare it bankrupt and we appeal now to shareable judgments—where, for God's sake, we do not mean by shared judgments shared with a majority or shared with any defined group. We can share judgments to our perdition with many but we must make an appeal beyond that sphere!

Arendt: I am afraid that I will have to answer. I am not going to go into the question of Kant's *Critique of Judgment.* Actually the question of the good doesn't arise and the question of truth doesn't arise. The whole book is actually concerned with the possible validity of these propositions.

Jonas: But it's not political.

Arendt: No, but I said only of the validity: whether one can transfer it to the political sphere is also one of the very interesting, but at this moment side, issues. And this, of course, I have done, and I have done it by simply taking Kant's late writing on politics. One of the main things here is a certain stand towards the French Revolution in Kant. But I am not going to go into that because it would lead us too far away from this question of the ultimates.

Now if our future should depend on what you say now— namely that we will get an ultimate which from above will decide for us (and then the question is, of course, who is going to recognize this ultimate and which will be the rules for recognizing this ultimate—you have really an infinite regress here, but anyhow) I would be utterly pessimistic. If that is the case then we are lost. Because this actually demands that a new god will appear.

This word (God) was a Christian word in the Christian Middle Ages, and permitted very great skepticism, but one had it in the ultimate instance, because it was God. But because this [God] had disappeared Western humanity was back in the situation in which it had been before it was saved, or salvaged, or whatever, by the good news—since they didn't believe in it any longer. That was the actual situation. And this situation sent them [i.e., the eighteenth-century revolutionaries] back scrambling for antiquity. And not as in some cases because you are in love with Greek verse or Greek songs as may be the case in my case. But that was not their motivation.

That is, they were in all nakedness confronted with the fact that men exist in the plural. And no human being knows what is *man* in the singular. We know only "male and female created he *them*"—that is, from the beginning this plurality poses an enormous problem.

For instance, I am perfectly sure that this whole totalitarian catastrophe would not have happened if people still had believed in God, or in hell rather—that is, if there still were ultimates. There were no ultimates. And you know as well as I do that there were no ultimates which one could with validity appeal to. One couldn't appeal to anybody.

And if you go through such a situation [as totalitarianism] the first thing you know is the following: you *never* know how somebody will act. You have the surprise of your life! This goes throughout all layers of society and it goes throughout various distinctions between men. And if you want to make a generalization then you could say that those who were still very firmly convinced of the so-called old values were the first to be ready to change their old values for a new set of values, provided they were given one. And I am afraid of this, because I think that the moment you give anybody a new set of values—or this famous "bannister"—you can immediately exchange it. And the only thing the guy gets used to is having a "bannister" and a set of values, no matter. I do not believe that we can stabilize the situation in which we have been since the seventeenth century in any final way.

F. M. Barnard: Would you then agree with Voltaire? You raised this question of God and to some extent a metaphysic which one may question *qua* metaphysic but which one may regard as extremely useful socially.

Arendt: Entirely agree. We wouldn't have to bother about this whole business if metaphysics and this whole value business hadn't fallen down. We begin to question because of these events.

Jonas: I share with Hannah Arendt the position that we are not in possession of any ultimates, either by knowledge or by conviction or faith. And I also believe that we cannot have this as a command performance because "we need it so bitterly we therefore should have it."

However, a part of wisdom is knowledge of ignorance. The Socratic attitude is to know that one does not know. And this realization of our ignorance can be of great practical importance in the exercise of the power of judgment, which is after all related to action in the political sphere, into future action, and far-reaching action.

Our enterprises have an eschatological tendency in them—a built-in utopianism, namely, to move towards ultimate situations. Lacking the knowledge of ultimate values—or, of what is ultimately desirable—or, of what is man so that the world can be fitting for man, we should at least abstain from allowing eschatological situations to come about. This alone is a very important practical injunction that we can draw from the insight that only with some conception of ultimates are we entitled to embark on certain things. So that at least as a restraining force the point of view I brought in may be of some relevance.

Arendt: With this I would agree.

Thinking About Society and Politics

Mary McCarthy: I would like to ask a question that I have had in my mind a long, long time. It is about the very sharp distinction that Hannah Arendt makes between the political and the social. It is particularly noticeable in her book *On Revolution,* where she demonstrates, or seeks to demonstrate, that the failure of the Russian and the French revolutions was based on the fact that these revolutions were concerned with the social, and concerned with suffering—in which the sentiment of compassion played a large role. Whereas, the American Revolution was political and ended in the foundation of something.

Now, I have always asked myself: "What is somebody supposed to do on the public stage, in the public space, if he does not concern himself with the social? That is, what's left?"

It seems to me that if you once have a constitution, and you've had the foundation, and you have had a framework of laws, the scene is there for political action. And the only thing that is left for the political man to do is what the Greeks did: make war! Now this cannot be right! On the other hand, if all questions of economics, human welfare, busing, anything that touches the social sphere, are to be excluded from the political scene, then I am mystified. I am left with war and speeches. But the speeches can't be just speeches. They have to be speeches about something.

Arendt: You are absolutely right, and I may admit that I ask myself this question. Number one, the Greeks did not only make war and Athens existed prior to the Peloponnesian War, and the real flower of Athens came between the Persian Wars and the Peloponnesian War. Now what did they do then?

Life changes constantly, and things are constantly there that want to be talked about. At all times people living together will have affairs that belong in the realm of the public—"are worthy to be talked about in public." What these matters *are* at any historical *moment* is probably *utterly* different. For instance, the great cathedrals were the public spaces of the Middle Ages. The town halls came later. And *there* perhaps they had to talk about a matter which is not without any interest either: the question of God. So what becomes public at every given period seems to me utterly different. It would be quite interesting to follow it through as a historical study, and I think one could do it. There will always be conflicts. And you don't need war.

Richard Bernstein: Let's admit the *negative* side of a persistent thesis in your work: that when men confuse the social and the political there are devastating consequences in theory and in practice.

Arendt: Okay!

Bernstein: But you know darn well that—at least, for us, now—one can't consistently make that distinction! Although we can appreciate the distinction, the two are inextricably connected. It's not good enough to answer Mary McCarthy's question by saying that in different times we have to look at exactly what comes into the public realm. It's a question of whether you can dissociate or separate the social and the political consistently now.

Arendt: I think that is certain. There are things where the right measures can be figured out. These things can really be administered and are not then subject to public debate. Public debate can only deal with things which—if we want to put it negatively—we cannot figure out with certainty. Otherwise, if we can figure it out with certainty, why do we all need to get together?

Take a town-hall meeting. There is a question, for instance, of where to put the bridge. This can be decided either from above, or it can be done by debate. In case there really is an open question where it is better to put the bridge, it can be decided better by debate than from above. I once assisted such a town-hall meeting in New Hampshire, and I was very impressed by the level of sense in the town.

On the other hand, it seems to me also quite clear that no amount of speeches and discussions and debates—or what is unfortunately taking their place: research committees, which are an excuse for doing nothing—that none of these things will be able to solve the very grave social problems which the big cities pose to us.

Or take another example. We have the last remnant of active citizen participation in the republic in the juries. I was a juror—with great delight and with real enthusiasm. Here again, all these questions are somehow *really* debatable. The jury was extremely responsible, but also aware that there are *different viewpoints*, from the two sides of the court-trial, from which you could look at the issue. This seems to me quite clearly a matter of *common public interest*.

On the other hand, everything which can really be figured out, in the sphere Engels called the administration of things—these are social things in general. That they should then be subject to debate seems to me phony and a plague.

C. B. Macpherson: Are you telling us what a jury or a town meeting can handle is political, and everything else is social?

Arendt: No, I didn't say that. I gave these only as examples of where in everyday life things come up which are *not* social, and which really *belong* in a public realm. And I gave the town-hall meeting and the jury as examples of the very few places where a non-spurious public still exists.

Albrecht Wellmer: I would ask you to give one example in our time of a social problem which is not at the same time a political problem. Take anything: like education, or health, or urban problems, even the simple problem of living standards. It seems to me that even the social problems in our society are unavoidably political problems. But if this is true, then, of course, it would also be true that a distinction between the social and the political in our society is impossible to draw.

Arendt: Let's take the housing problem. The social problem is certainly adequate housing. But the question of whether this adequate housing means integration or not is *certainly* a political question. With every one of these questions there is a double face. And one of these faces should not be subject to debate. There shouldn't be any debate about the question that everybody should have decent housing.

George Baird: From an administrative point of view, the British government described as inadequate a huge percentage of the housing stock of Britain in a way that makes no sense to a large proportion of the inhabitants who actually live there.

Arendt: I think this example is helpful in showing this double face of which I have talked in a very concrete way. The political issue is that these people love their neighborhood and don't want to move, even if you give them one more bathroom. This is indeed entirely a debatable question, and a public issue, and should be decided publicly and not from above. But if it's a question of how many square feet every human being needs in order to be able to breathe and to live a decent life, this is something which we really can figure out.

. . .

Michael Gerstein: It seems to me that one is forced to act politically, to deal with concrete situations and concrete problems. And insofar as one is forced to make those kinds of decisions then the question of class, the question of property, the question of the future of a society becomes a very concrete problem and one can't anymore deal solely in terms of abstractions such as bureaucracy or abstractions such as centralization. These seem to me to reveal the basically de-politicized character of your thought which I found very disturbing when I read your work. Hearing you here today disturbs me even further, because fortunately—or unfortunately— we are forced to act in the world and we are going to have to know what the world looks like.

Arendt: These are the problems of so-called "mass society." I say so-called "mass society" but it is unfortunately a fact. Now, I would like to know why you believe that words like class and property are less abstract than bureaucracy and administration or the words I use. They are exactly the same. All these belong to the same category of words. The question is only can you point to something very real with these words. These words either have a revealing—or disclosing—quality or they haven't.

If you think that bureaucracy has no disclosing quality— which means the rule by the bureau, and not the rule by men, nor the rule by law—then I believe you haven't really lived in this world long enough. But believe me bureaucracy is a reality much more so today than class. In other words, you use a number of abstract nouns which were once revealing, namely, in the nineteenth century, and you do not even bother to examine critically whether they still hold or whether they should be changed, or anything of that kind.

Property is another question. Property is indeed very important, but in a different sense than the one in which you think about it. What we should encourage everywhere is property—of course, not the property of the means of production, but private property strictly. And, believe me, this property is very much in danger, either by inflation, which is only another way of expropriating a people, or by exorbitant taxes, which is also a way of expropriation. It is the sweeter way to expropriate—instead of killing all of them. These processes of expropriation you have everywhere. To make a decent amount of property available to every human being—not to expropriate, but to spread property—then you will have some possibilities for freedom even under the rather inhuman conditions of modern production.

.   .   .

Mary McCarthy: Actually you do have the tendency now—I am not talking about the Soviet Union—in some of the eastern states towards private property in exactly the sense you mean: without ownership of the means of production. It seems to me that, so far as I can look ahead, socialism does represent the only force for conservation, and, in fact, represents a conservative force in the modern world.

Arendt: I said the means of production should not be in the hands of a single man. But who owns it then instead? The government.

A few years ago, in Germany, the left demanded the nationalization of the Springer Press, the right-wing press. Springer is only one man, and, of course, he has a certain amount of power over public opinion through certain methods, etc. But he does not have the accumulated power and means of violence which a government has. So the left would have given their government the whole power of Mr. Springer, which, of course, would have been a much greater power: a government-directed press. I mean even that freedom which Springer has got to grant because of competition—because there are other newspapers which will tell what he prefers not to tell—even this kind of freedom would have disappeared.

So, if you talk about the ownership of the means of production: the first who inherited it was the government itself. Now the government itself was, of course, much stronger than any single capitalist could be. And, if it's a question of the worker, it turned out that they could strike—and the right to strike is, of course, a very precious right—against the single capitalist. But they couldn't strike against the government. So the few rights which the worker movement had actually acquired through long struggle since the middle of last century, were immediately taken away from them.

McCarthy: Consider the situation of the press in the United States: before the last election [1968] some sort of survey was made and I think it was something like 90 per cent of the U.S. press supported Nixon. So that you have an amalgam of the press and the government—or, at least the present government of the United States—in the form of the Republican Party—and it looks to me that you have got the same result in the United States at this time as you would have had in Germany had they expropriated Springer.

Arendt: If you were to expropriate the press you would have not 90 per cent for the government, but 100 per cent.

McCarthy: Not necessarily. For instance, in Holland television is nationally owned. (I think these things probably only work in small countries.) And they have an enormous range of political parties. Each political party has got its own TV channel or piece of a channel. And this functions. It is accepted by the people.

Arendt: Yes. But there you have laws which force the decentralization of this expropriation, of this accumulative process. The multi-party system in Holland acts as this mitigating factor, which they now try to introduce in some of the eastern countries. What we *will* have to do, by and large, is experiment.

McCarthy: Cheers!

.　　　.　　　.

C. B. Macpherson: Really, two of the statements Miss Arendt has made this morning about power seem to me outrageous. One was that Marx didn't understand power. And the other was that power is now in the bureaucracy.

It seems to me that one can hold that Marx didn't understand power only if you define power in some very peculiar way. And it strikes me that this is part of the pattern of Miss Arendt's thought. She defines a lot of key words in ways unique to herself: you know, social *versus* political (a rather special meaning to the word "social"), force *versus* violence (a quite special meaning to the word "force"). . . .

Arendt: No, power *versus* violence. I am sorry.

Macpherson: Power and violence, sorry. Action (a unique definition of "action"). This intellectual practice—and it's a very enlivening practice, because it starts off, or should start off, all kinds of controversy—is still rather a curious practice: of taking a word that has perhaps more than one meaning in the ordinary understanding and giving it a very special meaning and then proceeding from there to reach striking, paradoxical conclusions.

Well, look, Marx didn't understand power, you say. What he understood, surely, was that power is in any society wielded by the people who control access to the means of production, the means of life, the means of labor. And that, in his terminology, was a class. Would Miss Arendt agree that the only reason a bureaucracy has what power it has—and I wouldn't agree with her that it has anything like the power she attributes to it—is because and only insofar as, and only in those countries where it has become a class—in Marx's sense, the people who control access to the means of production?

Arendt: I would not agree with this. What you consider my idiosyncratic use of words—I think there is a little more to it, of course. We all grow up and inherit a certain vocabulary. We then have got to examine this vocabulary. And this not just by finding out how this word is usually used, which then gives as a result a certain number of uses. These uses are then legitimate. In my opinion a word has a much stronger relation to what it denotes or what it is, than just the way it is being used between you and me. That is, you look only to the communicative value of the word. I look to the disclosing quality. And this disclosing quality has, of course, always an historical background.

Macpherson: I look at the disclosing quality too, and that's why I say that such words as Marx's use of class, power, and so on were disclosing concepts.

Arendt: I didn't say the same about class. You see what I mean is, of course, the so-called superstructure. What Marx means by power is actually the power of a trend or development. This, he then believes, materializes, as it were, because this trend is utterly immaterial, in the superstructure, which is the government. And the laws of the government being the superstructure are nothing but mirrors of the trends in society.

The question of rule Marx did not understand and to a large extent that is in his favor because he did not believe that anybody wants power just for power's sake. This does not exist in Marx. Power in the naked sense that one person wants to rule another, and that we need laws in order to prevent that, this Marx didn't understand.

You know, somehow Marx still believed that if you leave men alone—society corrupts man—and change society, man will reappear. He will reappear—God, protect us from it: this optimism, runs throughout history. You know, Lenin once said he didn't understand why criminal law should exist, because once we have changed circumstances everybody will prevent everybody else from committing a crime with the same matter-of-courseness as every man will hurry up to aid a woman who is in distress. I thought this example of Lenin so very nicely nineteenth-century, you know. All this we do not believe any longer.

Macpherson: But surely Marx saw as clearly as, say, James Mill that men want power over others in order to extract some benefit for themselves from that power. It's not power for its own sake. It's power to extract benefit.

Arendt: Yes, but you know this power to extract benefit for profit's sake . . .

Macpherson: Not necessarily just profit, any benefit.

Arendt: But we don't know how great a percentage of the population would do it just for fun and without thinking about it. That is, Marx always thought that what we see as human motivations, more or less, are actually the motivations of trends. And trends, of course, *are* abstractions. And I would doubt whether they exist of themselves. The trend of a white wall is to get dirty with time, unless somebody appears and redecorates the room.

Macpherson: It is certainly true that Marx was interested in trends, that he was interested in the laws of motion of the society, and so on. But I don't recognize Marx in your picture of him having turned the trend into some kind of real force all by itself and then reading it back.

Arendt: Well, we cannot sit down here and read Marx! But this seems to me quite obvious and it comes, of course, from Hegel. Hegel's world spirit reappears in Marx as man as a species-being. In each case you have ruled out or counted out the plurality of men. There are not many men whose acting together and against each other finally results in history. But there is the one giant noun, and this noun is in the singular and now you ascribe everything to this noun. This I believe, is really an abstraction.

Hans Morganthau: Let me say a word about the basic misunderstanding of power by Marx. Marx organically connected the desire for power with the class division of society. And he believed that with this class division removed in a classless society the struggle for power—the desire for power—would of itself disappear. This is the prophecy of the *Communist Manifesto* when the domination of man by man will be replaced by the administration of things. But this is a Rousseauist misconception of the nature of man, of the nature of society, and of the nature of power. And what I find particularly interesting is that in this misconception of power, nineteenth-century Marxism and nineteenth-century liberalism are brothers under the skin. They believe the same thing.

.   .   .

Albrecht Wellmer: I have another question concerning the importance of certain distinctions in your work, or, what Mary McCarthy called "the medieval element" in your thinking. It is quite clear that many of these distinctions have proved extremely fruitful with regard to criticizing ideological fixations: particularly those fixations which represent the prevailing of nineteenth-century traditions. For instance, in the theory of Marx.

On the other hand, I am puzzled by a certain kind of abstractness of these distinctions. I always have the feeling that these distinctions are designating limiting cases to which nothing in reality really corresponds. I wonder about the nature of these constructs, or ideal types, or concepts, which designate limiting cases.

What I want to say is that there might be a certain Hegelian element missing in your thinking.

Arendt: Sure!

Wellmer: I want to give a tentative interpretation of the way in which you draw distinctions like work and labor, the political and the social, and power and violence. Could it not be that these alternatives designate not permanent possibilities of mankind—at least, not in the first place—but the extreme limits between which human history extends: namely, the human being as an animal and the utopia. So that if, for instance, every labor would have become work, if the social would have become a public or political topic, in *your* sense, and if violence had been abandoned in favor of power, in your sense again, then apparently, this would be the realization of an utopia.

Now, I wonder whether the fact that you are not quite conscious of the utopian element in your thinking explains why you relate in such a strange way to the critical or socialist or anarchist traditions of thinking. I have the feeling that this is precisely the reason why you never can give an adequate account either of these traditions, or of something like critical theory, and of the relation of your theory to these traditions.

Arendt: I may be unaware of the utopian element. This is one of the things that strikes me as quite possible. I don't say "yes": I just say it's quite possible. But if I am unaware of it, for heaven's sake, I *am* unaware of it. And no psychoanalysis from the side of the *Frankfurter Schule* will help. I really am not in a position to answer you right now—I have got to think that over.

At least you see the one thing which I also see as questionable: namely if I don't believe in this or that theory, why don't I write a refutation of it? I will do that only under duress. That is my lack of communication. I do not believe that this has anything to do with abstractness.

Wellmer: My question got lost. May I reformulate my question? What would you say to an interpretation of your distinctions by which the one alternative would designate the limiting case of animality and the other limiting case would designate the full realization of humanity?

Arendt: I would say that by these fancy methods you have *eliminated* distinction and have already done this Hegelian trick in which one concept, all of its own, begins to develop into its own *negative*. *No it doesn't!* And *good* doesn't develop into *bad*, and *bad* doesn't develop into *good*. There I would be adamant.

You know I have a great respect for Hegel. So that's not at issue. Just as I have a great respect for Marx. And I am, of course, also influenced by all these people whom, after all, I read. So don't misunderstand me. But this would be precisely the trap—in my notion—into which I refuse to go.

.   .   .

Hans Morganthau: The question has been raised about centralization, which runs directly counter to democracy if it is pushed far enough.

Arendt: I think this question is very complicated. I would say on the first level there is indeed all over the world a certain rebellion, almost, against bigness. And I think this is a healthy reaction. And I myself share it. Especially because this bigness and centralization demands these bureaucracies. And the bureaucracies are really the rule by nobody. And this nobody is not a benevolent nobody. We cannot hold anybody responsible for what happens because there is really no author of deeds and events. It is really frightening. So I share this to a very large extent. And this, of course, spells decentralization. And I also think that this country [U.S.A.] can remain or become a powerful country only if there are many sources of power. That is, if power is being divided as it was in the original notion of the Founding Fathers, and before that the notion—not so clear, but still—the notion of Montesquieu.

But if all this is said—and my sympathies are there—and you know I have this romantic sympathy with the council system, which never was tried out—that is something which builds itself up from the grass roots, so that you really can say *potestas in populo*, that is, that power comes from below and not from above —if all that is said, then we have the following: after all, the world in which we live has to be kept. We cannot permit it to go to pieces. And this means that "administration of things," which Engels thought such a marvelous idea, and which actually is an awful idea, but which is still a necessity. And this can be done only in a more or less central manner.

And on the other hand this centralization is an awful danger, because these structures are so vulnerable. How can you keep these up without centralization? And if you have it, the vulnerability is immense.

The American Constitution as an Ideal Type

Ed Weissman: We have just been told that there is this distinction to be drawn between the theorist and the activist in an important way. We've just been told that there is a basic incompatability between the activist and the theorist. . . .

Arendt: No, not between the men, between the activities.

Weissman: Right. And implicit in all you've said is a basic intellectual commitment to some sort of idealized picture of the American Constitution and the American experience. This strikes me as the most unshakable sort of a commitment which is basic to so much of what you say that you need not ever bring it up explicitly.

When you do speak of the American Constitution you make what seems to me some assumptions about it which I would like to ask you about. It strikes me that in some respects you misinterpret the American Constitution in the exact same way that Montesquieu misunderstood the British Constitution. It's the same kind of intellectual transference as well. Basically what he saw in the British Constitution was not, in fact, a real separation of powers at all, but simply a temporary stand-off between an old society and a new, which had an institutional reflection. Now you take this notion of the separation of powers and transfer it to the American republic.

But once you do away with the stand-off between the old society and the new, you wind up with the British monarchical situation all over again, when the institutions represent mere interests. So it is no accident that we wind up with the current American administration [1972]. It was inevitable that we'd wind up with an elective king, Nixon, with Kissinger, who, of course, becomes a typical minister to the Crown in the old sense of the term.

Arendt: Well, of course, I did something like Montesquieu did with the English Constitution in that I construed out of [the American Constitution] a certain ideal type. I tried to back it up a little better than Montesquieu did with historical fact, for the simple reason that I do not belong to the aristocracy and therefore do not enjoy this blessed laziness which is one of the main characteristics of Montesquieu's writings. Now whether this is permissible is another question, which would lead us too far here.

Actually we all do that. We all make somehow what Max Weber called the "ideal type." That is, we think a certain set of historical facts, and speeches, and what have you, through, until it becomes some type of consistent rule. This is especially difficult with Montesquieu because of his laziness, and it is much easier with the Founding Fathers because they were extraordinarily hard workers, and so they gave you everything which you wanted.

I do not believe in your conclusions: this inevitability which would lead us from the American Revolution to Mr. Kissinger. I think that even you, schooled in the school of necessity, and trends, and inevitability of historical laws, should see that this is a little abstruse.

. . .

C. B. Macpherson: I was interested in Miss Arendt's position in relation to the traditions. I take it the idea is that she has rejected the tradition of Hobbes and Rousseau, and she has accepted the tradition of Montesquieu and the Federalists. I can understand this, but it raises a puzzle because there is one very important thing that it seems to me the Hobbes tradition and the Federalist tradition have in common. That is their model of man as a calculating individual seeking to maximize his own interest. Bourgeois man is the model. And the model of society that follows when you put in the additional assumption is that every man's interest naturally conflicts with everybody else's. Surely both traditions had that model of man and model of society in common. Now if Arendt rejects one tradition and accepts the other, the question is what does she do about what they had in common? Does she accept or does she reject the model of bourgeois man?

Arendt: I do not believe that the model of man is the same for the two traditions. I agree that the model of man which you described is the bourgeois and I agree that this bourgeois, God knows, is a reality.

But if I may, I want to talk now about the model of man in this other tradition. The tradition of Montesquieu that you mentioned could really go back to Machiavelli and Montaigne, and so on. They ransacked the archives of antiquity precisely in order to get a different kind of man. And this kind of man is not the bourgeois, but the citizen. This distinction between *le citoyen* and *le bourgeois* remained, of course, throughout the eighteenth century because it became such a central way of talking and thinking about these things during the French Revolution, and lasted up to 1848.

I think I could express it in a slightly different way. I would say that after the absolute monarchy had become so absolute that it could emancipate itself from all other feudal powers, including the power of the church, a really great crisis came. What came was the reemergence of real politics, as in antiquity—as I see the revolutions.

You see I went back to Greek and Roman antiquity only half because I like it so much—I like Greek antiquity but I never liked Roman antiquity. I went back, nevertheless, because I knew that I simply wanted to read all these books that these people had read. And they read all these books—as they would have said—in order to find a model for this new political realm which they wanted to bring about, and which they called a republic.

The model of man of this republic was to a certain extent the citizen of the Athenian *polis*. After all we still have the words from there, and they echo through the centuries. On the other hand the model was the *res publica,* the public thing, of the Romans. The influence of the Romans was stronger in its immediacy on the minds of these men. You know Montesquieu didn't only write *L'Esprit des Lois* but also wrote about *la grandeur* and *la misère* of Rome. They were all absolutely fascinated. What did Adams do? Adams collected constitutions as other people would collect stamps. And a large part of his so-called collected works are nothing but excerpts and partly of no great interest.

They taught themselves a new science and they called it a new science. Tocqueville was the last who still talked about that. He says for this modern age we need a new science. He meant a new science of politics, not the *nuova scienza* of the previous centuries, of Vico. And that is what I actually have in mind. I don't believe that something very tangible comes out of anything which people like me are doing, but what I am after is to think about these things not just in the realm of antiquity, but I feel the same needs for antiquity which the great revolutionaries of the eighteenth century felt.

.   .   .

F. M. Barnard: I really would like to know what evidence there is for saying that there is this distinction between interests and opinions in the Founding Fathers' vision of democracy.

Arendt: At the moment I cannot quote anything. The distinction is, number one, the notion of group interests, which are always there, and opinions, where I have got to make up my mind. This distinction is clearly there. You have it in the constitution itself: the legislature [the House of Representatives] was supposed more or less to represent the interests of the inhabitants; the Senate, on the contrary, was supposed to filter these interests and to come to some kind of impartial opinions which would relate to the commonweal.

This distinction between the two institutions is of course very old. It follows the Roman *potestas in populo, auctoritas in senatu*. The Senate in Rome was deprived of power. The Senator in Rome was only there to give his opinion. But this opinion had some kind of authority insofar as this opinion was not inspired by the *potestas* of the populace. They were called *maiores*. In this sense they were representing the constitution of Rome, re-tying it, or connecting it with Rome's past. So the Senate had an altogether different function in the Roman republic than the populace.

And this is at the back of the thinking of the Founding Fathers, who knew this very well. And that is also one of the reasons why they were so extremely interested in having a Senate —much more interested than any European thinker ever was. They felt that they needed to filter the opinions which arise immediately from interested parties through a body which is one step or two steps removed from this direct influence.

·   ·   ·

Now let me talk for a moment about the relationship between violence and power. My simile, so to speak, when I talk about power is "all against one." That is, the extreme of power is all against one. Then no violence is necessary to overpower the one. The extreme of violence is the opposite: one against all. The one guy with the machine gun who keeps everybody in a state of perfect obedience, so that no opinion is necessary any longer, and no persuasion.

There is no doubt that violence can always destroy power: if you have the minimum of people who are willing to execute your orders then violence can always reduce power to sheer impotence. We have seen that many times.

What violence can never do is to generate power. That is,

once violence has destroyed the power structure then no new power structure springs up. This is what Montesquieu meant when he said that tyranny is the only form of government that carries the seed of destruction within itself. After having depowered everybody in the realm through tyranny, there is no longer any possibility for a new power structure to serve as a sufficient basis for the tyranny to go on—unless of course the whole form of government is changed.

If you look at power without any violence from the subjective side of being forced, then the situation of all against one is probably psychologically even stronger than the other situation of one against all. For in the situation in which someone puts a knife to my throat and says, "Your money or I'll cut you," I, of course, obey immediately. But in terms of my power I remain as I was because, while I obey, I don't agree. But if you have the situation of all against one it is so overpowering that you actually can get at the guy. He can no longer keep his position even though he does not yield out of violence. So unless limited by laws this would be unlimited majority rule.

And the Founding Fathers, as you know, were afraid of majority rule—they were by no means for pure democracy. Then they found out that power can be checked only through one thing, and that is power—counterpower. The balance of power checking power is an insight of Montesquieu, which the drafters of the constitution had very much in mind.

Political Thinking Without a Bannister

Hans Morganthau: What are you? Are you a conservative? Are you a liberal? Where is your position within the contemporary possibilities?

Arendt: I don't know. I really don't know and I've never known. And I suppose I never had any such position. You know the left think that I am conservative, and the conservatives sometimes think I am left or I am a maverick or God knows what. And I must say I couldn't care less. I don't think that the real questions of this century will get any kind of illumination by this kind of thing.

I don't belong to any group. You know the only group I ever belonged to were the Zionists. This was only because of Hitler, of course. And this was from '33 to '43. And after that I broke. The only possibility to fight back *as a Jew* and not as a human being—which I thought was a great mistake, because if you are attacked as a Jew you have got to fight back as a Jew, you cannot say, "Excuse me, I am not a Jew; I am a human being." This is silly. And I was surrounded by this kind of silliness. There was no other possibility, so I went into Jewish politics—not really politics—I went into social work and was somehow also connected with politics.

I never was a socialist. I never was a communist. I come from a socialist background. My parents were socialists. But I myself, never. I never wanted anything of that kind. So I cannot answer the question.

. . .

I never was a liberal. When I said what I was not, I forgot [to mention that]. I never believed in liberalism. When I came to this country I wrote in my very halting English a Kafka article, and they had it "Englished" for the *Partisan Review*. And when I came to talk to them about the Englishing I read this article and there, of all things, the word "progress" appeared! I said: "What do you mean by this? I never used that word," and so on. And then one of the editors went to the other in the next room and left me there and I overheard him say, really in a tone of despair, "She doesn't even believe in progress!"

. . .

Mary McCarthy: Where do you stand on capitalism?

Arendt: I do not share Marx's great enthusiasm about capitalism. If you read the first pages of the *Communist Manifesto* it is the greatest praise of capitalism you ever saw. And this at a time when capitalism was already under very sharp attack especially from the so-called right. The conservatives were the first to bring up these many criticisms, which later were taken over by the left, and also by Karl Marx, of course.

In one sense Marx was entirely right: the logical development of capitalism is socialism. And the reason is very simple. Capitalism started with expropriation. That is the law which then determined [the development]. And socialism carries expropriation to its logical end and is therefore in a way without any moderating influences. What today is called humane socialism means no more than that this cruel tendency which was started with capitalism and went on with socialism is somehow tempered by law.

The whole modern production process is actually a process of gradual expropriation. I therefore would always refuse to make a distinction between the two. For me it is really one and the same movement. And in this sense Karl Marx was entirely right. He is the only one who really dared to think this new production process through—this process which crept up in Europe in the seventeenth, and then eighteenth, and nineteenth century. And so far he is entirely right. Only it is hell. It is not paradise that comes finally out of it.

What Marx did not understand was what power really is. He did not understand this strictly political thing. But he saw one thing, namely, that capitalism, left to its own devices, has a tendency to raze all laws that are in the way of its cruel progress.

Also, the cruelty of capitalism in the seventeenth, eighteenth, and nineteenth centuries was, of course, overwhelming. And this you have to keep in mind if you read Marx's great praise of capitalism. He was surrounded by the most hideous consequences of this system and nevertheless thought that this was a great business. He was, of course, also Hegelian and believed in the power of the negative. Well I *don't* believe in the power of the negative, of the negation, if it is the terrible misfortune of other people.

So you ask me where I am. I am nowhere. I am really not in the mainstream of present or any other political thought. But not because I want to be so original—it so happens that I somehow don't fit. For instance, this business between capitalism and socialism seems to me the most obvious thing in the world. And nobody even understands what I am talking about, so to speak.

I don't mean that I am misunderstood. On the contrary I am very well understood. But if you come up with such a thing and you take away their bannisters from people—their safe guiding lines (and then they talk about the breakdown of tradition but they have never realized what it means! That it means you really are out in the cold!) then, of course the reaction is—and this has been my case quite often—that you are simply ignored. And I don't mind that. Sometimes you are attacked. But you usually are ignored, because even useful polemic cannot be carried through on my terms. And you may say that this is really a fault of mine.

You said kindly enough that I want to share. Yes, that is true. I do want to share. And I do not want to indoctrinate. That is really true. I do not want anybody to accept whatever I may [think]. But, on the other hand, this kind of ignoring the main literature in my own field is something that should be held against me at some point, I think. And, well, you know, I don't reflect much on what I am doing. I think it's a waste of time. You never know yourself anyhow. So it's quite useless. But this I think is a real fault, and not just a lacuna. This would cut much deeper if one said, "Why don't you read the books of your colleagues?" or, "Why do you do it very seldom?"

.   .   .

There's this other thing, which Draenos brought out. You said "groundless thinking." I have a metaphor which is not quite that cruel, and which I have never published but kept for myself. I call it thinking without a bannister. In German, *Denken ohne Geländer*. That is, as you go up and down the stairs you can always hold onto the bannister so that you don't fall down.

But we have lost this bannister. That is the way I tell it to myself. And this is indeed what I try to do.

. . .

This business that the tradition is broken and the Ariadne thread is lost. Well, that is not quite as new as I made it out to be. It was, after all, Tocqueville who said that "the past has ceased to throw its light onto the future, and the mind of man wanders in darkness." This is the situation since the middle of the last century, and, seen from the viewpoint of Tocqueville, entirely true. I always thought that one has got to start thinking as though nobody had thought before, and then start learning from everybody else.

. . .

Mary McCarthy: This space that Hannah Arendt creates in her work and which one can walk into with the great sense of walking through an arch into a liberated area and a great part of it is occupied by definitions. Very close to the roots of Hannah Arendt's thinking is the *distinguo*: "I distinguish this from that. I distinguish labor from work. I distinguish fame from reputation." And so on. This is actually a medieval habit of thought.

Arendt: It is Aristotelian!

McCarthy: This habit of distinguishing is not popular in the modern world, where there is a kind of verbal blur surrounding most discourse. And if Hannah Arendt arouses hostility, one reason is because the possibility of making distinctions is not available to the ordinary reader. But to go back to the distinctions themselves—I would say that each one within this liberated area, within this free space—each distinction was like a little house. And, let us say, fame is living in its little house with its architecture, and reputation is living in another. So that all this space created by her is actually furnished.

Hans Morganthau: Sounds like a low-income housing project!

Arendt: And without any federal subsidy!

McCarthy: And I think that the chance of invigoration and oxygenation does combine with some sense of stability and security. And that is through the elaboration, the marvelous, shall we say, unfolding of definitions. Each of her works is an unfolding of definitions, which of course touch on the subject, and more and more enlighten it as one distinction unfolds (after another). But there is also this stability in which fame lives in its mansion, or little house, and labor lives in its, and work in another, and the political is strictly segregated in its house from the social.

Arendt: It is perfectly true what you say about distinctions. I always start anything—I don't like to know too well what I am doing—I always start anything by saying, "A and B are not the same." And this, of course, comes right out of Aristotle. And for you, it comes out of Aquinas, who also did the same.

· · ·

I would like to say that everything I did and everything I wrote—all that is tentative. I think that all thinking, the way that I have indulged in it perhaps a little beyond measure, extravagantly, has the earmark of being tentative. And what was so great in these conversations with Jaspers was that you could sustain such an effort, which was merely tentative, which did not aim at any results, for weeks.

It could happen to us that I would arrive—I would stay there for a few weeks—and on the first day we hit on a certain subject. One such subject I remember was *ein gute Vers ist ein gute Vers*, which I had said. A good line of poetry is a good line of poetry, meaning by this that it has a convincing force of its own, which he didn't quite believe. And the point for me was to convince him that Brecht was a great poet. This one line was enough for us for two weeks, two sessions every day. And we came back to it again and again.

The disagreement was never quite resolved. But the thinking about such a thing itself became immensely richer, through this exchange, as he said "without reservations," that is, where you don't keep anything back. You don't think, "Oh, I shouldn't say that, it will hurt him." The confidence in the friendship is so great that you know nothing can hurt.

Elisabeth Young-Bruehl

A CHRONOLOGICAL BIBLIOGRAPHY OF THE WORKS OF HANNAH ARENDT (1906–1975)

I n the first section of this bibliography, Arendt's books and booklets in American and German editions are listed; in the second section, articles and book reviews. Arendt's columns (under the title "This Means You") and articles for the German-language newspaper *Aufbau* (New York) from 1941 through 1945 and her nine untitled brief book notices for *Jewish Social Studies* (New York) from 1942 through 1953 are not listed. Articles that appeared in German but not in English are listed; otherwise, only the English versions of articles are given. The list of German articles from before the Second World War may not be complete. Brief notes indicate which articles were republished as parts of books, but they do not indicate which of the republished articles underwent substantial revision before republication. Thanks are due to Lawrence May for his help in preparing this bibliography.

I. BOOKS

1929
Der Liebesbegriff bei Augustin. Berlin: J. Springer, 1929.

1948
Edition of Bernard Lazare, *Job's Dung Heap.* New York: Schocken Books, 1948.

Sechs Essays. Heidelberg: L. Schneider, 1948. (Reprinted in *Die Verbogene Tradition,* 1976, see below.)

1951

The Origins of Totalitarianism. New York: Harcourt, Brace & Co., 1951. Second enlarged edition: New York: The World Publishing Co., Meridian Books, 1958. Third edition, with new prefaces: New York: Harcourt, Brace & World, 1966, 1968, 1973. German editions: *Elemente und Ursprünge totaler Herrschaft.* Frankfurt: Europäische Verlagsanstalt, 1955, 1958, 1961, 1962. (British title: *The Burden of Our Time.*)

1955

Edition of Hermann Broch: *Dichten und Erkennen, Essays,* two volumes of Broch's *Gesammelte Werke.* Zurich: Rheinverlag, 1955 (now Frankfurt: Suhrkamp). (Arendt's introduction, translated by Richard and Clara Winston, appeared in *Men in Dark Times.*)

1957

Fragwürdige Traditionsbestände im politischen Denken der Gegenwart. Frankfurt a.M.: Europäische Verlagsanstalt, 1957. (Four essays, all included in *Between Past and Future.*)

1958

The Human Condition. Chicago: University of Chicago Press, 1958; (Doubleday/Anchor, 1959). German edition: *Vita activa oder von tätigen Leben,* Stuttgart: Kohlhammer, 1960; Munich: Piper, 1967.

Karl Jaspers: Reden Zur Verleihung des Friedenpreises des Deutschen Buchhandels. Munich: Piper, 1958. (Reprinted in *Men in Dark Times.*)

Rahel Varnhagen: The Life of a Jewess. London: East and West Library, 1958. American edition: *Rahel Varnhagen: The Life of a Jewish Woman.* New York: Harcourt Brace Jovanovich, 1974. German edition: *Rahel Varnhagen: Lebensgeschichte einer deutschen Jüdin aus der Romantik.* Munich: Piper, 1959 (Ullstein Verlag, 1975).

Die Ungarische Revolution und der totalitäre Imperialismus. Munich: Piper, 1958. (Included in 1958 American edition of *The Origins of Totalitarianism.*)

1960

Von der Menschlichkeit in Finsteren Zeiten: Gedanken Zu Lessing. Hamburg: Hauswedell, 1960. Munich: Piper, 1960. (Later the first essay in *Men in Dark Times.*)

1961

Between Past and Future: Six Exercises in Political Thought. New York: The Viking Press, 1961. Revised edition, including two additional essays, 1968. (Four essays in *Fragwurdige Traditionsbestände im Politischen Denken der Gegenwart,* 1957, see above.)

1962

Edition of Karl Jaspers' *The Great Philosophers.* New York: Harcourt, Brace & Co., 1962 and 1966 (volumes I and II).

1963

Eichmann in Jerusalem: A Report on the Banality of Evil. New York: The Viking Press, 1963. Revised and enlarged edition, 1965. German edition: *Eichmann in Jerusalem: Ein Bericht von der Banalität des Bösen.* Munich: Piper, 1964.

1965

On Revolution. New York: The Viking Press, 1963. Revised second edition, 1965. German edition: *Über die Revolution.* Munich: Piper, 1963.

1968

Men in Dark Times. New York: Harcourt, Brace & World, 1968.
Edition of Walter Benjamin's *Illuminations,* translated by Harry Zohn. New York: Harcourt, Brace & World, 1968. (Introduction to this volume collected in *Men in Dark Times.*) German edition: Frankfurt: Suhrkamp, 1965.

1970

On Violence. New York: Harcourt, Brace & World, 1970. (An expanded version of "Reflections on Violence" [1969].) German version: *Macht und Gewalt.* Munich: Piper, 1975.

1971

Walter Benjamin—Bertolt Brecht: Zwei Essays. Munich: Piper, 1971. (Both essays included in *Men in Dark Times.*)

1972

Crises of the Republic. New York: Harcourt Brace Jovanovich, 1972.
Wahrheit und Lüge in der Politik: Zwei Essays. Munich: Piper, 1972. (The two essays, "Lying in Politics" [1971] and "Truth and Politics" [1967], first appeared in English, see below.)

1976

Die Verborgene Tradition: Acht Essays. Frankfurt: Suhrkamp, 1976. (Six of these essays appeared in 1948 as *Sechs Essays,* the other two are "Zionism Reconsidered" [1945] and "Aufklärung und Judenfrage" [1932]).

1978

The Jew as Pariah: Jewish Identity and Politics in the Modern Age. Edited and with an Introduction by Ron H. Feldman. New York: Grove Press, Inc., 1978. (A collection of articles on Jewish issues written between 1942 and 1966.)

The Life of the Mind. New York: Harcourt Brace Jovanovich, 1978. (Two volumes of an uncompleted work, posthumously published, edited by Mary McCarthy.)

II. ARTICLES

1930

"Augustin und Protestantismus," *Frankfurter Zeitung,* no. 902 (12 April 1930).

"Philosophie und Soziologie. Anlässlich Karl Mannheim, 'Ideologie und Utopie,'" *Die Gesellschaft* (Berlin), VII (1930), pp. 163–76. (Reprinted in *Ideologie und Wissenssoziologie.* Darmstadt: Wissenschaftliche Buchgesellschaft, 1974).

"Rilkes Duineser Elegien," with G. Stern, *Neue Schweizer Rundschau* (Zurich), XXIII (1930), pp. 855–71.

1931

A review of Hans Weil's *Die Entstehung des deutschen Bildungsprinzips* in *Archiv für Sozialwissenschaft und Sozialpolitik* (Tübingen), LXVI (1931), p. 200–205.

1932

"Adam Muller-Renaissance?" *Kölnische Zeitung,* no. 501 (13 September 1932) and no. 510 (17 September 1932).

"Aufklärung und Judenfrage," *Zeitschrift für die Geschichte der Juden in Deutschland* (Berlin), IV/2–3 (1932). (Reprinted in *Die Verborgene Tradition.*)

"Berliner Salon" and "Brief Rahels an Pauline Wiesel," *Deutscher Almanach für das Jahr 1932* (Leipzig), pp. 175–84 and 185–90.

"Freidrich von Gentz. Zu seinem 100. Todestag am 9 Juni," *Kölnische Zeitung*, no. 308 (8 June 1932).

"Sören Kierkegaard," *Frankfurter Zeitung*, no. 75–76 (29 January 1932).

1933

A review of Dr. Alice Rühle-Gerstel's *Das Frauenproblem der Gegenwart* in *Die Gesellschaft* (Berlin), x (1932), pp. 177–79.

"Rahel Varnhagen. Zum 100. Todestag," *Kölnische Zeitung*, no. 131 (7 March 1933). (Reprinted in *Judische Rundschau*, no. 28/29 [7 April 1933].)

1942

"A Believer in European Unity," *Review of Politics*, iv/2 (April 1942) pp. 245–47. (A Review of P. R. Sweet, *Friedrich von Gentz: Defender of the Old Order*).

"From the Dreyfus Affair to France Today," *Jewish Social Studies*, iv (July 1942) pp. 195–240. (Reprinted in *Essays on Antisemitism*, Conference on Jewish Relations, 1946, and used in *The Origins of Totalitarianism*, Part I.)

1943

"Portrait of a Period," *The Menorah Journal*, xxxi (Fall 1943), pp. 307–14. (Review of *The World of Yesterday: An Autobiography* by Stephen Zweig.)

"We Refugees," *The Menorah Journal*, xxxi (January 1943), pp. 69–77.

"Why the Crémieux Decree Was Abrogated," *Contemporary Jewish Record*, vi/2 (April 1943), pp. 115–23.

1944

"Concerning Minorities," *Contemporary Jewish Record*, vii/4 (August 1944), pp. 353–68. (Used in *The Origins of Totalitarianism*, Part II.)

"Franz Kafka: A Revaluation," *Partisan Review*, xi/4 (Fall 1944), pp. 412–22. (Reprinted in *Sechs Essays* and *Die Verborgene Tradition* in German.)

"The Jew as Pariah: A Hidden Tradition," *Jewish Social Studies* vi/2 (February 1944), pp. 99–122.

"Our Foreign Language Groups," *The Chicago Jewish Forum*, iii/1 (Fall 1944), pp. 23–34.

"Race-Thinking before Racism," *The Review of Politics*, vi/1 (January 1944), pp. 36–73. (Used in *The Origins of Totalitarianism*, Part II.)

1945

"Approaches to the 'German Problem'," *Partisan Review*, XII/1 (Winter 1945), pp. 93–106.

"The Assets of Personality," *Contemporary Jewish Record*, VIII/2 (April 1945), pp. 214–16. (Review of Meyer W. Weisgal, ed., *Chaim Weismann*).

"Christianity and Revolution," *The Nation* (22 September 1945), pp. 288–89.

"Dilthey as Philosopher and Historian," *Partisan Review*, XII/3 (Summer 1945), pp. 404–06. (Review of *Wilhelm Dilthey: An Introduction* by H. A. Hodges.)

"Imperialism, Nationalism, Chauvinism," *The Review of Politics*, VII/4 (October 1945), pp. 441–63. (Used in *The Origins of Totalitarianism*, Part II.)

"Nightmare and Flight," *Partisan Review*, XII/2 (Spring 1945), pp. 259–60. (Review of *The Devil's Share* by Denis de Rougemont.)

"Organized Guilt and Universal Responsibility," *Jewish Frontier* (January 1945), pp. 19–23. (Reprinted in Roger Smith, ed. *Guilt: Man and Society*. New York: Doubleday/Anchor, 1971.)

"Parties, Movements and Classes," *Partisan Review*, XII/4 (Fall 1945), pp. 504–12. (Used in *The Origins of Totalitarianism*, Part II.)

"Power Politics Triumphs," *Commentary*, 1 (December 1945), pp. 92–93. (Review of Feliks Gross, *Crossroads of Two Continents*.)

"The Seeds of a Fascist International," *Jewish Frontier* (June 1945), pp. 12–16.

"The Stateless People," *Contemporary Jewish Record*, VIII/2 (April 1945), pp. 137–53. (Used in *The Origins of Totalitarianism*, Part II.)

"Zionism Reconsidered," *The Menorah Journal*, XXXIII (August 1945), pp. 162–96. (Translated into German for *Die Verborgene Tradition* and reprinted in M. Selzer, ed. *Zionism Reconsidered*. New York: Macmillan, 1970, pp. 213–49.)

1946

"Expansion and the Philosophy of Power," *Sewanee Review*, LIV (October 1946), pp. 601–16. (Used in *The Origins of Totalitarianism*, Part II).

"French Existentialism," *The Nation* (23 February 1946), pp. 226–28. (Anthologized in *One Hundred Years of the Nation*.)

"The Image of Hell," *Commentary*, II/3 (September 1946), pp. 291–95. (Review of *The Black Book: The Nazi Crime Against the Jewish People* compiled by the World Jewish Congress *et al.* and *Hitler's Professors* by Max Weinreich.)

"Imperialism: Road to Suicide," *Commentary*, 1 (February 1946), pp. 27–35.

"The Ivory Tower of Common Sense," *The Nation* (19 October 1946), pp. 447–49. (Review of *Problems of Men* by John Dewey.)

"The Jewish State: 50 Years After, Where Have Herzl's Politics Led?" *Commentary*, I (May 1946), pp. 1–8.

"The Nation," *The Review of Politics*, VIII/1 (January 1946), pp. 138–41. (Review of J. T. Delos, *La Nation*, Editions de l'Arbre, Montreal.)

"No longer and Not Yet," *The Nation* (14 September 1946), pp. 300–302. (Review of *The Death of Virgil* by Hermann Broch, tr. by J. S. Untermeyer.)

"Privileged Jews," *Jewish Social Studies*, VIII/1 (January 1946), pp. 3–30. (Reprinted in Duker and Ben-Horin, *Emancipation and Counteremancipation*. New York: Ktav Publishing House, 1947).

"Proof Positive," *The Nation* (5 January 1946), p. 22. (Brief review of Victor Lange, *Modern German Literature*.)

"The Streets of Berlin," *The Nation* (23 March 1946), pp. 350–51. (Review of Robert Gilbert, *Meine Reime Deine Reime*.)

"Tentative List of Jewish Cultural Treasures in Axis-Occupied Countries," *Supplement to Jewish Social Studies*, VIII/1 (1946). (This was prepared by the Research Staff of the Commission on European Jewish Cultural Reconstruction headed by Arendt.)

"Tentative List of Jewish Educational Institutions in Axis-Occupied Countries," *Supplement to Jewish Social Studies*, VIII/3 (1946). (This was also prepared by the Research Staff of the Commission on European Jewish Cultural Reconstruction headed by Arendt.)

"The Too Ambitious Reporter," *Commentary*, II (January 1946), pp. 94–95. (Review of *Twilight Bar* and *The Yogi and the Commissar* by Arthur Koestler.)

"What Is Existenz Philosophy?" *The Partisan Review*, XIII/1 (Winter 1946), pp. 34–56.

1947

"Creating a Cultural Atmosphere," *Commentary*, IV (November 1947), pp. 424–26.

"The Hole of Oblivion," *Jewish Frontier* (July 1947), pp. 23–26. (Review of *The Dark Side of the Moon*, anonymous.)

1948

"About Collaboration" (a letter), *Jewish Frontier*, XV (October 1948), pp. 55–56.

"Beyond Personal Frustration: The Poetry of Bertolt Brecht," *The Kenyon Review*, X/2 (Spring 1948), pp. 304–12. (Review of *Selected Poems* by Bertolt Brecht, tr. by H. R. Hays; an article based on this review, printed in *Die Neue Rundschau*, LXI (1950), pp. 53–67 was translated for P. Demetz, ed., *Brecht*. Englewood Cliffs, N.J.: Prentice-Hall, 1962, pp. 43–50.)

"The Concentration Camps," *Partisan Review*, xv/7 (July 1948), pp. 743–63. (Anthologized in *Partisan Reader, 1945–1953* and used in *The Origins of Totalitarianism*, Part II.)

"Jewish History, Revised," *Jewish Frontier* (March 1948), pp. 34–38. (Review of *Major Trends in Jewish Mysticism* by Gershom Scholem.)

"The Mission of Bernadotte," *The New Leader*, xxxi (23 October 1948), pp. 808, 819.

"To Save the Jewish Homeland: There Is Still Time," *Commentary*, v (May 1948), pp. 398–406.

1949

"The Achievement of Hermann Broch," *The Kenyon Review*, xi/3 (Summer 1949), pp. 476–83.

" 'The Rights of Man': What Are They?" *Modern Review*, iii/1 (Summer 1949), pp. 24–37. (Used in *The Origins of Totalitarianism*, Part II.)

"Single Track to Zion," *Saturday Review of Literature*, xxxii (February 5, 1949), pp. 22–23. (Review of Chaim Weizmann, *Trial and Error: The Autobiography of Chaim Weizmann*.)

"Totalitarian Terror," *The Review of Politics*, xi/1 (January 1949), pp. 112–15. (Review of *Forced Labor in Soviet Russia* by David J. Dallin and Boris I. Nicolaevsky.)

1950

"The Aftermath of Nazi Rule, Report from Germany," *Commentary*, x (October 1950), pp. 342–53. (Anthologized in *The Commentary Reader*.)

"Mob and the Elite," *Partisan Review*, xvii (November 1950), pp. 808–19. (Used in *The Origins of Totalitarianism*, Part III.)

"Peace or Armistice in the Near East?" *The Review of Politics*, xii/1 (January 1950), pp. 56–82.

"Religion and the Intellectuals, A Symposium," *Partisan Review*, xvii (February 1950), pp. 113–16. (Reprinted as a part of *Partisan Review*, Series III, 1950, pp. 15–18.)

"Social Science Techniques and the Study of Concentration Camps," *Jewish Social Studies*, xii/1 (1950), pp. 49–64.

1951

"Bei Hitler Zu Tisch," *Der Monat*, iv (October 1951), pp. 85–90.

"The Imperialist Character," *The Review of Politics*, xii/3 (July 1950), pp. 303–20. (Used in *The Origins of Totalitarianism*, Part II.)

"The Road to the Dreyfus Affair," *Commentary*, xi (February 1951), pp. 201–203. (Review of *Anti-Semitism in Modern France* by Robert F. Byrnes.)

"Totalitarian Movement," *Twentieth Century*, 149 (May 1951), pp. 368–89. (Used in *The Origins of Totalitarianism*, Part III.)

1952

"The History of the Great Crime," *Commentary*, XIII (March 1952), pp. 300–304. (Review of *Bréviaire de la Haine: Le IIIê Reich et les Juifs* by Leon Poliakov.)

"Magnes, The Conscience of the Jewish People," *Jewish Newsletter*, VIII/25 (24 November 1952), p. 2.

1953

"The Ex-Communists," *Commonweal*, LVII/24 (20 March 1953), pp. 595–99. (Reprinted in *The Washington Post*, 31 July 1953.)

"Ideology and Terror: A Novel Form of Government," *The Review of Politics*, XV/3 (July 1953), pp. 303–27. (Included in the 1958 edition of *The Origins of Totalitarianism*. A German version appeared in *Offener Horizont: Festschrift für Karl Jaspers*. Munich: Piper, 1953).

"Rejoinder to Eric Voeglin's Review of *The Origins of Totalitarianism*," *Review of Politics*, XV (January 1953), pp. 76–85.

"Religion and Politics," *Confluence*, II/3 (September 1953), pp. 105–26. (Cf. Arendt's reply to criticism of this article in *Confluence*, pp. 118–20.)

"Understanding and Politics," *Partisan Review*, XX/4 (July–August 1953), pp. 377–92.

"Understanding Communism," *Partisan Review*, XX/5 (September–October 1953), pp. 580–83 (Review of Waldemar Gurian, *Bolshevism*.)

1954

"Europe and America: Dream and Nightmare," *Commonweal*, LX/23 (24 September 1954), pp. 551–54.

"Europe and America: The Threat of Conformism," *Commonweal*, LX/25 (24 September 1954), pp. 607–10.

"Europe and the Atom Bomb," *Commonweal*, LX/24 (17 September 1954), pp. 578–80.

"Tradition and the Modern Age," *Partisan Review*, XII (January 1954), pp. 53–75. (Drawn from a series of lectures delivered at Princeton as the Christian Gauss Seminars in Criticism, 1953, and used in *Between Past and Future*.)

1955

"The Personality of Waldemar Gurian," *The Review of Politics*, XVII/1 (January 1955), pp. 33–42. (Reprinted in *Men in Dark Times*.)

1956

"Authority in the Twentieth Century," *The Review of Politics*, xviii/4 (October 1956), pp. 403–17.

1957

"History and Immortality," *Partisan Review*, xxiv/1 (Winter 1957), pp. 11–53.

"Jaspers as Citizen of the World," in P. A. Schilpp, *The Philosophy of Karl Jaspers*. La Salle, Illinois: Open Court Pub. Co., 1957, pp. 539–50. (Reprinted in *Men in Dark Times*.)

1958

"The Crisis in Education," *Partisan Review*, xxv/4 (Fall 1958), pp. 493–513. (Reprinted in *Between Past and Future*.)

"The Modern Concept of History," *The Review of Politics*, xx/4 (October 1958), pp. 570–90. (Reprinted in *Between Past and Future*.)

"Totalitarian Imperialism: Reflections on the Hungarian Revolution," *The Journal of Politics*, xx/1 (February 1958), pp. 5–43. (Reprinted in *Cross Currents*, viii/2 [Spring 1958], pp. 102–28, and added to the 1958 edition of *The Origins of Totalitarianism*.)

"Totalitarianism," *The Meridian*, ii/2 (Fall 1958), p. 1. (Arendt's reflections on *The Origins of Totalitarianism* at the time of its second edition.)

"What Was Authority?" in C. Friedrich, *Authority*. Cambridge, Mass.: Harvard University Press, 1959. (Reprinted in *Between Past and Future*.)

1959

"Reflections on Little Rock," *Dissent*, vi/1 (Winter 1959), pp. 45–56. (Included in same issue are criticisms by David Spitz and Melvin Tumin: in *Dissent* vi/2 [Spring 1959], pp. 179–81, Arendt replied to her critics; the article was reprinted in *The Public Life: A Journal of Politics*, iv/3–4 [May–June 1973], pp. 92–97.)

1960

"Freedom and Politics: A Lecture," *Chicago Review*, xiv/1 (Spring 1960), pp. 28–46. (Revised for *Between Past and Future*.)

"Revolution and Public Happiness," *Commentary*, xxx (November 1960), pp. 413–22. (Used in *On Revolution*.)

"Society and Culture," *Daedalus*, lxxxii/2 (Spring 1960), pp. 278–87. (Reprinted in *Between Past and Future*.)

1962

"Action and 'The Pursuit of Happiness,' " in *Politische Ordnung und Mensch-*

liche Existenz: Festgabe Für Eric Voeglin. Munich: Beck, 1962. (Used in *On Revolution.*)

"The Cold War and The West," *Partisan Review,* XXIX/1 (Winter 1962), pp. 10–20.

"Revolution and Freedom: A Lecture," in *In Zwei Welten: Siegfried Moses Zum Fünfundsiebzigsten Geburtstag.* Tel-Aviv: Bitaon Ltd., 1962. (Used in *On Revolution.*)

1963

"A Reporter at Large: Eichmann in Jerusalem," *The New Yorker,* February 16, 1963, pp. 40–113; February 23, 1963, pp. 40–111; March 2, 1963, pp. 40–91; March 9, 1963, pp. 48–131; March 16, 1963, pp. 58–134. (This five-part article, revised, was published as *Eichmann in Jerusalem: A Report on the Banality of Evil.*)

"Kennedy and After," *The New York Review of Books,* 1/9 (26 December 1963), p. 10.

"Man's Conquest of Space," *American Scholar,* XXXII (Autumn 1963), pp. 527–40.

"Reply to Judge Musmanno," *The New York Times Book Review,* VIII/4 (23 June 1963). (Arendt's exchange with Musmanno was reprinted in Freedman and Davis, eds., *Contemporary Controversy.* New York: Macmillan, 1966, pp. 312–17.)

1964

"*The Deputy:* Guilt by Silence," *The New York Herald Tribune Magazine* (23 February 1964), pp. 6–9. (Reprinted in *Storm over* The Deputy, edited by Eric Bentley.)

"Eichmann in Jerusalem," *Encounter* (January 1964), pp. 51–56. (An exchange of letters between Arendt and Gershom Scholem.)

"Nathalie Sarraute," *The New York Review of Books,* II/2 (5 March 1964), pp. 5–6. (Review of *The Golden Fruits* by Nathalie Sarraute, tr. by Maria Jolas.)

"Personal Responsibility under Dictatorship," *The Listener* (6 August 1964), pp. 185–87 and 205.

1965

"The Christian Pope," *The New York Review of Books,* IV/10 (17 June 1965), pp. 5–7. (Review of *Journal of a Soul* by Pope John XXIII, tr. by D. White; included in *Men in Dark Times.*)

"Hannah Arendt—Hans Magnus Ernzenberger: Politik und Verbrechen: Ein Briefwechsel," *Merkur* (April 1965), pp. 380–85.

1966

"The Formidable Dr. Robinson: A Reply to the Jewish Establishment," *The New York Review of Books*, v/12 (20 January 1966), pp. 26–30. (Arendt's response to letters about this article appeared in the March 17, 1966, issue.)

"A Heroine of the Revolution," *The New York Review of Books*, vii/5 (6 October 1966), pp. 21–27. (Review of *Rosa Luxemburg* by J. P. Nettl; included in *Men in Dark Times*.)

"Introduction," to Bernd Naumann, *Auschwitz*. New York: Praeger Pub., 1966. (Reprinted in Falk, Kolko and Lifton, eds., *Crimes of War*. New York: Random House, 1971.)

"The Negatives of Positive Thinking: A Measured Look at the Personality, Politics and Influence of Konrad Adenauer," *Book Week of The Washington Post* (5 June 1966), pp. 1 and 11. (Review of *Memoirs 1945–1953* by Konrad Adenauer, tr. by Beate Ruhm von Oppen.)

"On the Human Condition," in Mary Alice Hinton, ed., *The Evolving Society*. New York: Institute of Cybernetical Research, 1966, pp. 213–219.

"Remarks on 'The Crisis Character of Modern Society'," *Christianity and Crisis*, xxvi/9 (30 May 1966), pp. 112–14.

"What Is Permitted to Jove," *The New Yorker* (5 November 1966), pp. 68–122. (A study of Bertolt Brecht, reprinted in *Men in Dark Times*.)

1967

"Introduction," to J. Glenn Gray, *The Warriors*. New York: Harper & Row, 1967.

"Preface," to Karl Jaspers' *The Future of Germany*. Chicago: University of Chicago Press, 1967.

"Randall Jarrell: 1914–1965," in *Randall Jarrell, 1914–1965*. New York: Farrar, Straus & Giroux, 1967. (Reprinted in *Men in Dark Times*.)

"Truth and Politics," *The New Yorker* (February 25, 1967), pp. 49–88. (Reprinted in *Between Past and Future*, 2nd edition, and in David Spitz, ed., *Political Theory and Social Change*. New York: Atherton Press, 1967, pp. 3–37.)

1968

"Comment by Hannah Arendt on 'The Uses of Revolution' by Adam Ulam," in Richard Pipes, ed., *Revolutionary Russia*. Cambridge, Mass.: Harvard University Press, 1968.

"He's All Dwight: Dwight MacDonald's *Politics*," *The New York Review of Books*, xi/2 (1 August 1968), pp. 31–33.

"Is America by Nature a Violent Society? Lawlessness Is Inherent in the Uprooted," *The New York Times Magazine* (28 April 1968), p. 24.

"Isak Dinesen: 1885–1962," *The New Yorker* (9 November 1968), pp. 223–36. (Reprinted in *Men in Dark Times.*)

"Walter Benjamin," *The New Yorker* (19 October 1968), pp. 65–156. Translated from the German by Harry Zohn. (Reprinted in *Men in Dark Times.*)

1969

"The Archimedean Point," *Ingenor*, College of Engineering, University of Michigan (Spring 1969), pp. 4–9, 24–26.

"Reflections on Violence," *Journal of International Affairs* (Winter 1969), pp. 1–35. (Reprinted in *The New York Review of Books*, xii/4 [27 February 1969], pp. 19–31. Expanded as *On Violence* and reprinted in *Crises of the Republic.*)

1970

"Civil Disobedience," *The New Yorker* (12 September 1970), pp. 70–105. (Reprinted in *Crises of the Republic,* and in E. V. Rostow, ed., *Is Law Dead?* New York: Simon and Schuster, 1971, pp. 213–43.)

Letter in reply to a review by J. M. Cameron, *New York Review of Books* xiii (1 January 1970), p. 36.

1971

"Lying and Politics: Reflections on the Pentagon Papers," *The New York Review of Books*, xvii/8 (18 November 1971), pp. 30–39. (Reprinted in *Crises of the Republic.*)

"Martin Heidegger at 80," *The New York Review of Books*, xvii/6 (21 October 1971), pp. 50–54. (Originally in German, *Merkur*, x [1969], pp. 893–902, tr. by Albert Hofstadter. Reprinted in English in Michael Murray, ed., *Heidegger and Modern Philosophy.* New Haven: Yale University Press, 1978.)

"Thinking and Moral Considerations: A Lecture," *Social Research*, xxxviii/3 (Fall 1971), pp. 417–46.

"Thoughts on Politics and Revolution," *The New York Review of Books*, xvi/7 (22 April 1971), pp. 8–20. (An interview conducted by Adelbert Reif in the summer of 1970, translated from the German by Denver Lindley; reprinted in *Crises of the Republic.*)

1972

"Nachwort," for Robert Gilbert's *Mich Hat Kein Esel im Galopp Verloren.* Munich: Piper, 1972.

"Washington's 'Problem-Solvers'—Where They Went Wrong," The *New York Times* (5 April 1972), Op-Ed page.

1974

"Karl Jaspers zum fünfundachtzigsten Geburtstage," in H. Saner, ed., *Erinnerugen an Karl Jaspers*. Munich: Piper, 1974, pp. 311–315.

1975

"Home to Roost," *The New York Review of Books* (26 June 1975), pp. 3–6. (Reprinted in S. B. Warner, *The American Experiment*. Boston: Houghton Mifflin, 1976, pp. 61–77, with Arendt's comments.)

"Remembering Wystan H. Auden," *The New Yorker* (20 January 1975), pp. 39–40. (Reprinted in *The Harvard Advocate*, cviii/2–3, pp. 42–45; and in *W. H. Auden: A Tribute*. London: Weidenfeld & Nicholson, 1974/5, pp. 181–187.)

1977

"Public Rights and Private Interests," in Mooney and Stuber, eds., *Small Comforts for Hard Times: Humanists on Public Policy*. New York: Columbia University Press, 1977. (Response to a paper by Charles Frankel in the same volume.)

"Thinking," *The New Yorker* (21 November 1977, pp. 65–140; 28 November 1977, pp. 135–216; 5 December 1977, pp. 135–216). This three-part article comprises the first volume of *The Life of the Mind*, 1978.

1978

"From an Interview," with Roger Errera, *The New York Review of Books* xxv/16 (26 October 1978), p. 18.

Notes on the Authors

Melvyn A. Hill is an associate professor in the Division of Social Science at York University, Toronto.

Elisabeth Young-Bruehl is an associate professor of letters in the College of Letters, Wesleyan University. She is presently at work on a biography of Hannah Arendt.

Bernard Crick is professor of politics at Birkbeck College, University of London. He is the author of *Political Theory and Practice* (1974).

Mildred Bakan is an associate professor in the Department of Philosophy and the Division of Social Science at York University.

Bikhu Parekh is a senior lecturer in the Department of Politics at the University of Hull, England.

Kenneth Frampton is an architect and an architectural historian. He is a fellow of the Institute of Architecture and Urban Studies, New York, and a member of the faculty of the Graduate School of Architecture and Urban Planning, Columbia University. He is the author of *A Critical History of Modern Architecture.*

Robert W. Major is a consultant on urban affairs and a writer presently living in New York City.

Peter Fuss is a professor in the Department of Philosophy at the University of Missouri, St. Louis.

James Miller is an associate professor of government at the University of Texas at Austin. He is the author of *History and Human Experience: From Marx to Merleau-Ponty* (University of California, 1979) and the editor of *The Rolling Stone Illustrated History of Rock and Roll.*

Stan Spyros Draenos teaches at York University. He has recently completed a study of psychoanalytic theory entitled "Freud and the Odyssey of Enlightenment: The Self-Encounter of Man through Science."

J. Glenn Gray is the author of *The Warriors: Reflections on Men in Battle; the Promise of Wisdom; Hegel and Greek Thought;* and *Understanding Violence and Other Essays,* as well as numerous articles. He served as general editor for the works of Martin Heidegger, published in English by Harper & Row. He was professor of philosophy at Colorado College, Colorado Springs, until his death in 1977.

Michael Denneny is an editor at St. Martin's Press, New York, an associate editor at *The Christopher Street Magazine* and the author of *Lovers: The Story of Two Men.*

Index

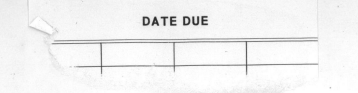

DATE DUE